7A
NB

THE BALLAD OF
BLIND TOM

Blind Tom in 1882

THE BALLAD OF
BLIND TOM

Deirdre O'Connell

OVERLOOK DUCKWORTH
New York • Woodstock • London

This edition first published in the United States in 2009 by
Overlook Duckworth Peter Mayer Publishers, Inc.
New York, Woodstock & London

NEW YORK:
The Overlook Press
141 Wooster Street
New York, NY 10012

WOODSTOCK:
The Overlook Press
One Overlook Drive
Woodstock, NY 12498
www.overlookpress.com
[for individual orders, bulk and special sales, contact our Woodstock office]

LONDON:
Duckworth
90-93 Cowcross Street
London EC1M 6BF
inquiries@duckworth-publishers. co.uk
www.ducknet.co.uk

Cataloging-in-Publication Data is available from the Library of Congress

Book design and type formatting by Bernard Schleifer
Manufactured in the United States of America
ISBN 978-1-59020-143-5
ISBN 978-0-7156-3837-8
FIRST EDITION
10 9 8 7 6 5 4 3 2 1

To Jasmine, Indigo and David

Contents

SONGS,

Sketch of the Life,

OF

BLIND TOM

THE MARVELOUS MUSICAL PRODIGY,

THE NEGRO BOY PIANIST

WHOSE RECENT PERFORMANCES AT THE

Great St. James' and Egyptian Halls, London, and Salle Hertz, Paris,

HAVE CREATED SUCH A PROFOUND SENSATION.

*Blind Tom's concert program, which contains a biographical note
that is the source of as many fictions as facts.*

Fragments

———◆———

WHEN *The New York Times* REPORTED BLIND TOM'S DEMISE IN HOBOKEN, New Jersey in 1908, it was the fourth time in twenty years his death had been announced. And still the mourners at his funeral weren't convinced it was the right man. The piano virtuoso had been entertaining the American public with his dazzling feats of mimicry and memory since the Civil War after all, and the body in the coffin seemed too young.

But as the wheezy melodeon ground out a tortured *Nearer My God To Thee* opinion suddenly shifted Tom's way. A deafening clap of thunder drowned out the tormented hymn. The skies broke open and a glorious tempest whipped the trees in the chapel yard, their branches clattering the stain glass windows. A thunderstorm requiem, *The Times* reporter noted, to befit the genius of a composer whose music echoed nature's rattle and hum. What the reporter did not realize was that this was not an isolated incident, but rather the final act of a life-long conversation between Tom and the natural world.

For years after Tom's death, at least three or four Blind Toms were doing the rounds in dime circus freak shows across the country. Stumbling towards the piano, eyes rolled back, tongue lolling, arms outstretched like a hulking bear—only to utterly transform the moment their fingers touched the ivory. A divine ravishment flowing through their fingers, the music rising in heavenly tones (if the piano was in tune). He was a freak too good to leave mouldering in an unmarked grave. As the years passed and the last of the Tin Pan Alley generation followed the Civil War's into eternity, all that remained of this man who never forgot was a scattered collection of memories. Fragments. Time erases us all and Blind Tom was hovering on the cusp of oblivion.

I first came across one such fragment during a visit home to Sydney, Australia in 1993 (I was then living in London) when a friend, artist Martin Sharp, showed me an entry in his 1920 edition of *The Encyclopedia of Aberrations*. The entry was "Moronic Genius" and detailed the phenomenal musical memory of Thomas Wiggins, a Georgia-born slave who assigned to his curious memory the music, sounds and voices of this turbulent time. Concertos, spirituals, sentimental ballads. Thunderstorms, weaponry, trains. Conversations, sermons, political speeches. He repeated everything just as he heard it, replete with hand gestures and poise—but only a superficial understanding of the impact "slavery," "abolition" and "secession" had on him.

Martin asked me to look up Blind Tom in The British Library when I returned to London. I did, unearthing an 1868 concert program that compared his genius to Mozart's along with a handful of less-than-impressed concert reviews. Somewhere between maestro and charlatan, idiot and genius, was the real Blind Tom.

Six months later, chance brought a holiday to Washington, D.C. and after a quick nose through the index at the Library of Congress, I was lost to Blind Tom. Here, I discovered a mine of information, including Dr. Geneva Handy Southall's pioneering thesis. What emerged was not just a snapshot of Tom, but an all too disturbing picture of his masters and guardians desperately plotting ways to hold onto their Golden Goose.

A career in chains? Perhaps. Once Tom's master discovered that the worthless runt he had purchased out of pity was a musical prodigy, he lost no time in licensing the eight-year-old to a Barnum-style showman, under whom Tom raised thousands of dollars for the Confederate War effort. Emancipation failed to deliver Tom from the shackles of slavery, his master's son merely morphing into the role of guardian and manager. Legally adjudged insane, Tom spent much of his life in perpetual motion, performing to packed houses across the continent—the profits of which financed his guardian's extravagant lifestyle.

Back in London I set to work writing—what? A biography, novel, documentary? What was the right format to fit this mixed bag of tour dates, concert reviews, lawsuits and judgments; this social history of slavery, war, emancipation? Why did it seem like I was re-telling the history of nineteenth century America? Slowly the true nature of the problem dawned on me. My manuscript was more con-cerned with the people around Tom than Tom himself. The pages I was filling dealt with other people's stories as if Tom was a bit play-er in his own life. I still did not understand my subject; had not yet come to grips with the enigma of Blind Tom.

Determined to crack this nut, I headed to the United States for an unofficial sabbatical in the country's vast public libraries, colleges and archives and dug up a mountain of material, much of it bearing the stamp of two factually erratic articles that had been endlessly reworked and repeated over the century. Yet hidden amongst the repeats were some highly prized originals: a wonderfully candid and eclectic collection of eyewitness accounts.

Scores of people, from Tom's master's grandson to Mark Twain, to soldiers, schoolteachers, booking agents and musicians had at some point written to magazines and journals describing their encounters with him. In the 1950s two writers attempted to publish books on him. I stumbled across both their research boxes, each holding even more first-hand accounts. Case studies written by psychologists, phrenologists and music professors all fleshed out, in striking detail, a picture of Tom—not the prodigy or the legend—but the man.

I learnt, for instance, that when Tom wasn't playing the piano he leaned his body forward, balanced on one leg and jumped—huge gravity-defying leaps that no one could explain or commercially exploit. When Tom traveled by train he hissed, clattered and whis-tled along in unison, his entire body transformed by the locomotive. When alone, he entertained imaginary characters—serving them tea and swapping the day's news. That in his hometown of Columbus, Georgia, folks believed that during the Fireman's Parade the spirit of the drum entered Tom's mother's ecstatic body and "marked" the unborn baby inside. Priceless glimpses and tidbits that confirmed to me that Tom was truly one in a hundred million.

Now I had no excuse. I had in hand an anarchic, hilarious, quirky, mythic, tragic picture of Blind Tom—the stuff of greatness. But still I procrastinated, unable to solve the enigma. The sum of his parts was still undefined—an unwieldy, often contradictory, collection of frag-ments. However, some themes began to emerge.

From the prevailing view of the nineteenth century Southern planter—guided by the dictates of white superiority—came a recurring image of Tom as bestial or sub-human. An "idiotic" African consigned to the basest level of the racial hierarchy.

In complete contradiction to this, the African-American mytho-magical worldview perceived Tom as a Spirit Child. A child born with second sight whose mimicry and music powered a lifelong dialogue with the divine beings residing in nature.

From modern science came an understanding of the autistic experience. Here Tom can be understood as a mentally afflicted child who, in his hypersensitive state, was unable to pull the disparate elements together to perceive a coherent world.

These three core images of Tom—sub-human, divine, fragmented —opened up a dialogue through which his relationship with race, power, the irrational and memory could be investigated. A dialogue that extended beyond Tom himself to illuminate aspects of the political and social fabric of America.

The image of fragmentation also found resonance in my experience. For ten years I lugged around the world two archive boxes that contained bits and pieces of facts about Blind Tom. The pieces of this crazy misshapen jigsaw refused to lock neatly into places—some pieces stood in stark contradiction to each other while others monotonously repeated themselves. This situation was a little like Tom himself who, in his autistic aloneness, experienced the world as an ever-disintegrating, fractured place: a vast repository of unconnected facts—some focused on obsessively, others repeated *ad nauseam*. A place only made whole by gravity-defying leaps and, of course, music.

Why not then accept the fragments for what they are: a collection of pieces. Embrace the holes, the contradictions, the outright lies and distortions and thankfully the shiny nuggets of truth. For what binds this story into any meaningful whole are not the politics of the day, or the machinations of those close to him (though they are part of the intriguing story I am about to tell), but a central image of a complex man who listened to the turbulent world around him and reflected it in sound.

PART ONE

THE SEEN AND THE UNSEEN

Cover of The Oliver Gallop, *a piece composed by Tom at the age of 10 and named in onor of his manager, Perry Oliver.*

- 1 -

A Good Breeding Woman

"GEORGIA FIELD-HANDS ARE NOT AS ACCURATE AS JEWS IN PRESERVING their genealogy; they do not anticipate a Messiah," opined Rebecca Harding Davis in an 1862 *Atlantic Monthly* article. "This idiot-boy is only 'Tom.' Just a mushroom growth—unkinned, unexpected, not hoped for, owning no name to purify and honor and give away when he is dead."[1]

Forty years later, "Blind Tom" was a name shrouded in myth, a byword for inexplicable, reclusive, oddball genius. Social commentators would casually declare that "Edison was the Blind Tom of the science world," certain that their readers understood exactly what they meant.[2] The names Thomas Greene, Thomas Bethune and Thomas Wiggins meant little to anyone except the person with a legal claim on the prodigy. But the slave's Christian name, Thomas, was different. It was born of a game. Two games, in fact: one of matrimony, the other a matter of survival.

Wiley Jones's slave woman Charity was known throughout Muscogee County as a good breeder, and now at the age of forty-eight she was having another. On May 25th, 1849 in Columbus, Georgia, she gave birth to anywhere between her twelfth and twenty-first child. After contemplating the baby for a moment, she figured it would be right for the master's daughter to choose the name. Valeria Jones accepted the honor with gusto. For the seventeen-year-old it was an excellent opportunity to play on the heartstrings of her tormented beaus. This time it was Major Grimes's turn to take hope, for the name she chose was his own: Thomas.[3]

This account of Thomas's naming, as told by Valeria's son Walter D. Lamar, is blissfully unaware of the fear and anxiety surrounding the child's entry into the world. It is also oblivious to that fact that Valeria was not the only woman plying her charms. Charity was also busy buttering up her master's daughter—for if anyone could sway Master Wiley Jones, it was daddy's little girl.

When Charity first looked into her newborn's eyes and saw that there were no more whites in them than there were to the back of her hand, her first reaction was fear.[4] Fear that Master Wiley Jones would not be pleased: fear of his retribution. Perhaps an old Granny midwife tried to allay her anxieties, convince her that this was cause for celebration: among the slaves, blindness and oddly colored eyes were signs that a child had the gift of "second sight," with the vision to know things seen and unseen. But when Charity saw her master greet the news with a tightened jaw, she knew her son's destiny was hanging by a thread. "Wiley Jones was very disappointed," his grandson explained many years later, "he feared the blind boy would become a useless burden."[5] Charity's granddaughter, Elnora Walker, remembered what the implications of this "disappointment" were: "Charity always carried the newborn with her because the whites had threatened to kill him because he was blind."[6]

Few disabled children born into slavery survived into adulthood. With no registrar of births or census information to draw on, it is difficult to ascertain what percentage of slaves were disabled, although the evidence may be conspicuous in its absence. The Georgia Slave Narratives, a vast oral history project conducted by white interviewers in the 1920's, contains two hundred and fifty interviews with former slaves, most of them written in a black Southern dialect that is part accurate and part stereotypical. The only reference to disabled slave children in them concerns a blind brother and sister, the children of two runaways who, for years, hid out in a cave. Eventually they were recaptured and "it warn't long fore bofe of dem chillun was daid."[7] From illness or a pillow pressed over their faces while their parents were working in the fields? Who can say.

Another narrative tells of an intellectually disabled slave, a "half-crazy," "crack-brained" man whose sister-in-law watched as an overseer beat him to death, too helpless to intervene.[8] Unless the slaves' disabilities were unusual enough to increase their value—as in the case of Millie and Christina, the conjoined twins from North Carolina who, in 1852, were sold as infants to a circus showman for $10,000—only a handful of slave owners were prepared to take on the additional expense to feed and clothe someone they could neither work nor sell. "The blind, lunatics, and idiots all would be a tax on the slave master," lectured one abolitionist. "It would be for his interest to shorten their days."[9]

The abolitionist may call it murder, but to the planter it was simply the fate of any runt. The "defective" infant's end would come quietly, humanely—another death in an age of high infant mortality—and neither his tender-hearted wife nor his daughter need be any the wiser. But a runt who had been named by the daughter of the house could not be so easily discarded. Like most privileged white seventeen-year-olds, Valeria's interests lay not in the welfare of the family chattel, but on balls, operas, picnics, weddings, moonlight steamboat cruises and—as the social season wore on—no longer the attentions of Major Grimes but rather those of the dashing Henry James Lamar, the man she would marry the following year. So absorbed was she in her game of matrimony, she was unaware of the grace her naming power bestowed on the slave child or that Charity's invitation was simply a tactic to curry favor and good-will.

A VIOLENT LOVE OF DANCE

In the months leading up to Thomas's birth, Charity passed her days on the Georgia farm preparing meals for her master's family and rearing children of her own. Some nights she fell onto the old hay mattress in the slave cabin exhausted. Other nights, she joined Valeria in the music room of the big house and danced.

Columbus may have been a thriving frontier town—its warehouses laden with cotton, its stores crammed with imported goods—but it was still a rough and tumble place. Fortunately, for a night of frivolity and music, Valeria needed to look no further than the family cook. Charity had been something of a "strut gal" in her heyday—a title given to the plantation's best dancers—and Valeria was an accomplished pianist. Together, they worked up a storm.[10] "They played on the piano in the evenings," reported Walter D. Lamar, "and frequently had Charity to dance for them, a duty that fell lightly on the shoulders of the Negro, who violently loved not only to dance but the music. She took advantage of every opportunity to hear the piano and seemed enchanted with its melodies."[11]

But as with the story of Thomas's naming, this tale has another side. A Louisiana slave named Solomon Northrup tells of the nights when he "had" to dance for his cruel, drunken master. "No matter how worn out and tired we were, there must be a general dance. There must be no halting or delay, no slow or languid movements; all must be brisk, and lively, and alert. . . . Bent with excessive toil and feeling rather as if we could cast ourselves upon the earth and weep, many a night in the house of Edwin Epps have his unhappy slaves been made to dance and laugh."[12] While Valeria was never known to be drunken or cruel, Charity was dancing for the same reason as Northrop: she had to, although any resentment was carefully masked with her famously sunny disposition.

Apart from an evangelical few who were deeply offended by the frivolities of secular dance, white folk in this golden age of minstrelsy were tickled pink watching the contortions, high kicks and flings of their slaves. "Twas too utterly ridiculous to be true," wrote a Charleston journalist of one such display. The couple "began to quickstep with body thrown far back in cake-walk style and the audience applauded in screams."[13] The custom of holding one's body stiffly erect is as uniquely European as the knee-flexed, bent body stance is African, and the Cakewalk was the slave's deeply ironic response to the rigidity of their white masters. Slavemasters have described these dances as "rude" and "grotesque," a reflection of their servants' incapacity to comprehend the subtleties of a more highly evolved civilization. The joke, however, was squarely on them, the master class unable to tell as to who was being ridiculous and who was being ridiculed.

But there was more to be gained than the quiet satisfaction of poking fun at the white folks. "Playin' up to master" was a stock tool-in-trade for many slaves and Charity certainly knew that the more she made Valeria and her friends laugh, the more flamboyantly she worked her feet from her legs, legs from her trunk, shoulders from her arms, the more favors would be bestowed on her. She knew she was playing a game that was complex and inscrutable and that Valeria had only the vaguest idea of the rules.

Valeria's naming honor, then, was as strategic as Charity's sunny disposition—a clever tactic to encourage the master's daughter to cuddle and delight in the blind newborn. How then could she allow her father to kill it? The tactic worked—but not for long. Eight

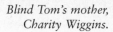

*Blind Tom's mother,
Charity Wiggins.*

months later, while Valeria was deliriously preparing for her upcoming wedding, Wiley Jones delivered some brutal news: Charity and her family were to be sold on the auction block. He had debts to settle and, one way or another, he was getting rid of that runty child.

CARRIED OFF

Wiley Jones's plan to sell the slave family was, for Charity, yet another separation in a lifetime of separations—herself, her husband and her children had been "carried off" by one master or another. "Many died heart-broken by reason of it," recalled one slave. Others longed for freedom hoping to reclaim a wife, husband or child. A mother would see her baby again.[14] If Charity's actions are anything to go by, she too nursed dreams of reunion. On three well-documented occasions she battled to keep her kinfolk close, leveraging to her advantage whatever resources she had at her disposal. However, like most slaves, the rest of her life story has been largely obliterated, leaving only a few fragments from which we can begin to imagine a life scarred by separation.

The fact of Charity's first, and possibly most harrowing, separation is based on two dates. In 1801 she was born in Virginia, yet by the early to mid twenties had somehow landed in Baldwin County, Georgia.[15] While the specifics of her journey are lost to time, countless others who trod the same path remembered the dehumanizing hardship.

In the first few decades of Charity's life, King Cotton was in ascendancy but while Georgia and the Carolinas were booming, Virginia was in economic decline. Decades of tobacco production had sucked her soils dry and thousands of once productive acres now lay abandoned. Close to ruin, the planters' only remunerative income came from their slaves. "Virginia was a slave breeding state and niggers were sold off jes' like stock," remembered one Georgia slave.[16] "In dem days so many families were broke up an' some went one way and der others went t'other way; and you nebber see them no more," recalled another. "Virginia was a regular slave market."[17]

In the odd instance, planters journeyed to Virginia to make their purchases but, by and large, slavetraders brought them to Georgia in "speculator droves." Englishman J. S. Buckingham was shown two auction houses in Georgia that dealt exclusively with Virginian slaves and watched families being broken up with "no more thought than separating a colt from its dam."[18] Somewhere amidst those auction houses and speculator droves was young Charity and while she may not have been victim to such brutality again, the threat of enforced separation would ever haunt her.

Matrimony triggered Charity's next separation, although the union was not her own. After one, maybe two, decades of relative stability on James A Wiggins's farm in Baldwin County, she was carried off again. When Master Wiggins gave his daughter Mary Emiline away in marriage in the fall of 1829, property and rings were exchanged. The groom Wiley Jones entered married life knowing that, along with a feather bed and fine saddle horse, a good breeding woman and a number of children were now his chattel.[19]

In addition to the dowry, Wiley Jones also received a parcel of land from the government of the United States after they removed the remnants of the Creek Nation from their ancestral lands along the Chattahoochee River and laid it off into lots: the skeleton frame of what would become the city of Columbus, in the county of Muscogee.[20] By means of a lottery, Wiley Jones secured in 1832 a twenty-acre block, ten miles out of town along the Stagecoach Road. As he and his wife suffered the bone-jarring, one hundred-mile journey west, he did so not in the egalitarian spirit of a frontiersman but as an aspiring aristocrat, certain he was planting more than cotton. A great civilization that would one day rival Greece or Rome was rising in the South and he would rise with it.

In the back of the wagon, perhaps walking in file behind it, were Charity Wiggins and the youngest of her brood. This moment has been celebrated by a local history of the city: the arrival in Columbus of "the slave, Charity Wiggins, who later had a number of children, among them the sightless negro Blind Tom."[21] However good taste did not permit any mention of the children who came with her, or the ones who were left behind. By thirty-one, Charity could easily have given birth to at least six children and some of these, plus the man she called her husband, were a world away in Baldwin County. Amongst Charity's descendants this knowledge still survives. "Charity Wiggins had another set of children," reported Blind Tom's great-grandniece, Emma Jefferson. "They were Mullins. There was Dora Mullins, Matilda Mullins and Weya Mullins. And my grandmother was Matilda's daughter."[22] In 1884, Charity would tell a lawyer the names and ages of all her living children and listed an additional four children who were born before 1832.[23]

Once in Columbus, Wiley Jones lost no time in pairing Charity up with Mingo, a field worker owned by a neighbor named Myles Greene.[24] Little is known of Mingo's early life. Born in 1796 in North Carolina,[25] his name suggests a Santa Dominican background, his mother perhaps one of the thousands of slaves brought by their masters to America from the island after a core of runaway slaves launched a bloody voodoo-fuelled revolt. Shortly after its founding, Greene brought Mingo to Columbus with him, eventually selling him—possibly years after he and Charity had started a family—to Wiley Jones.[26]

Charity greatly pleased her master, producing a swarm of children. The precise size of that swarm varies from one account to another. Wiley Jones's grandson, Walter D. Lamar, asserts that Blind Tom was Charity's twelfth child. A Professor of Medicine learned from Tom's second master's son that he was the fourteenth child of a father who had eighteen children.[27] A nameless letter found in the Georgia Archive claims that Tom was the sixteenth of nineteen children,[28] while a concert program states Tom was the last of twenty-one children. The list Charity herself gave her lawyer in 1884 places Tom as the ninth surviving child of twelve. In 1902, 100-year-old Charity was asked to name all her children. "She counted them slowly off on her fingers; but the aged mind was unable to recall all the names at the moment. Some of them died in slavery times she said."[29]

And some, if not left behind in Baldwin County, were sold off by Wiley Jones in Muscogee County when they were "just about grown." For it is an indisputable fact that of the dozen or more children Charity brought into the world, only two still lived with her in 1849, the year Tom was born. Dora, Matilda, Weya and the others seem to have been sold on: some to local families, others to the limits of an ever-expanding frontier. As any planter could tell you, there was more profit in slave trading than cotton and a few sales a year would nicely subsidize Jones's comfortable lifestyle and enable him to live the life of a Southern gentleman—or at least, the illusion of it.

IDLE SUPERIORITY

The industry of the frontiersman is legendary and English writer J.S. Buckingham—as he suffered the stagecoach journey from Macon to Columbus in 1842—noted the toils and privations of poor settler families as they worked to clear and cultivate the land. On arriving at his Columbus hotel, an unusual sight met him. Despite being all but empty, not a single room in the hotel was prepared and the entire building—barely a decade old—was in dire need of repair. He attributed the situation to the idle superiority of the gentlemanly master, life-long indolence of his wife and grinding indifference of his slaves.[30]

Perhaps a similar air of regal shiftlessness pervaded Wiley Jones's fine house. Although he owned somewhere between twelve and fifteen slaves,[31] eighteen years after acquiring his twenty-acre block, only five acres had been cleared—a paltry amount considering the labor force he had at his disposal.

Another fact suggests that a sense of injustice and powerlessness smoldered in his slaves quarters. On July 4th, 1844, Jones's mixed race house servant set fire to his house in revenge for being barred from the Fourth of July frolics and seeing a young man she was

A notice placed by Tom's master, Wiley Jones, announcing the sale of his house and slaves.

sweet on—or so she confessed after being whipped and imprisoned.[32] Whatever inspired her to strike the match, she clearly loathed her master.

Wiley Jones was a man well capable of cruelty. When nine of his servants went under the hammer in 1850,[33] the advertisement he ran in *The Columbus Times & Sentential* simply listed the skills of his "very likely and very valuable Georgia raised Negro slaves."[34] Unlike other auction notices that specified that their Negroes "will be sold in families," nothing indicated any intention to sell his slaves off in family units. To maximize his returns, each one was to be sold off separately. This same market principle was to be applied to Mingo, Charity, their two daughters and blind baby son.

Some in the city found the matter of breaking up slave families distasteful. True Southern Gentlemen did not—like money-grubbing Yankees—dabble in slavery for the "profit in it," they did not sell slaves to settle debts. They owned slaves because God had entrusted them with a paternal duty to care for a race of people whom "He made exempt from all moral restraints or moral requirement." The ethos was reinforced by Southern preachers who, while lambasting the abolitionist from the pulpit each Sunday, nevertheless recognized that a slave had a transcendental spirit and was entitled to, at least, the right to their own life and salvation.

Such calls to *noblesse oblige* fell on deaf ears—and not just those of Wiley Jones. It was a well-known secret that in 1858, a number of local businessmen made a killing in the illegal African slave trade, selling seven hundred and fifty men and women procured at $3 each for $600 a piece.[35] Columbus itself enjoyed the financial fruits of a buoyant slave trade. Demand was high, slave labor driving not only cotton but the city's steel mills and factories. As a boy, slave Rias Body often saw human chattel herded down Broad Street to the old slave mart. Prospective buyers, accompanied by doctors, would then feel, thump and sprint them to test their health. "A young or middle-aged Negro man well-trained in some trade often sold for $2000 to $4000 in gold," recalled Body. "Women and runty Negro men commanded a price from $600 up. A good breeding woman could sometimes sell for as high as $1200."[36]

Most of these slaves ended up on plantations and farms to the south or west. By the mid-nineteenth century, Georgia-born slaves could be found working in the newly acquired lands of Texas, Alabama and Louisiana and laying the tracks of a railroad network that would link the South. Such prospects struck "horror" into their hearts, reported J.S. Buckingham, for the "farther they go, the harder they are worked and the worse they are used."[37]

This was the future Charity and her family now faced. As devastating as their pending separation may have been, she could at least entertain hopes that someone half-decent might buy her husband and two young girls. But who—she must have agonized—would want to buy her blind baby son? His death seemed certain.

Every Inch a
Southern Gentleman

—————•—————

As the sun dropped below the horizon, the damp December chill clung to two figures impassively waiting by the side of Stagecoach Road, their eyes fixed to its western approach. Finally a buggy appeared. At its helm was General James Neil Bethune, one of Columbus's most respected citizens. He recognized the couple flagging him down as his neighbor's field hands, so pulled over, already suspecting the reason why.

Mingo and Charity told him what he—indeed the whole town—already knew. Wiley Jones was selling them to settle his debts and they feared that the auction block would destroy them. *But you, General Bethune*—they deferentially shuffled—*you could save us.* Before they had even finished, Bethune was shaking his head. He was not a planter but a lawyer and newspaperman, and with no cotton to pick had no need for field hands. He wished them good luck and continued on his way.

But a few days later, Bethune swung by Wiley Jones's place and purchased the entire family. His grandson later recalled: "When Grandpa drove into the yard with the five Negros, Grandma, who had not been told of Grandpa's intentions, threw up her hands and cried, 'James, how could you? You know we have more than I can take care of'."[1]

Mrs. Bethune may have been infuriated with her husband—but was she really that surprised? According to those who knew him best she would, by now, have grown used to his capricious whims. The question is, how did Mingo and Charity know that he was the man who would offer them the protection their master did not? Why did they think he would part with a few thousand dollars that he did not seem to have and acquire a slave family that he did not seem to need?

A CHAMPION OF FREEDOM

There was nothing half-hearted about James Neil Bethune, though no one could ever predict the direction of his passions. He once famously caused quite a stir in Columbus after the city council passed an ordinance restricting the time and place a farmer could sell his produce. In full view of the County Hall, he deliberately defied the act, baiting the powers that be to enforce it. They did. Bethune was arrested, thrown into a "loathsome prison" and convicted of the misdemeanor.

The old warhorse battled the charge all the way to the Georgia Supreme Court, arguing his case at every step. "It is not the size of the violation but the principle behind it," he insisted. "The question involves whether the citizen has any right to personal liberty; whether he has any rights at all, whether this is a free government or unlimited despotism."[2]

The citizens of Columbus followed every development, thanks to the vast coverage it received in *The Corner Stone*, a newspaper edited, owned and printed by one J.N. Bethune. So when the judges saw fit to overturn his conviction, it was front page news and Bethune returned from Macon in a blaze of glory. As he stepped off the train, drums pounded, cannons fired and crowds cheered. His unwavering courage was eulogized in impromptu speeches ("the most odious tyrannical ordinance ever attempted to be imposed upon a free people"), and was met with modest replies ("I have done only what I thought it was my duty to do"). Columbus's "champion of freedom" was then bundled into a fine carriage, a band of musicians leading his triumphant parade through the city.[3]

Everything about General Bethune pointed to a man of great principle and a maverick ruled as much by his heart as his head. "He was a man of ardent convictions and dauntless courage," remarked one commentator, "but was known as well for his generous impulses and tender sympathies, in spite of the rugged and severe manner and austerity with which he has always tried to cloak his real nature."[4]

Unlike Charity and Mingo's broken ancestry, Bethune's heritage could be traced back more than two centuries to John Bethune, the fifth Laird of Balfour on Scotland's Isle of Skye. Educated, landed and professional—a family of doctors, lawyers, church ministers and military officers—in service to the ruling MacDonald clan, the Bethunes enjoyed enormous prestige and privilege until Bethune's grandfather inherited an estate burdened with debt. The family was penniless.[5]

Like thousands of other impoverished gentlemen, Bethune's father —John McEacharn Bethune—migrated to the United States in the hope of restoring his family's lost fortune. He settled in Georgia and was appointed the state's Surveyor General, a high profile, though financially restricted, profession that put him in as much contact with the chiefs of the Indian Nations as the powerbrokers in Milledgeville. Despite their limited means, the Bethunes possessed something that no amount of money could buy: a cavalier pedigree (well, almost).

The South was forged by the spirit of the English Cavalier. When the puritanical Oliver Cromwell defeated King Charles in the English Civil War of 1651, a band of Royal Cavaliers fled to Virginia, eventually rising to become its most extravagant and opulent elite. It was fortuitous for John McEacharn Bethune that the Chief of the MacDonald clan had the good sense to form a political alliance with King Charles because, ten thousand miles and two hundred years down the track, this association was the basis to the family's claim that they were descended from Cavalier stock.

James was duly "reared as became his birth," studying law at the University of Georgia, a college famed for its narrow and autocratic regime and one that "did not fail to appear in the careers of Southern leaders."[6]

"He was every inch a Southern Gentleman," remembers one neighbor.[7] Indeed General Bethune (who acquired the almost obligatory moniker after the Indian Wars of 1828) upheld political positions that were more in keeping with the oligarchic interests of a planter, than of a lawyer and newspaperman struggling to get a slice of the American dream. Perhaps, on some level, Bethune did not want democratic initiatives like public education and women's suffrage diluting the power of his cavalier pedigree. He saw himself as a gentleman in the classical Greek sense of the word: one whose natural function was social and political participation. Treasurer of the City Council, founding member of the Lyceum and the Bank of Columbus, Bethune rubbed shoulders with heavyweights like Senator Walter Colquitt and Judge Henry L. Benning, yet he had no real stake in King Cotton and possessed only a fraction of their wealth.

In 1836, at the age of 33, Bethune married the daughter of a Columbus businessman, though in this too he bucked convention. His bride, Frances Gunby, was 31 years old—an old maid by the standards of the day—and a schoolteacher. Over the next fourteen years, she bore him seven children—three boys and four girls—and the farmhouse he named *Solitude* was transformed into a "lively" household with a strong musical flavor: each child either sang or played an instrument, or both. (Although, for fear of being branded a "sissy," the boys flatly refused to play the piano).

Solitude was also home to a number of slaves, though how many is unclear. There was a house servant named Maria and a driver named George but there must have been more: cooks, houseboys, farm workers, nurses to raise the children—although each child was not assigned a personal maid as was often the custom in wealthy families. Overall, the Bethunes' assets and income were modest—$4,000 according to the 1850 census[8]—one acquaintance described them as "very respectable people who had known more prosperous times—but they were poor then."[9]

Poor and respectable but fervent and eccentric. Even Bethune's colleagues were startled by his "forceful and original" ideas.[10] He had no time for party politics unless they were his own and in 1860, he ran for Congress on the Free Trade and Direct Taxation ticket. It was an issue that had rattled him for years. Ever since the 1823 sectional crisis over the Tariff of Abominations—during which cries for "secession" and "state rights" were often heard—Bethune had debated, pamphleteered, editorialized and campaigned to expose the injustices of a system that taxed a Southern man, not on the property he owned, but on the foreign goods he consumed. It was, in Bethune's words, the "systematic robbery of one class of citizens for their purpose of enriching the other and corrupting both."[11]

There was some economic basis to his outrage. Three-quarters of all American exports—cotton, rice, tobacco, flour, hemp—came from the South-western states while the vast majority of imports came through the North, arriving in the South at greatly inflated prices. Bethune's solution was not to industrialize the South—a proposition that, he believed, would "lure this blessed high civilization into vice, corruption and crime"—but to ban the Custom House. The North's refusal to do so was perceived as an act of aggression and from this point on, Bethune publicly called for Georgia's immediate secession from the Union: "It is in our interest to separate from the North and their interest to hold onto us. Why do we sacrifice our interest for theirs? They are the superior and we the inferior, and we are slaves."[12]

For a slave-owning man to declare himself the victim of slavery, the object of "despotism," "robbery" and "persecution" was a peculiarly Southern perception that baffled J.S. Buckingham. "The strangest contrast was often observable in the columns of the same paper," he remarked, "one page teeming with proof of the ultra-democratic or extreme republican views of the editor, and the other advocating the most uncontrolled despotism over the slave population, and deprecating any interference with the 'cherished institutions' and 'constitutional rights of the South.'"[13]

Here Buckingham identifies an intriguing contradiction that Bethune encapsulated *par excellence*. At its heart was the theological equivalent of a mixed metaphor. The "law of nature" governing the white race was free will, while the "law of nature" governing the black race was pre-determinism.

"What is slavery?" Bethune asked his readers. "It is a class of laborers controlled not by government, for like children, it is too large for government to manage. This class of laborers are incapable of taking care of themselves, so are controlled by individuals who are not only capable of taking care of them but interested in doing it."[14] Following this logic, unbridled libertarianism was a right God had bestowed on European people as sure as servitude was the rightful place of the African. In a curiously southern twist, buttoned down Calvinism and the Age of Enlightenment sat comfortably side by side, not only in the pages of the same newspaper, but in the mind of its editor.

THE SIN OF SLAVERY

When Mingo and Charity approached General Bethune in the dying months of 1849, a sectional crisis featuring the slogans "states rights" and "secession" was threatening to tear the Union apart. It was an issue that so enraged the "champion of freedom" that he would spearhead a campaign to sever all "entangling alliances" with the

North. "Southern rights on the auction block of political expediency were always being knocked down to the highest bidder," he railed at a meeting of the faithful, declaring his readiness to march up to the Mason Dixon line with his coffin on his back and demand his rights or die getting them.[15] Admittedly, there was more talk than walk but there was plenty of it, all focused around a single issue: slavery.

California's attempts to gain admission into the Union had destabilized the precarious balance between North and South and unleashed a torrent of vitriol and grandstanding. In the war of words leading up to the Compromise of 1850, southerners accused abolitionists of attempting to "incite the slaves to rebellion, bring about the massacre of the whites and the annihilation of their property."[16] Abolitionists hit back, damning all slaveholders as sinners who would burn in the hellfires of eternity, and accusing them of possessing less virtue than all the brothels in New York City.

To cast such slurs on men who prided themselves on their respectability was heady stuff. Yet the message was clear: if these good God-fearing men opposed prostitution, why did they refuse to condemn a system where women were bought and sold, with no legal rights as people, wives and mothers? Why did they participate in a morally depraved system that violated the sanctity of family life?[17]

Accusations like these would have stung Bethune. As a thinker, editor and southern patriot, he had spent long hours contemplating the abolitionist's charge and, through astute observation and the application of economic principle, could systematically rebuke each one. He did not deny the Africans had moral rights. As his 1855 editorial argued, *slavery* was their right:

> Set the stakes down around any part of the earth containing four million of the laboring class and compare them with the four million southern slaves. A laborer may receive $40 per year but how does this compare to wholesome food, comfortable clothing, lodging, medical attention and nursing? The wages of other laborers stop when they get sick.
>
> Talk about the sin of holding them in bondage! Better far consider the sin of discarding them and thrusting them out from their present condition of ease, comfort, happiness and prosperity into conditions of misery and destitution. . . . They are part of our people; they have been raised up with us; they have the right to their present condition and we have no right to deprive them of it.

*General James Neil Bethune,
who purchased Blind Tom and
his family out of pity.*

Keeping the supply of black labor tight keeps prices high, as high as the attachment between the slave and his master. [Masters] do not wish to break up the family ties and often make large sacrifices rather than do it. It is to this feeling mainly that the slave is indebted for his condition.[18]

Here the aristocrat in Bethune reigns resplendent. There is no talk of slave-trading, profits or even chattel. They are not "our property" but "our people:" an integral and much loved part of the South. The classic virtues of a Southern Gentlemen can be ticked off one by one: tolerant, dignified, moderate, well-reasoned, broad-minded, non-puritan and courteous. A man who embodied the spirit of *noblesse oblige*: the obligation of the strong to sustain the weak.

Of course reality was mocking this ideal. The brutal truth was that Masters were breaking up slave families—and right in his backyard. So when Mingo and Charity flagged down his buggy that winter evening and confronted him with the human cost of that mockery, Bethune was deeply troubled by their plight. In the ensuing days, as he sat alone in his well-stocked library at *Solitude*, he teased out the reasons why.

What made Mingo and Charity's case different from the thousands of other sales in Columbus every year was the presence of a

blind baby. A runt. A useless burden. Wiley Jones had wanted him
dead and and that is exactly what he would be after the auction. For
all his talk of paternalism, Bethune implicitly knew that the institution of slavery offered protection only to the productive and nothing
to those who were, in essence, the weakest of the weak. Only the spirit of *noblesse oblige* could save the blind child and, if General Bethune
was worthy of his blood, it was his moral duty to protect him.

General Bethune's recollection of purchasing Mingo and Charity's
family is consistent with his grandson's version of the story with the
exception of one, rather unpalatable, detail: the auction.

Far from being acquired in a private sale a few days after the
roadside appeal, as his grandson suggested, Charity and Mingo had
to endure another month of anguish and uncertainty. One January
morning, they awoke (assuming they had slept at all) certain that this
day would be their last together. Like prisoners awaiting their execution, they lined up outside C.H. Harrison's slave mart in Broad Street
and smiled abundantly as prospective buyers examined them, presenting themselves as strong, healthy and fast workers. By now,
Charity was too old to convince anyone she was a good breeder but
could vouch that her daughters were fine stock. It was only the blind
baby who, even as a freebie, lacked any appeal. The child was doomed
until General Bethune slipped into back rows of the slave mart.

The General exuded an aura that gave Mingo and Charity cause
for hope. Unlike the shiftless Wiley Jones who was only out for himself, Bethune seemed active and industrious, dedicated to Georgia's
greater good. Perhaps they heard he was a fair, if imposing, master.
Perhaps too, they knew of his vocal opposition to the re-opening of
the African slave trade, a practice he described as "tainted with guilt
and with crime."[19] He was a man of high principle: a thinker and
writer who exposed hypocrisy and injustice.

Why else would he have turned up at C.H. Harrison's slave mart
on that fateful day: the auction block—that great abolitionist symbol of Southern barbarity—standing irrefutably before him? This,
perhaps, was his chance to right the wrongs of slavery. "I attended
the sale and purchased the whole family," he later reported. "Tom at
that stage was eight months old and simply regarded as an encumbrance."[20] It was a selfless act of redemption—though little did he
realize it would prove the best deal of his life.

No Ordinary Child

ON A MOONLESS FROSTY NIGHT, IF NOT FOR THE SOFT EMBERS IN THE fireplace, the cabin would be inky black. If not for the holy terror babbling, twisting, and turning, the old hay mattress rustling like the northern wind, all would be at peace and Charity would be able to sleep. Out in the darkness, a hoot owl's unearthly cry hovered in the air. The three-year-old child hooted back with such precision that the harbinger of misfortune seemed like it was there in the room. Somewhere, a dog barked and the child lumbered out of bed, yapping like a hound, and pulled towards the door, determined to join the canine crew.

Apart from Tom, there wasn't a slave child in the two counties who dared wander the night for fear that the bogeymen Raw Head and Bloody Bones would get them. "Folkses done told us Raw Head and Bloody Bones lived in the woods and git little children and eat 'em up effen they got out in the woods atter dark!" remembered one slave.[1] It may have been only an old cow's skull draped in a hide, but it was the stuff of nightmares. This time-honored tactic to keep the little ones close to home was rendered useless on the blind child who had no fear—or no sense.

So when the squawks of an indignant chicken wrenched Charity from sleep, she sat bolt upright knowing that Tom was in the chicken coop, breaking eggs and whipping up the fowl. By the time she tracked him down, he would be out under the stars, wheeling around with a monotonous hum, hands rubbed together in satisfaction, convulsions of laughter and occasional snatches of conversation spouting from his mouth.[2] After stern words from the Mistress, Charity took to staying up one half of the night, her husband the other to keep watch on Tom.

Sleep deprivation and a burdened mind is a pernicious brew, and as Charity endured these endless nights, she must have brooded on the riddle that was her son. Somewhere along these trains of thought, the word "conjure" surely crossed her troubled mind. "De cunjur folks takes weeds and yarbs and fixes you so you can't sleep and can't eat and bark like a dog," said one Georgia slave about the plantation's medicine men and their magical powers.[3] Is that what had happened to Tom? Had someone fixed him with an evil curse? Or—as the Old Grannies believed—were the misty grey-blue cataracts that covered his eyes a sign of "second sight"? Could he see lost souls wandering the earth? Is that who he was talking to in the depth of the night?

But, as Charity once acknowledged, Tom had not always been like this. Apart from his blindness he was just like other babies—at first anyway. A few months after arriving at the Bethune farm things started to change. Impassive to her and the children around him, noises began to exert a controlling influence over him. Even by the age of three, he could scarcely walk and barely express his needs. Nothing existed for him beyond his everlasting thirst for sound.

On a small farm like *Solitude*, the older siblings usually helped their parents take care of the young. And though they were no more than ten, Tom's two sisters were shouldered with the responsibility of keeping him—and the two babies that followed him—confined to the yard. But at the twittering trill of a Pine Warbler, Tom would lope off into the thickly wooded forests that surrounded much of the farm. The frantic hollers for the missing child raised such alarm that Bethune's eldest son, Young Master John, once joined the search, combing the forest with his flute. Eventually its sweet sounds lured Tom home, though the incident put an end to any hope that the girls could keep tabs on the erratic child.

If Charity locked Tom in the cabin, chaos would ensue. Chairs would be dragged over the floor, plates rattled, pots and iron skillets banged against wooden bowls, pewter forks and tin cups with such deafening ferocity it would nigh on wake the dead. He would then turn on the younger children, biting and pinching them, laughing when they howled in pain. One time he nearly choked his younger brother to death and burnt his infant sister so badly that they feared for her life. She survived, but for the rest of her days sported a bald patch on the side of her head.[4]

Best for everyone was to keep Tom out of sight, away from the other slaves who held him in terror, far from his master who had not yet fully realized that the blind child was positively crack-brained. Safest place for him was a place they had often kept him: a high-sided wooden box.

THE WOODEN BOX

Historical diagnoses are an imperfect science at the best of times and the anecdotal evidence in Blind Tom's case presents challenges and contradictions. After assessing the sum total of evidence, one school of thought would point, with some confidence, to Early Infantile Autism. His echolalia, heightened sensory discrimination and ability to recall seemingly meaningless details alerting them to the possibility of an autistic spectral disorder, his striking lack of common sense clinching the verdict.

While other children lived in terror of Raw Head and Bloody Bones, the nightmarish legend failed to impress Tom one way or another. He had no concept of ghosts and haunts. In fact, he probably had little concept of anything but lived in a protracted infancy, and perceived not the whole object but its separate elements—a mass of objective sensory information that was never processed, filtered, censored or simplified into meaning. This raw sensory data was trapped in his mind and never entered the realm of language where it would have been imbued with individual and cultural reference points.[5] That is why his mother complained that he "did not have the knowledge of other children" and "could not be taught anything"; that was why he was unable to express his needs in words, those about him interpreting his whines and tugs as best they could. But how does it account for the "clear" and "distinct" voices that poured from his mouth? "Whatever words were addressed to him, he simply repeated in the tones in which they had been uttered; and would repeat conversations he had heard—sometimes for hours at a time."

The answer lies in the extraordinary sensory powers available to him. Tom's blindness had triggered a re-wiring of his brain. Functions that would ordinarily support the eye, were now redirected to the ear and magnified his sensitivity to sound. Coupled with this was a memory that was founded, not on words, but sensory information, aural pictures and sounds. If Tom's mind never filtered out this auditory data to create coherency and meaning, at least the detail was readily available to him, an astonishing array of it, and recalling the words and tonal shades of a conversation fifteen minutes in length was only the tip of a most remarkable iceberg.

The results were mind-boggling. Tom could sense the direction, humidity, pressure and rustle of the softest wind or detect the soundwaves of a coffee grinder as it bounced off a tin shed or rasped unimpeded out over the fields. In other words, he could tap into an acoustic landscape alive with vibration and recall it with sparkling precision.

Complicating this very persuasive diagnosis is the fact of Tom's blindness. Experts who work with the blind are quick to point out that children who are blind from birth and show no other brain dysfunction run a high risk of developmental retardation. Unable to perceive facial expressions and non-verbal cues, they need to feel out their world, and if they cannot, significant numbers retreat into themselves. The symptoms exhibited by this pathology—impaired social interaction, impaired communication, repetitive behavior, sleeping disorders, delayed language development, low frustration levels, fear and anxiety, hypersensitivity, echolalia and a remarkably good memory—are strikingly similar to autism. However, it is not Early Infantile Autism and the pathway to it is very different.[6]

I spoke to one expert who has worked closely with blind musical prodigies and he suspected that Tom's condition arose because he passed much of his day confined to a wooden box. Infants instinctively imitate the people around them and this key developmental building block was largely denied to the infant Tom. Trapped between the rough wooden slats, unable to interact with his siblings, he withdrew from the fabric of life and retreated into himself, imitating the only stimuli available to him: sound—the very sense that his remapped brain now fully supported. Lending weight to this interpretation is the case study of a non-autistic, sighted, musical savant who was kept in physical and social isolation from the day she was born. Of the scores of studies of musical savants conducted over the past half century, this is the one most similar to Tom.

Born one hundred years after Tom, "Harriet" was the sixth child in a musical Boston family. For the first two years of her life, she was confined to a crib placed directly against the grand piano. Virtually ignored, Harriet's main contact with the outside world was mediated through music and she would bang her head against her crib until she could hear it. By seven months she could hum, with perfect pitch, tempo and phrasing, *Caro Nome* from Verdi's *Rigoletto*.

At the age of two, her mother fell ill and a nurse was hired to take care of her. For the first time, Harriet was allowed to walk around and play with other children. Impossible to control, she destroyed all she could lay her hands on, terrorizing and eventually killing two of the family cats, delighted as they screeched in pain. She was prone to escape, sneaking out of the house, invariably heading for some nearby mud flats to listen to the ooze suck at her feet.[7]

The parallels are compelling: a world devoid of human contact yet filled with sound; stereotypic repetitive behavior; an inability to respond in a socially appropriate manner; and the niggling possibility that, with early intervention, these symptoms would never have developed in the first place. This last point lies at the heart of the diagnostic debate. Was Blind Tom born with a condition that gave him privileged access to lower levels of sensory information or was his developmental retardation and remarkable skill induced by blindness and social isolation? Although there is no decisive answer, the consensus of opinion leans towards the autism diagnosis but now and again, anecdotal evidence arises that flies in the face of it, and the niggling doubt starts to itch and one begins to think, well, maybe it was induced, maybe it was all down to that wooden box.

Either way, both diagnoses go only part of the way to explain the phenomenon of Blind Tom. Even in this age of celebrity savants, no other savant has attained the level of fame Tom achieved during his lifetime. Certainly, many have risen to prominence but many more have met fates similar to Harriet's. A pianist of great passion and scope, she spent twenty-five years of her life working the kitchen of a Boston hospital preparing salads, all of them arranged exactly the same—an indication that a host of other influences shaped Tom's life as he banged his head against the wooden box.

CLEAR ACROSS THE FIELDS

Compared to the northern states, which positively buzzed with the hum of industry, the South was very, very quiet. "Society seems to be asleep, man to be idle" wrote one man of life south of the

Mason Dixon[8]—referring to the white planter, of course. Swelling and fading into the pastoral quietude, marking the progression of the day, the cycle of the year, came sounds so intrinsically linked to the region that white folk unconsciously lumped them in with nature: the strains of slave labor, hand tool and song.

From first light, when the conch's bellow stirred the slaves to work ("That shell could be heard for five miles"[9]) to bedtime, when the Nurse sang a deep soulful lullaby to her white charge, still too young to understand the sorrow behind her words ("Black sheep, black sheep, where you left yo' lammy?"[10]); to wash day when women with battling sticks pounded out a rousing song; to market day when the cart-driver, with free-form profanity, hollered and cursed the oxen for plunging into the creek instead of crossing the bridge ("it was enough to make a preacher lose his best religion"[11]).

Harvest time was marked by the distant song of field hands picking cotton late into the night; winter nights by the women's laments set to the whir and clack of the spinning wheel and loom ("I can hear dem spinnin wheels now, turnin' roun' an' sayin' hum-m-m-m, hum-m-m-m"[12]). Death, by the moan-studded hymns of a slave funeral procession wheeling its way down the burial grounds.[13] Pure abandoned eccentricity, by a fruit vendor in downtown Columbus declaring his produce: *Dew-beh-ree, dew-beh-ree, dew-beeeeeeeeeeeeh-ree.*[14] Quintessential Southern glamour by the paddleboats pulling out of the docks, the moment made perfect by the harmonies of the roustabouts on the lower decks.[15]

White folks were confounded. How was it possible—they beseeched their servants—to join in a song they had never heard before and sing it like they had known it all their lives? Without waiting for an answer, they concluded that their servants were "natural" musicians and their music "artless" and "unscientific," as instinctual as the whistle of the whip-poor-will or the cheeky fanfare of the white-eye vireo.

Organic, spontaneous, and communal the slave's music may have been—"natural" it was not. For centuries, African culture exalted verbal improvisation and the spoken arts. The songs of the slaves—with their overlapping call and response and complex rhythms that were anchored in movement and dance—were expressions of an ancient tradition that had at its heart a common musical language: a vast repository of lyrics and tunes that could be mixed and matched and improvised upon so that old songs were constantly re-created anew.[16]

A selection of Plantation Melodies *composed by Blind Tom and released as sheet music in 1881.*

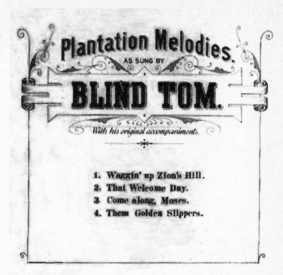

In the void of his blank box, Tom was shaped by the sounds of the South. He breathed it in like the air, the convergence of hand tool and song marking his entry point into the world of music. A concert program from 1868 contains a biographical note—a comprehensive, close-up portrait of the turbulent child with only a few allusions to the frustration of his parents—that comes close to acknowledging how these farmyard sounds affected Tom, but fails to connect the dots. "His mother usually did the churning," it reports. "He would whine and tug at her, until she would stand him on a stool and permit him to go to work and was perhaps the only person who ever sought butter churning as a source of pleasure."[17]

Missing from this account is the song that inevitably accompanied the plunging dasher and viscous squelch of buttermilk in motion. One slave's childhood memory of butter churning was firmly rooted in its hypnotic rhythm. "De fust work I done wuz churnin' an' I loved ter do 'hit kase I loved milk and butter so good. I'd dance an' dance 'round dat old churn, churnin' and churnin' 'till de butter wuz come."[18] Chances are, Charity and her strangely gifted son were doing precisely the same.

Dancing brought psychic relief to many a slave's life. The Saturday night breakdowns, for many, made the relentless toil of the week bearable, and slaves were known to walk up to fifteen miles to attend these weekly frolics or one of the cornshuckings, log-rollings, quiltings and festive celebrations that dotted each year. At some point, the sound of the fiddle, trumpet and banjo must have reached Tom's ears. "De Sat'day nigh dance wuz jist de finest ting we wanted in dem days," remembers a woman of Tom's age. "My brother was de captain of de quill band an' dey sure could make you shout an' dance til you wuz nigh 'bout exhausted."[19] Quills—panpipes fashioned out of reeds—were just one of the plantation band's homemade instruments. Fiddles were carved from gourds, long wooden handles served as necks, strings were made from cat gut while horse tails were stretched into bows.[20] Add to this bones, tin buckets and broom straws and the band was complete.

As an adult, Tom was seen to play mostly European music, as if he was untouched by his African roots and slave upbringing, but somewhere along the line these home-made instruments came up on his radar. Tom's great niece, Julia Lee, remembers visiting their "peculiar" uncle who delighted all seven children by playing on a rub board and old tin pan that was cut out in sections and strung with three or four knuckles. "He used this in his concert," along with other "odd instruments"[21]—a feature that newspaper reviews failed to mention and a pattern that was consistent with other African-American elements of his shows.

Critics and reviewers either underplayed or overlooked Tom's plantation melodies, deeming them inconsequential. "As to Tom's improvisations, there was no musical merit whatever; they were generally mere echoes of plantation songs," wrote one man of ten-year-old Tom's musical efforts while another lumped his "wild, barbaric racial laments" in with his imitations of nature.[22] But amongst black members of his audience, such moments were heartily appreciated. His piano imitations of "the sweet sounds of the guitar and the janglier banjo" were said to have "delighted the 'gallery gods' beyond measure and they were loud in their applause"—an indication of Tom's grounding in the music of the slaves.[23]

However there was one sound, familiar to most slaves, that Tom did not necessarily enjoy. In cabin and woods, slaves would gather at night, their voices lifted in ecstatic worship, shouting praises unto the Lord.

SILENCE IN CHURCH

A decade after the Great Revival of the 1830's and 40's that saw thousands of black and white folk flock to tent meetings to loudly and ecstatically embrace salvation, relative calm was restored or—as in the case of the Southern Methodist Church—imposed. The frantic scenes that were instrumental in establishing the Wesleyan church were quietly forgotten and replaced with more respectable services. It was not by shrieks and hysterics that one deepened one's faith now, but by reason and reflection. And so congregations gathered in hushed reverence and passively listened to the intellectual discourse of their preacher.

It was a development that even General Bethune found unwelcome. He wrote an editorial criticizing the new preacher for replacing the spirituals—a much-loved feature of services that, while segregated, saw black and white worship together—with the subdued drone of the hymnals. "It did not sound to us like the full rich notes of Sister Shorter, nor the trumpet tones of Brother Jepson—and we think it would be a long time before the old sisters of the Church would get happy enough to shout. Singing, particularly when it is done with the spirit, is one of the most profitable portions of public worship, but we never felt it more fully than on last Sunday."[24]

For the slaves, the hymns only reminded them of what they had lost. They were forbidden to "shout" at formal church services, so, far from the supervising eyes of masters and patrollers, secretly staged their own. "A large pot was always placed against the cabin door to keep the sound of the voices from escaping," Columbus-born Mary Gladdy told an interviewer in the 1920s. "Then the slaves would sing and pray and relate experiences all night long. Their great soul-hungering desire was freedom [and] every person attending felt the spirit of the Lord touch them just before day."[25]

That intensity of emotion struck anyone who witnessed such meetings. "The mutterings, the ejaculations, grew louder, more dramatic until suddenly I felt the creative thrill dart through the people like an electric vibration," observed a white Virginian woman. "Then, up from the depth of some sinner's remorse and imploring came a pitiful little plea, a real moan, sobbed in musical cadence."[26] "A rhythm was born almost without reference to the words that were being spoken by the preacher," reported another. "It seemed to take shape almost visibly, and grow. I was gripped with the feeling of a mass-intelligence, a self-conscious entity, gradually informing the crowd and taking possession of every mind there, including my own."[27]

Like the constricting pull of a wave that rises, collapses and releases its energy, worshippers would break into chorus upon chorus of "utterly indescribable, almost unearthly" spirituals studded with shouts, sobs, cries and pained, pleasured wails. If Blind Tom was enraptured with the squawk of a chicken, then this was manna from heaven. The question is, was he even there?

While spiritually empowering, prayer meetings were highly risky affairs. Patrollers scoured the district each night for unsupervised gatherings, convinced that an insurrection was brewing. Secrecy was vital and children could only attend under the strictest conditions. "Dem chillun couldn' talk till dey got home" remembered one former slave. "If you talk you get a whippin' from de ole lady nex' night. Ole Granny whip 'em."[28] The punishment meted out by the elder slave woman was harsh, but it was not without cause. Masters were known to grill slave children, hoping to discover what was really going on in the quarters and more than once, childish prattle resulted in a whipping for an adult engaged in a forbidden activity.[29]

Blind Tom's concert program reports, with certain satisfaction, that the rod was not spared on Charity's children. The task of teaching the intricate, subtle and often contradictory rules of the plantation hierarchy fell largely upon the mother's shoulders and the switch was a foolproof way of teaching those rules and strengthening the memory.[30] If Charity attempted to beat these lessons into Tom, her efforts ended in abject failure. Even if she never laid a finger on him, it was by now abundantly clear "he did not have the knowledge of other children"—he could not be taught. As wild as his antics may have been, his play differed from that of her other children. There was no role playing or pretense, no distinction between "I" and "you," let alone "us" and "them." Rather than force Tom to conform to the rules, his people would have to adapt to him. If he was the one most likely to recount to the master's children "their great soul-hungering desire" for freedom in its full unedited glory, then nothing but the most flattering references to Master's family could be uttered in his earshot. The implications were serious: if he was heard parroting the potentially seditious words of the black preacher then the consequences would be catastrophic for everyone. The upshot for the child who posed such a threat must have been even more isolation.

TEARS OF ECSTASY

As the Bethunes often reminded the public, they were a musical family: Francis Bethune and her children were all either "instrumentalists, vocalists or both."[31] Though Charity battled to keep young Thomas away from her master's family, the pull of their music was simply too great.

The pure resonant vibrations of a flute inspired fifteen-month-old Tom to drag and crawl his way out of the yard, through the woods to a shady stream where seventeen-year-old John Bethune wiled away a summer's afternoon. Like a serpent hypnotized by its charmer, Tom rose to his feet and, balancing himself on John's knees, swayed to the flute's hypnotic modulations.[32] It was a moment John later described as Tom's entry into "unwritten history." In fact it was the converse—the legend was now being written.

Also assigned to posterity was the moment five-year-old James Bethune "climbed into Tom's box to play with him and began singing a popular song of the day. He was dumbfounded to hear Tom sing it after him, with tune and words complete and accurate."[33]

Tom's first contact with the Bethune daughters—Mary, Cherry, Susan and Fanny—cemented his gifts in the consciousness of the family. Unlike their brothers, the girls lived a largely interior life, excluded from both the domestic arts (considered the realm of servants) and academia (considered the realm of men). Music offered one of the few creative outlets available to them, and any break to their demure routines took on an enormous significance:

> The daughters of Mr. Bethune were singing a popular air when upon closing they thought they heard a voice, at a short distance repeating the chorus. For mere amusement they repeated one stanza of the song. Again the strange voice echoed the words, but this time not in soprano but alto. Upon looking out the window Blind Tom, then a youth scarcely three years of age, was seen lying flat upon his back, his sightless orbs bathed in a flood of tears—tears, not of grief, but of ecstasy. The harmony of the moment had touched a corresponding chord in his soul, and he could not restrain the tears. Instantly was the poor black boy brought into the mansion, and song after song proved only one thing, and that was the budding of his imitative genius.[34]

Imagine how flattered the Bethune girls felt to elicit "tears of ecstasy" from the child. Here was something that reached beyond social pleasantries and dreams of matrimony—here was passion.

After that, the quartet became a quintet. Whenever the girls struck up a melody, as they did on the veranda most summer nights, Tom was never too far away, chiming in with his "strong, soft, and melodious" voice and astonishing them all when he broke into a "fine seconds." "He don't have to learn any tunes," they enthused to their father, "he knows them all; for as soon as we begin to sing, he sings right along with us,"[35] an indication of the extent to which the toddler had absorbed the music of the antebellum world: a vast repository of black work songs, white ballads and minstrel hits or sometimes a seamless amalgam of all three.

Charity welcomed the Bethune girls' interest in her son. Generous as General Bethune had been, Tom's survival still hinged on his continued benevolence. His newfound favor with the young mistresses now meant that he had a certain currency: a value, meager though it was, that lifted him above the status of runt to plaything. As Charity knew from her dancing days with Valeria Jones, gifts and privileges would inevitably follow. It was a small but welcome comfort, though never did she imagine that, one day, Tom would see himself as more a member of the Bethune family than his own.

- 4 -

Unwritten Legend

———◆———

IN 1853, THE BETHUNES PURCHASED A PIANO AND, FROM THE MOMENT it first sounded, Tom was drawn to the Big House. The tone of the hammers striking the strings had a "peculiar and most remarkable effect on him," recalled one of the Bethune lads. "At first he stood spellbound, then his eyes began to roll, his fingers to twitch and his body to sway back and forth when suddenly he convulsed with emotion and the contortions of his body was something painful to behold." The introduction was not complete before he was permitted to touch and smell each key—his nose as important as his fingers in discerning this musical elephant.[1] And then he was removed from the room and his re-entry blocked. Barred from the house, he took up unofficial residency either outside the parlor room window or directly under the piano beneath the house.

But the levee could not hold back the flood. The moment the music stopped, Tom's bid to get the piano was relentless. He was forever stealing inside, determined that these moments of harmonious rapture would never end.[2] But the "little nuisance" was not welcome. The Bethune girls objected most strongly to his presence. "It was not exactly proper, according to high Southern ideas, for a half-naked picaninny to come uninvited into the mansion" and they were concerned it would cause talk.[3] Somehow Charity and Mingo had to drive home the message that the Master's house was strictly off limits. All they could do was confine him to the box and sit up half the night, taking turns to watch him.

But the four-year-old's determination outstripped them all. The first few unwelcomed visits produced a cacophony as Tom banged away at the keys with his fists, forearms and elbows—anything that would make a sound. Slipping in and out of the discord, an occasional three note refrain may have been heard, or a wild approximation of a melody's shifts and turns. But, with surprising speed, his efforts became more refined until one day, when the family was at dinner, Tom crawled into the parlor and began to play a simple melody that one of the girls had been practicing earlier that day. No one paid much attention, everyone assuming it was a member of the family. They were naturally astonished when they discovered it was Charity's blind son at the piano, although this did not stop them from unceremoniously booting him from the room.[4]

This version of events—relayed by Charity—is largely consistent with the story journalist Henry Watterson heard, admittedly second hand but, significantly, before the Blind Tom publicity machine kicked in. The family were out of the room when they heard the piano tinkle, "they ran back and to their amazement, saw the chubby little black monkey on the stool, banging away for dear life, and yet not without sequence and rhythm, trying to repeat what they had just been playing and singing."[5]

Nine years on, however, this story was almost unrecognizable. Tom's lust for the piano was matched by his management's urge to mythologize a single watershed moment: the star-spangled moment the prodigy was born! The widely read 1862 *Atlantic Monthly* article describes a four-year-old with almost superhuman powers. One summer night, it avows, his master's family was awoken by the sound of music in the drawing room:

> . . . not only the simple airs, but the most difficult exercises usually played by his daughters, were repeated again and again, the touch of the musician being timid, but singularly true and delicate. Going down, they found Tom, who had been left asleep in the hall, seated at the piano in an ecstasy of delight, breaking out at the end of each successful fugue into shouts of laughter, kicking his heels and clapping his hands. This was the first time he had touched the piano.

With stroke of a pen, Tom's clumsy stab at sequence and rhythm becomes a triumphant fugue played with delicacy and truth, a distortion that subsequent versions of the story were loath to correct. The

1865 concert program insists that although Tom's hands were "not yet sufficiently developed to cover an octave" he repeated a difficult aria "even to the perception of a fault."[6] In 1868, the concert program was revised and the discovery story was calibrated with the *Atlantic Monthly's* version of events plus a small concession to the truth: "his performance, though necessarily very imperfect, was marvelously strange; this was his first known effort at a tune [and] he played with both hands, and used the black as well as the white keys."

Putting aside the "first known effort" claim, Tom's midnight visit may very well have taken place. Yet perhaps the watershed it marked was not Tom's discovery of the piano, but General Bethune's discovery of Tom. Buried away in his Columbus office, his mind burdened with sectional politics, he barely registered his children's incomprehensible reports about the "strange picaninny." But now, with the child and the piano before him, the pieces fell into place. The realization dawned like a rose-petal sun bursting over the horizon: the "useless encumbrance" he had purchased out of pity had an extraordinary musical gift.

This Herculean moment became the written legend's spectacular Act I finale and was repeated so often that anything less seemed disappointing. The mid-western novelist Willa Cather captured the legend in her 1918 novel *My Ántonia*, with a character named Blind Samson d'Arnault who was almost certainly based on Blind Tom:

> When he was six-years-old he began to run away from home, always taking the same direction. He felt his way through the lilacs, along the boxwood hedge, up to the south wing of the Big House, where Miss Nellie d'Arnault practiced the piano every morning. This angered his mother more than anything else he could have done; she was so ashamed of his ugliness that she couldn't bear to have white folks see him. Whenever she caught him slipping away from the cabin, she whipped him unmercifully, and told him what dreadful things old Mr. d'Arnault would do to him if he ever found him near the Big House.
>
> But the next time Samson had a chance, he ran away again. . . . Through the dark he found his way to the Thing, to its mouth. He touched it softly, and it answered softly, kindly. He shivered and stood still. Then he began to feel it all over, ran his finger-tips along the slippery sides, embraced the carved legs, tried to get some conception of its shape and size, of the space it occupied in primeval

night. It was cold and hard, and like nothing else in his black universe. He went back to its mouth, began at one end of the keyboard and felt his way down into the mellow thunder, as far as he could go. He seemed to know that it must be done with the fingers, not with the fists or the feet.

He approached this highly artificial instrument through a mere instinct, and coupled himself to it, as if he knew it was to piece him out and make a whole creature of him. After he had tried over all the sounds, he began to finger out passages from things Miss Nellie had been practicing, passages that were already his, that lay under the bone of his pinched, conical little skull, definite as animal desires.

This eroticized re-telling of the "discovery" perpetuates some useful myths: the primitive African, the "unmerciful" and neglectful mother, who beats her senseless son because she is so "ashamed of his ugliness." It is a scenario that begs for the intervention of a cultivated and appreciative benefactor to rescue Tom and nurture his strange gifts.

Indeed, the next step in Tom's legend could not have happened without the autocrat's blessing: the four-year-old was promptly removed from his family's quarters and lodged in the Bethune house. The General's motivations were both logical and charitable to him. "I suggested to my family that since he had a capacity for music and it would amuse him and them, to let him have free access to the instrument." "The child is music crazy, poor little thing," his son remembers him saying, "Let it enjoy itself. Perhaps it may learn to play one day and make its life bearable." His daughters could protest all they liked, General Bethune was determined to "cultivate the germs he had seen" and see what they would bring forth.[7] The dejected bundle of rags, once banned from stepping any further than the scullery, now had the run of the house—the parlor walls stained with a trail of his muddy fingerprints that led all the way to the piano, where he would sit for hours and play.[8]

EIGHTH WONDER OF THE PLANTATION

As long as there were still Indians around it was hard for high-minded Georgians to convince themselves they were anywhere else but a frontier, observed one young man.[9] But Columbus's finest families worked hard at maintaining the illusion of civility until the tedium began to grate. So when something unusual happened—something that confounded the social order—it stirred up a monumental to-do and soon the Bethune homestead was besieged with visitors eager to witness the "eighth wonder of the plantation." Two such visitors were Mr. "C Sharp" (the name he gave to the *Atlanta Constitution)* and his new wife "Miss Fannie" who was a friend of the Bethune girls and familiar face in the house. The couple had recently returned from their honeymoon and opened their visit with a duet on the piano and flute:

> At the first sound of the music, Tom came rushing into the parlor in a single garment, so common amongst the "little niggers" in the south and while the music was going, he fell down upon the floor, rolled over, turned somersaults, clapped his hands and groaned and went through diverse motions as if really in pain from the pleasure the music gave him.
>
> As the last note was played, he sprang up, rushed to my wife and, pushing at her, cried out eagerly: "Miss Fannie, please git away; I wants to play dat tune!" And jumping on the piano stool, he played it off perfectly, although I know he had never heard it until that moment, for it had only been recently published and had not yet come south.[10]

Tom's new found status as the "family pet" meant more than unlimited access to the piano, a fine feather pillow and good food. An entire world opened up. Over dinner one night, Bethune—with great gusto and scientific rigor—hypothesized that, since Tom had as much sense as a horse or dog, he could be taught to associate actions with words, as long as one used precisely the same term to express the same idea. He thereupon arose from the table and approached Tom, ordering him to "sit down," at the same time physically sitting him down on the floor. Next, he told him to "get up," lifting Tom to his feet. The results were immediate, the motion forever linked to the instruction. After that, everybody began to teach him something. Present him with an object and tell him its name, he would feel it, smell it, pronounce its name and never forget it.

Tom flourished as he began to hear, smell, feel and proclaim his world. The tactile stimulation his slave parents were unable to offer him was now replaced with the attentions of seven excitable children. His vocabulary blossomed and the child who could barely express his own needs, now began to exhibit a flair for language, sometimes asking questions in poetic but highly idiosyncratic ways—

"Did you ever drink Italian water sweetened with stars?"[11]

Just how well Tom understood his world continued to surprise the Bethunes. "His power of judging the lapse of time was as remarkable as his power of remembering and imitating sounds," the Bethunes noted with measured excitement. On the hour, every hour, he could be found in front of the grandfather clock and as soon as the strike had passed, he would set up a cry and leave.[12]

But Tom was not in the house to keep time. According to an 1895 *Washington Post* article, Bethune personally oversaw this musical education, purchasing a piano especially for the boy and installing it in his Columbus office. "Every morning Charity would dress Tom up and bundle him in his master's carryall and every day the little fellow would play the piano. General Bethune would hire wandering musicians to come and play for Tom and the prodigy would go into spasms of delight and would repeat everything that he heard."[13]

A touching story yet ultimately overstated. The author of the article is playing politics as by 1895 the family had every good reason to exaggerate the paternal care Bethune showered on his slave. Twenty years earlier, however, he was happy to credit his children with kick-starting Tom's formal musical education. It was Bethune's eldest son John who oversaw his lessons with musicians in the town: members of the Columbus Amateur Orchestra perhaps, or the black-faced performers from Campbell's Ethiopian Minstrels who toured Columbus at least once a year.[14]

Eldest daughter Mary ("one of the gentler, sweeter members of a somewhat turbulent family") devoted herself to teaching Tom all she knew on the piano (which, by some accounts, was not much), as did the girls' music teacher Professor George W. Chase.[15] During their lessons as Tom would lie beneath the piano then pop up and repeat a piece note for note, word for word.

Tom learned at an astonishing rate. And why not? His immersion into the world of sound and music was to the exclusion of everything else. The congeries of constant practice, an all-consuming passion and a hypersensitive ear produced startling results. Soon, he began composing his own pieces. "He would run and jump about the yard a little while, come back and play something of his own. Asked what it was, he replied, 'It is what the wind said to me,' or 'what the birds said to me,' or 'what the trees said to me,' or what something else said to him," remembered the Bethunes' cousin, Oscar Jordan.[16]

THUNDERSTRUCK

Thunderstorms are an electric rite of spring in Georgia, the high drama of the skies: a volatile, wild and utterly compelling climax after the oppressive heat and humidity of the day. For hours a muffled growl echoes tantalizingly across the southern expanse, the promise of release building with the darkening skies. Fat purple clouds then usher in a cool breeze and the occasional heavy raindrop: a quiet relief until the first deafening crack of the big guns. Then the hammer strikes the anvil, charges of white neon plug the earth and the stallion-led chariot careers through the sky. The storms assaulted the senses with such power, it seared the memory and begged Blind Tom to channel it into the keys of the piano.

One specific aspect of nature's mighty symphony engrossed Tom. It could be heard only in a forgotten corner of the Bethune homestead where a large tin gutter ran from the roof to within a foot of the ground. During a hard rain, water trickled down in soothing musical tones, and it was here that little Tom could be found the minute the skies broke open—flat on his back, arched over the drain and locked into the gentle downstream gurgle as it mixed with the sporadic tick tick tick of the drops. According to the 1868 concert program, after one exceptionally severe thunderstorm, Tom listened to the drain then "went to the piano and played what is now known as his *Rain Storm* and said it was what the rain, the wind and the thunder said to him. The perfection of the representation can only be fully appreciated by those who have heard the sounds of the falling water upon the roofs, and its running off through the gutters."[17]

And thus, Tom's first major composition was born, conceived at the tender age of five. "Listen to his own *Rain Storm*," wrote a music critic in 1882, "and you shall hear first the thunder's reverberating peal, and anon the gentle patter of the rain drops on the roof. Soon they fall thick and fast coming with a rushing sound. Again is heard the thunder's awful roar, while the angry winds mingle in the tempestuous fray. After a while, the tempest gradually ceases; all is calmness; and you will look with wonder upon this musical musician, and marvel that the pianoforte can imitate so closely the sounds made by the angry elements."[18]

But is this truly a reflection of the child's musical abilities? If so, then it is a towering achievement. The problem is that until the release

A publicity photograph to promote the release of Rain Storm *in 1865.*

of the sheet music in 1865—ten years after the inspirational thunderstorm—such praise was conspicuous in its absence.

In 1854, a Georgia woman enthusiastically chronicled six-year-old Tom's visit to her town. "I heard him play a sweet wild piece which he said the birdy sang to him (he is fond of such natural sounds). He calls it The *Red Bird Waltz*, another he said was *The Rain Waltz*. The gentleman who had charge of him said he would sit for hours and seem to listen to the falling rain—he says it talks to him."[19] With second billing to the red bird, the rain waltz heard by the lady is hardly his infant masterpiece. Besides which, *Rain Storm* is not a waltz. Indeed until he was sixteen, this "masterpiece" barely rates a mention (as compared with the open mouthed flummox that followed his performances of *Yankee Doodle* on one hand, *Dixie* on the other, while singing *The Fisher's Hornpipe*).

Throughout his early career, Tom performed a novelty-styled "musical feat" named *What the Wind, Thunder, and Rain said to Tom*.[20] Loose and unformed, one pundit described the prodigy's "ability to produce the sound of falling rain, the sounds of hail, the sounds of wind blowing through the trees" as "startling."[21] And this seems to be the piece that Tom composed when he was five years old.

RAINDROPS & PIANOFORTE

A little-quoted *Washington Post* article, most likely gleaned from Bethune's youngest son James, tells of a night after an usually heavy rainstorm when

> the inmates of the house were aroused from their slumbers by a sound which seemed a confused medley of raindrops and pianoforte. Creeping softly down the stairs they beheld Blind Tom bending eagerly over the piano. He would strike one and then another chord until he had produced the exact harmony which he sought, then, springing from the piano stool would grope his way through an open window onto the verandah and, placing his ear close to the gutter, which extended along the side of the house, listened intently for a moment. Having caught the tone desired, he would hurry back to the piano and, after a few trials, reproduce it with wonderful accuracy. This he continued going back and forth from the piano to gutter until at last was composed the entire selection.[22]

Aspects of this composition—the article confirms—were later embodied in the piece *Rain Storm*.

The most striking difference between *What the Wind, Thunder, and Rain said to Tom* and *Rain Storm* is that the first is a soundscape, a sequence of notes documenting a particular moment in time. There is no deeper meaning or underlying symbolism, it is exactly what it is—the sound of water trickling down a drain during a storm. The second is a genre-driven descriptive piece, conceived with more than a nod to the hugely popular storm piece in Gioacchino Rossini's opera, *William Tell*. In both pieces, a bright jaunty melody, dainty trills and brooding tremolo depict the rise and fall of a generic storm—sunshine, raindrops, wind, wild thunder and lightning before calm is once again restored—all which serve to reaffirm a single overarching idea: the Laws of Nature that order our universe can withstand even the most chaotic storm.

Although Tom was alive when Romanticism was in vogue, his instincts ran contrary to its spirit. A reaction to the onslaught of industrialism, Romanticism eulogized sentiment over reason, the symbolic over the real and the poet over the scientist. Cloying and maudlin at worst, rhapsodic and transcendental at best, this intrinsically nostalgic movement was searching for a truth that the modern world had somehow obliterated. "How they used to read things into music!," despaired music critic Harold C. Schonberg. "Music to the Romantics was part of the Mystery, it had Meaning or Meanings, an Idea or Ideas, that were bound up with Nature, the Soul, Life. Music expressed states of mind and feelings, and it had to have a program, explicit or implicit."

Even though Tom was only five years old, it was already clear that his musical instincts were at odds with the times. His compositions were, to his audiences, nothing more than a curious amalgam of sounds, atmospheric and formless as if suspended in time and space. One hundred years later, concert halls would house symphonies of the modern age where pianists would bang the bass keys with forearms and elbows to conjure up the sounds of factory and forge but, for now, these pure atmospheric soundscapes were outside the realm of music.

Somewhere along the line Tom was steered away from these as yet unnavigated musical shores and schooled in the conventions of the Romantics, but his urge to document the world as he heard it, unencumbered by popular taste and convention, would remain a hallmark of his style. It was, and continues to be, the most exciting aspect of his compositions. A writer who was privy to a private performance by eleven-year-old Tom purposefully distinguished his more conventional compositions—"a few light marches and gallops that were simple and plaintive enough, but with easily detected traces of remembered harmonies" from the "startling beauty and pathos" of his "strange, weird improvisations." Broken, wandering fragments of everyday sounds: "droll pieces whose cadences mimicked the sleepy lapping of the river waters, the bucolic call of the woodcock, the quail and the dawn greeting meadow lark enchanted even those usually indifferent to music."[23]

Though Tom's music amused, astonished, and perplexed the white folks who crowded into the Bethunes' parlor, for them his musical echoes of nature had little significance beyond aesthetics and entertainment. But the black slaves, peering through windows and doors, detected in Tom—not a musical prodigy—but a child whose musical revelations rekindled a connection with the great spirits of Africa, reminding them that a profoundly sacred universe lay no further than the farmyard and fields.

Second Sight

"To cut the storm in two, you go out into the yard with a double-edged axe and chop up the ground. Or split the sky with the stick of a spade," recounted one former slave.[1] Three hundred years of slavery had reduced Shango, the great West African god of thunder and lightning whose emblem was the double-edged axe, into this curious folk custom. Wrenched from its cosmological underpinning, few remembered why it was so, and local white historians simply added it to a long list of quaint and incomprehensible superstitions.

Just down the Chattahoochee in Catholic Louisiana, a lavish display of candles, incense, vestments and saints blended seamlessly with African theology to create Voodoo. In Protestant Georgia, the slaves had little more than the Trinity, the Devil, and the heroes of the Old Testament on which to hang the complex pantheon of gods passed down from their forbearers. One slave woman, for instance, believed that she knew a man who was "kin ter the devil. He told me that he could go out 'hind the house and make some noise and the devil would come and dance with him. He sed the devil learned him to play the banjo and if you wanted to do anything the devil could do, go to a crossroad walk backwards and curse God."[2] The slaves may have called it Christianity, but as long as streams, rocks, trees, animals, crossroads, and thunder reverberated with manifestations of the

A representation of Shango, the Yoruba people's god of
thunder which is symbolized by the double axe on his head.

divine, vestiges of traditional African spirituality
continued to survive.

Slaves in and around Columbus were said to have
held Tom in fear but all that changed when his musical
gifts were discovered. "From the first hour of his musical
triumph," reported the 1865 concert program, "Tom was
regarded by the Negroes of the plantation upon which he
lived, and those of the surrounding country, as a spirit
from another world, and he was treated with the utmost
tenderness."[3] Such conclusions were by no means confined
to black folk: a clutch of white Southerners, notably women,
proffered similar views. "Blind Tom is not properly a
genius except in so far as that might mean that he is 'possessed of a spirit,'" speculated a lady of impeccable breeding
and refinement.[4]

So what exactly did she mean by "possession"? How
did "a spirit from another world" manifest itself? While
answers from Georgia slaves are thin on the ground, in
Haiti where the voodoo tradition has been well documented,
"possession" is seen as the fruit of an elaborate rite, overseen by a
priest, where worshippers—united by the sacred beat of the conga—
dance in a sinuous thread of undulating motion around a center
pole. Once a worshipper is "mounted" by a *loa* or divinity, a profound transformation takes place: his voice changes, words pour
from his mouth, sometimes prophecies, sometimes secrets he could
not have otherwise known. The entire body language alters and he
moves, speaks and behaves in the manner of the spirit or ancestor
that possesses him.[5]

The same manifestations were observable in Tom. Under the moon,
in the dead of night, he would twirl and hum and convulse with laughter. Suddenly his entire demeanor might change—his chest puff up, his
chin jut out and with authoritative boom announce this or that. Or he
might slump into an apathetic drawl, his body heavy with the burdens
of the mind, exactly like the local blacksmith or the blacksmith's long
deceased father. During storms, the crash of thunder and patter of
rain lulled him into an entranced state of indescribable joy, his body

a vessel through which the thunder spirit seemed to whisper its secrets. "It is what the wind said to me," or "what the birds said to me," or "what the trees said to me."[6] But this was more than a simple dialogue. He was in communication with the sky pantheon, revealing the essence of the thunder, the vibratory pattern of the rain.

At moments like these, Charity may have begun to fully appreciate a powerful experience she underwent when he was still in her belly. She related the story to General Bethune's niece, Lizzie, who also came to believe that when Tom's mother was still carrying him, a powerful force had entered her body and marked the unborn child.

As Tom was gestating in her womb Charity chanced upon the city's fire brigade, in full plumed regalia, parading up and down Broad Street. Behind them, six musicians kept them in their stride: two bass drums, two fife, two kettle drums, and if it was the same drum and fife band in 1848 as it was in 1859, they were "all colored except the last."[7]

The likelihood of this was reasonably good. As one music researcher discovered, Columbus had a tradition of black drum and fife music that harked back to slavery days and continued long after emancipation. In an age dominated by minstrelsy, their repertoire would have included not only the requisite marching songs, but a smattering of popular tunes that were either genuine slave folksongs or white imitations of them. So there is every possibility that the marching band that Charity—and Tom *in utero*—followed were black musicians playing African-American songs.

Perhaps too, there were moments when the drum became more prevalent than the fife, and the beats more syncopated and polyrhythmic. In an informal moment at the close of day, the strict regimentation may have broken down and the musicians began to dance and sway: the fife player calling out a line or two, the drummers responding with whoops and moans. It would not be unusual, then, for folks to dance—some for a moment, others until they shouted or dropped from exhaustion. Or some may have reacted like the man and woman a music researcher watched in Mississippi one hundred years later, who became "possessed by the drumming and crawled in the dust directly beneath the bass drum."[8]

Admittedly this is conjecture, but something musical that day struck Charity like a thunderbolt. Something powerful enough for her to return home in an "ecstasy of delight."[9] Something she only began to fully understand through her strange blind son's obsession with the piano. Slaves (and freak show promoters) would call the phenomenon "marking." It explained everything from character traits to birth defects: a white woman in Thomasville, for instance, gave birth to a son with "feet and hands just like a horse" because, while pregnant, she was "tickled at a horse with his tongue hanging out."[10] Other markings were more portentous. <u>Nat Turner</u>, the famed leader of the 1830 slave rebellion, believed his destiny was determined, in part, by the special markings on his head and breast. And Charity, it seems, believed that her son's peculiar passion for music had its roots in her wild dancing at the Columbus Fireman's Parade. She believed she was struck by an intense, rapturous energy that physically and psychically marked the unborn child.

FIXIN' MASTER

In the woods just south of Atlanta, lived an old blind root doctor known as Aunt Darkas who, at the break of day, could be found picking "any kind of root and herb she wanted. The Lord gave her power and vision."[11] By the look of things, the blind child Tom was blessed with his own inner vision and power. No longer living the life of a lowly slave, he had assumed his place in his master's house as if it were his birthright. He claimed kin with his master's family, calling "Little Miss Lizzie" his "cousin"—a lack of deference that was quite shocking to the ten-year-old girl but tolerated with bemusement by the rest of the family.

And this was only the start of his scandalous behavior. Tom, by his own admission, would slap people for teasing him. Lizzie, by her own admission, was one of those who teased. Is it possible that she was at the receiving end of one of Tom's clouts? Even if she escaped his wrath, it is to be expected that an autistic child will occasionally explode with crimson rage. How were the Bethunes to respond to excesses of their highly volatile slave child? Not by the rod, it seems. Or at least, not for very long. Tom's resentments were strong and if any physical punishment was inflicted on him, it would be neither forgotten nor forgiven— hardly the foundations of a lucrative show-business partnership. After a long, and possibly tortuous, system of trial and error, John and General Bethune hit on an "infallible formula of cajolery and flattery."

For the slaves outside who toiled from sun up to sun down in fear of the whip, this was astonishing. Wildcat frenzies that were rewarded with sweet talk and sugarplum, how did he get away with it? How was it possible? Their answer may well be found in another question: who else got away with it? There was only one type of person who did, the one shading himself under a tree while his black brothers and sisters toiled: the Conjurer.

Columbus was home to a number of Conjure men, their "secret doin's and carry ons" commanding fear and respect from black folk. *"Old Satan is a liar and a cunjorer too/ If you don't mind, he'll cunjor you,"* Mary Gladdy recited to a white oral historian, effortlessly slipping between the Christian and mytho-magical worldview. "These people were not intelligent but had highly sensitive minds," opined another local, Rias Body, who gave as wide a berth as possible to all such characters. But Frances Kimbrough sought out a hoodoo doctor in Muscogee County after a "fixin" from a jealous woman left her arm numb and useless. "Neither gave her any trouble again."

Countless more references dot the Georgia Slave Narratives but none compare with William Wells Brown's recollections of a fearsome, one-eyed conjurer named Dinkie who "wore a snake's skin around his neck, carried a petrified frog in one pocket, and a dried lizard in the other" and despite every effort, his master "couldn't work him, couldn't whip him, couldn't sell him."[12]

> No one could remember the time when Dinkie was called upon to perform manual labor. He was not sick, yet he never worked. [He] hunted, slept, was at the table at meal time, roamed through the woods, went to the city, and returned when he pleased, with no one to object, or to ask a question. The whites, throughout the neighborhood, tipped their hats to the old one-eyed negro, while the policemen, or patrollers, permitted him to pass without a challenge. I once asked a negro why they appeared to be afraid of Dinkie. He looked at me, shrugged his shoulders, smiled, shook his head and said,—"Dinkie's got de power, ser; he knows things seen and unseen, an' dat's what makes him his own massa." It was literally true, this man was his own master.

One day these powers were put to the test. A clutch of anxious slaves watched as a brutal new overseer—determined to punish him for refusing to work—led Dinkie into a barn, "negro whip" in hand. Fifteen silent minutes passed before the barn door flew open and the overseer and conjurer emerged side by side: "the overseer to the field, and Dinkie back to his cabin."

In a world where the master's authority seemed absolute and slave's subjugation non-negotiable, here was evidence that black folk had access to forces that their masters could neither control nor understand. At the heart of the conjurer's power was an inversion of the prevailing order: if a Christian God could not save a good man from the evils of slavery, then who would? Dinkie's prayer to the "good and lovely devil" summed up the slave's metaphysical jam: "Before I got into your service, de white folks bought an' sold me an' my old wife an' chillen, an' whip me, and half starve me. Den I use to pray to de Lord, but dat did no good, coz de white folks don't fear de Lord. But dey fears you, an' ever since I got into your service, I is able to do as I please."

Even for those like Aunt Darkas who rejected the Devil and embraced the Lord, this same inversion was the source of their power. On what grounds did the oppressed and despised Africans conclude they were God's Chosen People destined for the Promised Land? Certainly not reason—after three hundred years of slavery there was no evidence the end was in sight. People knew because, after passing hours in ecstatic prayer, they felt it in their bones—a sensation state which neuro-psychiatrists would describe as paradoxical or ultra-paradoxical. This was the same paradox of the renunciate who experienced pain as intense mystical joy, of the yogi who experienced stillness as expansion, of the voodoo dancers who experienced darkness as white: the slave who experienced bondage as freedom.

It was not such a stretch then for the slaves to grasp the paradox of Blind Tom: a blind child with the gift of "vision," a senseless "idiot" revered for his powers of communication, a physically afflicted child deified as a transcendental spirit, a useless encumbrance worth his weight in gold. Although only a child, Tom's powers were already considerable. He had escaped the deprivations of the slave cabin for a life of comfort and luxury, knew no fear of white authority but embraced it with the same swaggering confidence as Dinkie and the other conjurers: invulnerable, invincible, "master to no man but himself."

However, the white master class wielded its own brand of magic, twisting words to create new meanings. As Bethune would later argue, Tom was as good as liberated from the shackles of slavery as "All his life he has accounted himself free."[13] And while there is a certain truth to this carefully worded statement, as time progressed it became abundantly clear that there was a world of difference between "feeling" free and "being" free.

The child prodigy Blind Tom who routinely played the piano for twelve hours a day

Star of the
Musical World

TOM'S MUSICAL EFFORTS IN THE BETHUNE HOMESTEAD WERE OCCASIONALLY rewarded with coins, which he—to his mother's consternation— would throw in the fire. Neither money nor his spiraling market value interested him, but like property prices in a boom, it was a topic that obsessed everyone else. One woman heard that Bethune turned down an offer of $100,000 for Tom. Incredulous neighbors cast their minds back to his price tag at the auction and thought how Wiley Jones—who was now living on the charity of his son-in-law— must be kicking himself.

The question now was when the asset was going to deliver a return. Not until he was eight years old insisted Etta Worsley, a Columbus historian whose claim that Tom made his stage debut in the Fall of 1857 at the local Temperance Hall has been cited as fact ever since. But one only needs to read a notice that appeared in an Atlanta newspaper shortly after the Temperance Hall performance, to know that his career was already underway:

THE GREAT STAR OF THE MUSICAL WORLD
AND THE PRODIGY OF THE AGE.
THE BLIND PIANIST
TOM

A Negro boy only eight years of age and as a Musical Genius is unrivalled! He has been visited by Members of em'nent Professors of Music, who have, without exception, pronounced him the most Wonderful Living Curiosity extant.[1]

Charity reckoned Tom was about three when he first began playing in public, an answer she never altered, no matter how many times she was asked: John Bethune taught him some pieces of music, then began exhibiting him before taking him away forever.[2] Other sources place Tom between four and five. A letter headed "Tuesday February 23" from a Georgia woman only known as "Mother," confirms that in early 1854, five-year-old Tom was touring the state with an unidentified gentleman and the young son of his master, presumably twenty-one-year-old John:

> Charlotte is standing in every position near and around me, so I can hardly write—she has already dictated more than would fill a sheet about a wonderful negro musician she went to hear and see— for she made good use of both faculty. I dare say the musical prodigy may be exhibited in Kingston—do take Jennie and Maffie.[3]

Throughout the following year, the musical prodigy continued to appear in towns throughout Georgia and neighboring states, performing under the name "Tom Greene"—the surname of Mingo's former master, Myles Greene. In November of 1855, a Milledgeville newspaper announced that "the Infant Pianist will be exhibited at Newell's Hall this evening. Of course everybody will go."[4] When Blind Tom arrived in Memphis some time later, Louis Hughes, the enslaved manservant of a wealthy Tennessee planter, remembers people from outlying towns and villages pouring into the city to hear him—if the regular trains were full, then they traveled by freight or on flat bottom cars. As Hughes drove his master's people home after the concert, they talked of nothing else but the boy. "He was indeed a wonder." So by October 1857—the date of his alleged debut—Tom had been on the stage for many years and was so popular that "Mother" was certain he would soon redeem the Bethune family's fallen fortunes.

But the transition from parlor to stage had not been easy. Tom was an obsessive and demanding child, whose interest in the piano did not extend to entertaining the general public. "Tom seemed to have but two motives in life: the gratification of his appetite and his passion for music," recalled one man after observing the prodigy during his off stage hours at a hotel. "I don't think I exaggerate when I state that he made the piano go for twelve hours out of twenty-four."[5] Tom would have played every waking moment if he could, and each day ended with a right royal battle as his keepers forced him to separate from his beloved piano. "Tom's nervous organization is excessively sensitive and he weeps whenever anything annoys him," noted a reporter. "Last evening, he cried bitterly at being taken from the piano. His other passion besides music is sugar plums and these will reconcile him to almost any disappointment."[6]

Staging a concert once, sometimes twice a day, required a great deal of cooperation from Tom, which was not always forthcoming. At every performance, John had to coax the reluctant child onto the stage, then shepherd him into position behind the piano. Tom's first urge, naturally, was to start playing, but no, he had to wait until the showman's announcements were over and John would physically hold back Tom's hands, while the child struggled and strained to make contact with the keys.

Furtive mutterings and desperate negotiations studded each show. Sometimes Tom would wander off the stage and had to be lured back, a supply of sugarplum always at the ready—although even this strategy was known to fail. The notion of interspersing each song with stage patter was not obvious to the child prodigy either. As soon as one tune ended, Tom would launch into the next and again, his hands needed to be clamped still. And John and the showman could never be sure if Tom would play the piece that had just been announced and in time, came to accept that the night's musical agenda would be dictated by Tom.

A feature known as the Audience Challenge was a more reliable affair. Here, an audience member was invited onto the stage to perform a piece of music that Tom, after a single hearing, would reproduce. "Lizzie played one of her hard pieces for him and he sat down after her and played it almost correctly," recalled Lizzie's sister, a girl only known as Sallie who was sufficiently impressed to attend all three of Blind Tom's shows.[7]

Such accomplishments seemed all the more dazzling because—as the girls were reminded at each concert—the prodigy was an "artless," "untaught," "natural" musician. "This boy has never received the advantages of instruction and manifests an intensity for the highest order of music," read an 1857 newspaper notice. "He has never had one moment's instruction, does not know a flat from a sharp, or the name of any key upon the instrument," other publicity material declared.

This fiction was to endure, not only throughout Tom's career, but throughout much of the history of African American show business. The notion that Africans were "natural musicians" was a common misconception amongst white people and one they were not prepared to change. To get a gig, many highly skilled black musicians were forced to tout themselves as untutored plantation Negroes playing the "music of nature, untrammeled by art or any degree of affectation."[8] "The African nature is full of poetry and song," pronounced *Dwights Journal* in 1856. "The Negro is a natural musician. He will learn to play an instrument more quickly than a white man. They have magnificent voices and sing without instruction."

Unlike most black musicians of the time, "heaven taught" Tom was not playing the "rude" harmonies of the minstrel but—if his management was to be believed—the most difficult works of the classical canon. The idea that any child could rattle them off was confounding enough but for a blind "idiotic" Negro child to do so struck at the heart of the racial hierarchy, pitting the "lowest rung of humanity" against the most "refined utterances of our highest civilization."

Long before Darwin, theorists were applying the evolutionary principle—the development of the simple into the complex and, by implication, of inferior into superior—to everybody and everything. Constructing elaborate race hierarchies was a favorite pursuit. "On Egyptian monuments the negros are so represented as to show that in natural propensities and mental abilities they were pretty much what we find them at the present day—indolent, playful, sensual, imitative, subservient, good-natured, versatile, unsteady in their purpose, devoted and affectionate," wrote Harvard's Professor Louis Agassiz, a leading advocate of polygenism, a theory that espoused that each race developed separately from one another—the Negro in Africa and the Caucasian in the lost continent of Atlantis.

According to this view, Tom was an "idiot" because generations of heathendom and barbarianism had dredged his brain clean of all traces of power or purity. "Physically, and in animal temperament, [he] ranks next to the lowest Guinea type. In intellect, reason or judgment, he is but one degree above an idiot," was the appraisal of one white abolitionist.[9] By all accounts, Tom could not have been further down the ladder. And yet, at the same time, he was the "greatest musical wonder of the age" who, after a few trials, could master "the difficult compositions of Beethoven, Mozart, Hertz, and others of equal reputation. Language can convey no adequate conceptions of his Wonderful powers. He must be seen and heard and will not fail to convince the most musical skeptic that he is unapproachable in point of Musical Talent."[10]

So was he? Well, his performances in Columbus, Athens or Augustus certainly elicited euphoric reviews, but the reporters' enthusiasm was more for the fashion and novelty in each city than the quality of his musicianship. Amid the wild superlatives, there was at least one skeptic, a professional pianist by the name of Otto Spahr, who was unmoved by Tom's alleged virtuosity.

Eight-year-old Tom played to the standard of the average schoolgirl, he adjudged. His repertoire was made up of simple schottisches, waltzes and polkas and variations on standards like *My Old Kentucky Home*, *Home Sweet Home,* and *The Maidens Prayer*. By chance, he and Tom were staying at the same hotel in Warrenton, Georgia and, as Spahr watched him play in the parlor, he began to suspect that the prodigy had been taught. Taking advantage of a quiet moment together, Spahr asked Tom who had taught him what piece. The guileless eight- year-old responded openly and honestly, clearly unaware of the implications of his words. "In some instances he [cited the] name of his mistress (Miss Betsy, I think he called her) at other times the name of some professor or some lady, mentioning in each case the names of persons and places without hesitation." (This breach was eventually closed. When, at sixteen, Tom was asked how he came to play so well, he responded "God taught me all these things. He used to back me. He taught me how to sing and how to play too.")

Tom's admission came as no surprise to Spahr who recognized in the child the makings a fine pianist—"a good musical ear and musical memory, a large hand, long and flexible fingers, long arms and, for one of his age, a powerful frame." Spahr also noticed that there were a number of keys that Tom was unfamiliar with, plus other gaps in his knowledge when he tested him:

I chose Strakosch's *Flirtation Polka* in the Key of 6 sharps and related keys. At first Tom could not find the keys at all. After repeated hearings he managed to reproduce some kind of semblance but still far from accurate. I then played the first movement of Beethoven's

Sonate (moonlight) in C sharp minor, and afterwards Charles Mayer's *Caprice On the Bellows*, op 61 in F sharp and half a dozen other keys. In neither of these pieces did he succeed at all, and had to give up, after a number of attempts. This proved to me, if proof had been needed, that teaching and experience were still necessary to him for the performance of such things.[11]

Even Tom would later concur with Spahr's assessment, admitting that when he first began to play "I couldn't get it out very well."[12] Henry Watterson—the young reporter and musician who met Tom a year or so later—also agreed. "The Bethune girls had taught him a few jingles which he rattled off on the piano. He knew nothing very complicated or very well. But he was blind and clearly an idiot, he was a prodigy."[13]

Which begs the question, if—as Otto Spahr contended—Tom was performing to the standard of the average schoolgirl, what was causing the wave of excitement and wonder wherever he performed?

SAME WORDS, SAME GESTURE, SAME EMPHASIS

Tom's strengths, according to all who appraised him, lay less in his musical abilities and more in his power of mimicry and memory. "I have seen him listen to [Congressman] Alexander N. Stephens and [Senator] Robert Toombs then go away and make the same speech in the exact same tones of the speaker, placing emphasis and gestures just as made by the speakers," reported John Bethune's cousin, Oscar Jordan. "We would listen from outside the room, his production of Toombs or Stephens was perfect."[14]

Tom had met the two giants of Georgia politics on their occasional visits to Columbus. They were curious to see the famous musical prodigy, so General Bethune organized a private performance for them at his city office but little did they realize that they too would be fodder for a Blind Tom act.[15]

Robert Toombs was built to be an orator: his body tapered from his shoulders to his feet, his arms and hands moved in graceful gesticulation and his powerful voice filled every nook and cranny of a room. The fire in his belly, fuelled as much by whiskey as by Georgia's fair name, had famously courted controversy. In Washington, he roiled anti-slavery senators, promising to call the muster roll of his slaves from Boston's abolitionist heartland. He cast aspersions on

Alexander Stephens and Robert Toombs, two giants of Georgia politics whose indiosycracies Tom had down to a tee.

their virility with taunts that Southern men could whip them with pop guns. As he spoke candidly in Jim Bethune's Columbus office, Tom was perhaps privy to a deliciously vicious assessment of his peers peppered, of course, with a few sly asides in praise his own glory.

Although "Little Aleck" Stephens was a man of no more modest inclinations, he was no less modest, with an ego inversely proportionate to his size. A lifetime of poor health had left him slight and sickly, with a voice some described as shrill and unpleasant. Like Toombs, he was a thorn in the side of both the Yankee abolitionist and the radical South, forever decrying northern tyranny while steadfastly refusing to jump the Union ship.

Add to the mix the ultra-secessionist sympathies of General Bethune, and Blind Tom was in for a night of unrivalled bluster and heat. It was a fly on the wall moment that was ripe for retelling—but also an affront to Stephens's and Toombs's inflated sense of honor. Consequently few were to savor Tom's innocent savaging of these political heavyweights. As readily as Robert Toombs lent himself to pasquinade, as precisely as Tom captured his physical and verbal idiosyncrasies, General Bethune had categorically banned any public rendition of the piece—even the Bethune boys were forced to listen to it from another room. Southern decorum being what it was, it was unthinkable for these pillars of the Georgia establishment to be lampooned and held up to public ridicule—especially from the mouth of a blind "idiotic" Negro child. That object of fun was to be "Uncle Charlie of Warm Springs."

SPRING WATERS

Although the advertisements play it down, comedy was a central part of Blind Tom's show. People reported that they laughed until their sides were about to split open. The source of much merriment was Tom's word for word, gesture for gesture impersonation of a slave and renowned comic in the district, known only as "Uncle Charlie." While most of his monologues were picked up surreptitiously, Tom it seems was taken to the nearby resort town of Warm Springs with the express purpose of hearing Uncle Charlie's outlandish and hilarious rant. Tom's recitation of it was to be the foundation of a showpiece known as the stump speech.

Stump speeches were fixtures of minstrel shows, appearing with undeviating certainty in the first part of the olio that built to the Act One finale. Here a blackfaced actor would assume the persona of a dim-witted old "darkey" who suffered from the great delusion that he possessed great intelligence. In his desire to share his pearls of wisdom, the misguided fool would stumble his way through countless malapropisms, jokes, puns and gags, and at one particularly incisive moment, fall off of his stump. But it wasn't all ridicule. Woven through the racist stereotyping could be genuine wit, sharp commentary and satire. "Bedren," announced minstrel's most famous star, Dan Emmett in the guise of a black preacher, "De text am foun' in de inside ob Job whar Paul draw'd him a pistol on 'Fressains, lebenteenth chapter and no 'tickular verse: 'Bressed am dem dat 'spects nuttin', kuz dey aint gwine to git nuttin'."[16]

Blind Tom's audience, well versed in the conventions of the minstrel show, roared and howled their way through "Uncle Charlie's" mock-scientific discourse on why the spring waters were so beneficial,[17] the eight-year-old replicating not only his witty banter and broad Southern dialect, but perplexed head turns, hapless shrugs and gulps. Unfortunately, the details of the act are lost to time but swathes of pundits (including an otherwise indifferent English critic) cite it as the highlight of the show. Perhaps it was the incongruity of the child embodying the countenance of the old man that so amused them or the utter sincerity that Tom brought to the performance. Perhaps, the real Uncle Charlie had pulled out all the stops the day Tom came to hear him, couching his barbed wit in a feigned naïveté—quietly undermining white scientific authority by rendering it absurd.

But the old uncle's stump speech was not the only convention borrowed from minstrelsy. Another character was to shape Blind Tom's career—albeit in more subtle ways—informing the way white audiences made sense of the child star.

JUMP JIM CROW

Twenty years before Tom was born, Thomas "Daddy" Rice—the as yet undiscovered star of the minstrel stage—chanced upon a misshapen elderly black stable hand cleaning out a pen. The man's right shoulder was deformed and drawn up high, his left leg was gnarled with rheumatism, stiff and crooked at the knee and, while he worked, he sang a mournful tune, each stanza rounded off with a "heel-a-rickin'" jump and rapid fire shuffle made all the more curious by his lame, twisted body. "*Wheel about and turn about and do jus' so / Eb'ry time I wheel about I jump Jim Crow.*"

In this strange mixture of pathos and humor, tragedy and farce, Rice recognized the makings of a stage act. He expanded the song, imitated the shambling gait of the unsuspecting slave and donned a pair of worn out oversized shoes, dilapidated coat and straw hat. Thus the long and lanky Daddy Rice gave birth to "Jim Crow." The awkward angularity of his lop-sided, earth-slapping, hand-clapping, thigh-patting dance—a curious mess of juba and jig—his upper body wildly gesticulating while his bow-legged feet slapped out the rhythm, left audiences crying with pained laughter.[18]

By the time Blind Tom's young star was rising in the middle of the century, Jim Crow was a fixture of every minstrel troupe in the country, with a popularity unequal to anything before or since, although by now any poignancy Daddy Rice had brought to the role had been subsumed in a series of distortions. His body was cockeyed and twisted, pulsating with the "natural rhythms" of this race. His face was wrung and stretched: nose, flared; eyes, close to popping out of their sockets; bottom lip, pendulous in the wide gaping grin of a fool. For Jim Crow was perpetually happy, always ready for a frolic and song, a crude simple slave who joyfully embraced his lowly place in the plantation hierarchy, oblivious to his own wretchedness.

And here was Blind Tom: "A wild, uncouth figure angular at all points which should be curved, and curved at all points that should present acute lines—loose jointed, thick lipped, sprawl footed with forehead almost covered by kinky locks, eyeballs prominent and distended, and an idiotic expression of countenance."[19] "Tom laughed and danced with many a shout—his saddening deformity being his least care. He was always cheerful, and never despondent."[20] "We see a boy with a decidedly African cast—low retreating forehead, flat spreading nose and projecting upper lip, with every mark of idiocy."[21] "Coal-black, with protruding heels, the ape-jaw, the sightless eyes closed, and the head thrown far back on the shoulder . . . his mouth wide open constantly; his great blubber lips and shining teeth were all you saw when he faced you."[22]

It was a perception almost hard wired in the public consciousness. Tom fulfilled the Jim Crow stereotype so convincingly, he could almost out-jump Jim Crow himself. Forever grinning and grimacing, his body entered the world of sound with a compulsive, ecstatic physicality that was blissfully immune to the pity, contempt, horror or amusement of those observing him. Throughout his life, Tom's autism was interpreted through prevailing racist stereotypes as incontrovertible "proof" that the Negro was a natural musician and that Africans were intellectually inferior to Europeans.

Yet people like Otto Spahr who had the opportunity to spend time with him knew there was no simple answer to the riddle of Blind Tom. He noted that Tom's responses to his many questions were "generally intelligent enough. In fact, had it not been for his queer antics and monkey motions, which were natural for one in his condition, he would have seemed like any other boy of his race and not at all idiotic."

As Tom's unofficial manager, young John Bethune oscillated between portraying Tom as a buffoon and emphasizing his dignity and humanity. The 1865 concert program he had a hand in devising describes Tom as "precocious," at times possessing the "air of a philosopher," other times exhibiting a "more than common amount of humor," and quite able to discuss the one issue that obsessed him —music. Sure, he had facial tics, a peculiarly jerky mode of expressing himself, a nervous gait and a complete inability to sit still for more than a second, but this was a far cry from the grotesque and bumbling fool he was widely perceived to be.

Perhaps these vacillations reflect John's ambiguous feelings towards Tom. From the moment he first encountered the infant on the riverbank that summer's afternoon as he played the flute, John's life began to veer from the path his father trod before him. He too had studied law at the University of Georgia and now dabbled in land speculation. Neither politically active, nor a member of the city's two militias (as most men from the city's "best families" were), he did not need a military rank to secure social status. Tom was his calling card, his invitation to the upper echelons of Georgia society. Touring the state with Tom had provided him with an elegant opportunity to escape his dreary legal career and be welcomed into the sumptuous parlors of the wealthy, influential, and just plain decadent—enticing new horizons for the playful, easy-going, good-times son of General Bethune.

For someone who played such a pivotal role in Blind Tom's life, John's voice can seem strangely absent: most press statements were issued by the elder Bethune, and none of his letters or diaries have survived—there is not even a photograph of him (though thankfully a sketch). But surely John was entertained—even inspired—by the child's fervent passions, oddball sense of humor, philosophical insights and uncensored physicality? Did he not then feel some obligation to defend Tom's honor? Whatever personal failings John Bethune may have been guilty of—and as time wore on they became abundantly clear—he never pandered to the lowest common denominator. In this age of wanton charlatanism, he walked a fine line between propriety and con. He knew (and perhaps his audience implicitly knew) that Tom was not the infant Mozart depicted in the newspaper advertisements, but the show's respectability was never compromised and never lapsed into a flagrantly exploitative freak show. The fashionable and elegant people of the South left his concerts, astounded and perplexed yet safe in the certainty they had been given quality entertainment.

John Bethune fashioned Tom's career with the same refinement he desired for himself. But just as he began flexing his show business muscle, his father made a decision that pulled the curtain on his newfound career. And like Charity before him, he was powerless to appeal.

The Showman &
The Magician

———◆———

SOMETIME DURING TOM'S 1857-58 WINTER TOUR OF GEORGIA, THE NINE-year-old played the southwestern town of Americus. Sitting comfortably in the VIP section of the grand old courthouse (which also served as a theater) was the town's first and so far only mayor, Perry H. Oliver, an enterprising man whose time on the soap boxes of Sumter County had given him a taste for life's bigger stages. As he watched John Bethune direct Tom's performance, his critical eye seized upon one missed opportunity after another and he began imagining how he would better utilize the freak potential of this "marvel of the age." Within weeks, he had abandoned his career in local politics, kissed his wife and young family goodbye, traveled to Columbus, negotiated a three year licensing deal with General Bethune and emerged as the new manager of "Blind Tom," the stage name by which the prodigy would forever be known.

The new arrangements must have come as quite a shock to twenty-six-year-old John Bethune, whose years of effort were just beginning to pay dividends. But his father had not brought him up to be a traveling showman and the lucrative agreement with Perry Oliver was the perfect opportunity steer John back towards a respectable legal career. But this was not Bethune's only reason—he needed the cash.

Four years earlier he had launched *The Corner Stone*, the first newspaper in the state to openly demand Georgia's immediate secession from the Union. Ever since then, his faith and fortitude had been put to the test. Riding home one winter's evening, his horse and buggy collided violently with a carriage and Bethune's leg was subsequently amputated (he quipped to his readers as he convalesced that he "literally had one foot in the grave").[1] The following year, his forty-year-old brother Benjamin died in the Bethune homestead, leaving his five children (including Cousin Lizzie) all crowding into the house.[2] Shortly afterwards his beloved wife Frances was struck by "a disease of a pulmonary nature" and died after a "severe and protracted" period of suffering.[3] (Bethune then channeled his grief into exposing the "tyranny" of the local Market Ordinance Act.)

The secessionist spleen that gave birth to *The Corner Stone* had not won many subscriptions and circulation was lukewarm at best— much of the heat lost when Tennessee's James Buchanan was voted President of the United States. Despite the hundreds of hours Bethune poured into the paper, returns were minuscule until the offer of an energetic mayor itching for a change of career. Fifteen thousand dollars over three years was no small onions.

Beyond a few scant details, not much is known about Perry Oliver's past. If not for his sojourn with Blind Tom, his name would have traveled little further than the Sumter County press. Within these confines he was well liked, or at least, well known for his "liberal, public-spirited, generous, and enterprising" enthusiasm, in particular his eagerness to share the lessons of his life with the young lads of the town, still green horned enough to believe him. Indeed by the time Perry Oliver died, many in Americus were of the opinion that he "was known throughout the world as the owner and exhibitor of the wonderful musical boy, Blind Tom." A remarkable achievement considering that the two barely left the South.[4]

But Oliver had always played fast and loose with the truth, with a penchant for poaching the details of other people's lives. An *Atlantic Monthly* writer walked away from an interview convinced that Oliver was a wealthy tobacco planter from Savannah and that Tom had been in his possession since birth. As Blind Tom's manager, he would spin yarns to the public, toy with their expectations and excite their sense of anticipation. Anything to fulfill the goal set by his role model P.T. Barnum: to get people "to think and talk, become curious and excited about the rare spectacle."[5]

A FINE SPECIMEN OF THE RICHEST BARNUMESQUE

Blind Tom was as resistant to stage direction under his new manager as he had been under John Bethune. It was the reach of the tour, the level of publicity and the rhetoric of the showman that made this show different. Now performing in the major cities across the South, Tom was playing to, and being challenged by, musicians far more accomplished than schoolgirl Sallie's older sister.

"In the fall of 1859, it was announced that Blind Tom was coming to visit our town," wrote one Mr. Weisel from an unidentified Georgia town to *Dwights Journal of Music*. "Immense showbills, a woodcut done in black ink representing a black boy seated at a huge piano and above and below it these words 'Blind Tom is coming' were pasted about. Succinct but unintelligible accounts of this wonderful boy had reached us when his talents were first discovered long before. We were on the *qui vive* to see this new candidate for fame. At last he came."[6]

Unbeknownst to Mr. Weisel, Perry Oliver had drawn on a raft of tactics pioneered by Barnum to ensure what "succinct but unintelligible accounts" had reached his ears. One inevitably concerned the miracle of the untutored genius who could reproduce any tune, no matter how complex, after a single hearing. "A Plantation Negro Boy, with one hour's instruction and perfectly blind from infancy plays more than 1100 pieces of music upon the piano with a copiousness of style and power, and brilliancy of execution, surpassing anything ever heard before," declared one newspaper advertisement.[7] But it would take more than this for readers well versed in humbug to be persuaded. Oliver needed these claims to be substantiated by independent reporters from reputable papers.

"We have just returned from seeing and hearing, at Mr. Stoddard's piano room on Calvert Street, a blind Negro slave boy, only ten years old," wrote one Baltimore critic. "Never have we witnessed such powers of imitation and improvising. They are instantaneously called into activity and without any seeming labor. One of the best pianists sat down and played a most difficult piece, involving the most complicated fingering and harmony. Little Tom took his place and repeated every note of it, *sur la champ*, and in the very same vigorous style."[8]

Other reports abounding in superlatives like "graceful," "exquisite" and "delicate" were re-published as far a field as Boston, New York and Chicago, their authenticity never in doubt.[9] Even the highly respected *Atlantic Monthly*—whose editorial independence was beyond reproach—endorsed Perry Oliver's claims:

☞ TOM! ☜

The BLIND NEGRO BOY PIANIST,

The Wonder of the World - The Marvel of the Age!

THE GREATEST LIVING MUSICIAN,

ONLY TEN YEARS OLD, and MASTER OF THE PIANO!

Playing Two Pieces of Music at Once!

AND CONVERSING AT THE SAME TIME.

PERFORMS WITH HIS BACK TO THE INSTRUMENT!

REPRODUCES THE MOST DIFFICULT MUSIC

AFTER ONCE HEARING IT.

He will also play the Secondo, or Bass, to any piece of Music that may be played with him by any one from the audience, without ever having heard it before and will then change seats and play the Primo. His own compositions have been pronounced Gems, by the best judges.

He Sings in German French, and English!

WITHOUT UNDERSTANDING EITHER LANGUAGE.

☞ This wonderful Negro Child—that is now attracting so much attention throughout the country, having played in Baltimore, for over five weeks, performing to upwards of FIVE THOUSAND PEOPLE during the last three days he was there, whose feats at the Piano baffle the most scientific and learned men in the land—was blind from birth, has never had one moment's instruction, does not know a *flat* from a *sharp*, or the name of any key upon the instrument; yet he plays the most difficult Operatic pieces, without ever striking a false note, not only brilliantly and beautifully, but with all the taste, expression and feeling of the most distinguished artist.

AT EACH OF HIS ENTERTAINMENTS HE WILL GIVE

INIMITABLE IMITATIONS

Of THE DRUM and FIFE, RAIL-ROAD CARS, GUITAR, &c.

WILL ALSO PLAY FROM THE OPERAS OF

Norma, Linda, Lucrecia Borgia, Trovatore, Somnambula, La Fille du Regiment, &c.,

TOGETHER WITH

MARCHES, WALTZES POLKAS, FANTASIAS, CONCERTAS,

Variations on Celebrated Airs, &c., and will Sing several pieces.

A CARD—The boy Tom was born in Georgia, and is only ten years old, and being perfectly blind was caressed and petted, as all negro children are about a plantation in the South, and more particularly those afflicted with so terrible an infirmity as the loss of sight. But when the veil of darkness was drawn over his eyes, as if to make amends, for the infliction upon the poor Negro Boy, a flood of light was poured into his brain, mysteriously even through the darkened portals, and his mind became an Opera of Beauty, written by the hand of God in syllables of music, for the delight of the world. The development of his ability, which is startling the musical firmament, was purely accidental. The boy being the pet of the family, had access to the parlor in which the Piano stood. The ladies in an adjoining apartment heard with surprise the instrument touched by no ordinary hand; entranced, they listened to the thrilling melody, and hastening to know who could produce such exquisite music, found the little plantation negro Tom, scarcely able to reach the keys, fingering them with the skill of an accomplished artist. Can anything be more wonderful than the history of this gifted negro boy? It is worthy of special mark, too, that in all his wonderful improvisations he has never been known in any instance to be guilty of repetition or plagiarism. He is presented to the public as a MUSICAL WONDER, surpassing everything hitherto known to the world as a MUSICAL WONDER.

TOM will use the magnificent piano presented to him by Wm. Knabe & Co., of Baltimore.

OPINIONS OF THE PRESS.

Our readers are aware that we are not apt to be taken with "wonders." Generally speaking, we have found them to be unmitigated humbugs. The charlatanism of itinerant exhibitors has made us suspicious of nearly all pretensions in the way of the marvellous, and we have therefore been careful not to commit ourselves to such Barnumisms as are constantly obtruding themselves upon editorial notice in a city like Baltimore.

For more than a week past, however, there has been a series of musical performances at Carroll Hall, in this city, which have certainly exceeded in interest, of a particular kind, anything we ever before witnessed. The performer is an exceedingly country negro boy, of apparently ten or twelve years of age; tall, but slender, having rather an idiotic expression of countenance when not excited by music, a stutterer in his efforts at conversation, and has been totally blind from his birth. Altogether, the appearance of the child, as indicative of talent of any kind, is about as unpromising as might in any case be found after a day's search among our colored population. Yet "Blind Tom," as he is familiarly called, is, perhaps, as great a *living* wonder as there is in the world at the present day. If Paul Morphy is entitled to rank with the foremost men of the world, because he can do what no other living man can do, then "Blind Tom" is equally worthy of public admiration, for in music he is as far excels, in some particulars, all other musical geniuses, as the celebrated chess player excels all others in the movements of the board.

But the reader is anxious to inquire, what are the facts in this marvellous case? We believe them to be these: Born on a plantation in Georgia, nothing was known of this boy's peculiar musical faculty until he was about six or eight years of age. A piano in the house of his master had frequently arrested the child's attention, and it was noticed that any performance upon it affected him to singular enthusiasm. But, of course, a piano was very properly, as would be supposed, a forbidden object to a little blind negro boy's touch. At midnight, on a certain occasion, however, the occupants of the house were startled by the sound of the instrument. Who could be playing it at that hour? On descending to the parlor to ascertain the cause of this unexpected serenade, there was "Blind Tom," playing away in triumphant possession, successful at his first effort. He was performing an air of the class familiar to the negroes of the plantation. Of course the surprising event made "Tom" a hero. Like Lord Byron, without the waking up, he "found himself famous." It was soon discovered that such was his imitative power in music, that after hearing the most elaborate and difficult pieces performed a few times, he could reproduce them with an accuracy as minute as it was astounding. He has had no instruction from musical teachers, and does not even know the name of the different notes in the scale.

On Saturday last we had the satisfactory test of "Tom's wonderful power of imitation. Repeated invitations had been given by Mr. Oliver, the gentleman to whom he belongs, to the effect that any gentleman or lady of the audience might play with "Tom" a duet, allowing four hands at the instrument, and although "Tom" might never have heard the piece, he would instantly play a correct accompaniment, and then changing seats with the principal, would reproduce the principal's part on the upper keys, no matter how long it might be. It happened that Mr. Otto Sutro was in the audience, a gentleman well known in this city as a musical teacher and composer, standing in the front rank of his profession. He walked to the platform, took his seat beside "Tom" and produced a brilliant melody, which, as the gentleman himself afterward informed us, was mainly an *improvisation*, so that "Tom" could not have heard it before. The boy went through it with courage and success. Had we not witnessed this feat, we could not have believed it possible.

Any piece heard by "Tom" seems to make the same impression on his brain that an object placed before a daguerrean instrument makes upon the plate which is to receive it. Once on his brain, it is soon at his finger ends. If the object before the daguerreotypist has defects upon it, the plate will show the defects. So, if the time, (for instance,) of the performer from whom "Tom" learns a piece is defective, the time for his reproduction will be correspondingly defective; and if the performer makes a false note in the piece, "Tom" will strike the same key precisely at the same chance when he renders it, unless it is so discordant as to shock his nicer sense of harmony. This should be borne in mind by those who bring to "Tom's" performances the critical taste which they would exercise in noting the skill of one whose life had been given to musical science.

Now the whole case must be considered. See, here is a blind black boy, with all the peculiarities of his race, full of tricks and antics, clapping his hands in childish glee when the audience applauds, cutting all manner of monkey shines—now shrugging his shoulders, now grimacing grotesquely, now awkwardly gesticulating, and soon looking supremely silly, in the blank simplicity of his unsophisticated boyhood—a real unmitigated specimen of a little uncultivated corn-field or cotton-plantation negro, feeling himself quite out of place before a refined and intellectual audience—yet whose power over the instrument, when his fingers once has touched it, is such that holds multitudes in speechless wonder, and behind whose nighttime halls is a storehouse of memory that carries apparently all the music he ever heard in his life. Not mere simple airs are they, but long and difficult compositions, requiring delicate skill of manipulation in expressive rendering. These are flung from his fingers with a strength and energy which show how perfectly the passion for music has the mastery of his whole being.

Whatever slight defects in *time* some of the boy's imitations may exhibit, the *time* of his own compositions is faultless; for "Tom" is not simply a mocking bird. He can *improvise* with astonishing success. One of his originals is a great favorite with the public. He calls it the "Oliver Gallop," in compliment to his master. It is sprightly in movement, flashing with brilliance, and while it partakes somewhat of the negro peculiarity of melody, is so charmingly rendered, that it never fails to bring down the house in a perfect storm of applause. Prof. Stoddard, of this city, is preparing it for publication. By the way, it is quite evident that "Tom" relishes a little of the motion of the cane and heel among the spectators, quite as well as some older and graver persons, who occasionally are called upon to stand in the presence of the multitude.

The fingering of "Tom" is unique. It is itself a proof that he has had no teacher. A scientific performer would crack his knuckles if he did not move his fingers with a more conventional and artistic grace. But "Tom's" is the fingering of nature, and whatever the Professors may say, it is beautiful, because it is natural. That so slight a hand, with so singular and yet so certain a motion, should bring from the instrument such stirring

---

An 1860 poster that first helped establish the myth of the untaught musical genius.

His master announced the exhibition closed, when a musician (who was a citizen of the town, by-the-way) drew out a thick roll of score, which he explained to be a Fantasia of his own composition, never published. The manuscript was some fourteen pages long,—variations on an inanimate theme. Mr. Oliver refused to submit the boy's brain to so cruel a test; some of the audience, even, interfered; but the musician insisted, and took his place. Tom sat beside him—his head rolling nervously from side to side—struck the opening cadence, and then, from the first note to the last, gave the secondo triumphantly. Jumping up, he fairly shoved the man from his seat, and proceeded to play the treble with more brilliancy and power than its composer.

So let the skeptics doubt, a persuasive body of evidence said otherwise.

But these were only half of the "succinct but unintelligible" tales to reach Mr. Weisel. Woven into many of these articles are base and grotesque descriptions that the respectability-conscious Perry Oliver would not have dared to utter. *The Atlantic Monthly* also feasted on descriptions of Tom sitting before the piano, "stretching out his arms full-length, like an ape clawing for food, answering some joke of his master's with a loud 'Yha! yha!' Nothing indexes the brain like the laugh; this was idiotic. 'Now, Tom, boy, something we like from Verdi.'"[10]

On the eve of the show, this was the image Perry Oliver wanted Mr. Weisel to see: not the genius but the beast. "As we passed the hotel where he was staying, we saw Tom looking out the window, going through the most ludicrous contortions of the face and attitudes of the body; at one time he would jump up and down as if on a springboard; then he would seize hold of the window sill and hang his head out and down as far as he could get it; then throw out his hands and feet for the brick wall, then place his ear to the wall as if listening—to what?—there was no music afloat—nothing but the noise incident to a large town."

Without daring to utter the distasteful "F" word, Oliver presented to the crowd who had gathered outside the hotel, a freak that would make Barnum proud. But if they wanted to know if his genius eclipsed the infant Mozart, if he could really sing in several languages, compose music that judges had pronounced beautiful, then good money needed to be handed over.[11]

In the hours leading up to Blind Tom's first concert in Mr.

Weisel's town, an intriguing mixture of rumor and fact had worked the public up into a frenzy of anticipation. The issue of whether the nine-year-old could meet expectations did not seem to bother Oliver in the slightest. The secret, as he well understood, was not in the actual experience but in the anticipation of it. By now, the suspense in the over-crowded hall was palpable. What could the crack-brained creature possibly play?

Well, according to musically literate Mr. Weisel, nothing but simple polkas, marches and scottishes that were "not over well done"—none of the promised Weber, Beethoven, augmented chords and fugues. Instead Tom attacked the piano in a most irregular fashion. First, he played *Yankee Doodle* with his left hand and *The Fishers Hornpipe* with his right, the two tunes blending together perfectly. Then he spun around and played it with his back to the piano—*The Fishers Hornpipe* with his left hand and *Yankee Doodle* on the right.

He was a cipher for the times too. Fifty years before the invention of the phonograph, Tom echoed the world back to his audience—railroad cars, drum and fifes and music boxes. In the early years of cinema, the mere image of a dolphin hurdling up and down a pool or an x-ray of a frog was enough to engross audiences. Similarly, the reproduction of commonplace sounds could enthrall antebellum audiences for entire minutes. "He imitated a locomotive about to start," reported Mr. Wiesel. "Taking the common chord of C he commenced to striking the *ppp* and slow, gradually accelerating the tempo and playing louder, while from his chest he puffed forth the steam thus: *tschoo tschoo!*"

Feats such as these failed to win Tom praise in *Dwights Journal of Music*, the champion of quality music. "Oh horrors," was Mr. Weisel's assessment. He had not attended the show to see novelties but to hear "The Greatest Living Musician: Only Ten Years Old and Master of the Piano." Where was the power, he wondered, the delicacy and brilliance of execution, the reproduction, after a single hearing, "of the most difficult pieces"?:

> The pretensions put forward by the handbills were not "commanded by a scrutiny of scientific and musical skeptics" for we could not persuade Mr. Oliver to allow Tom to reproduce a given piece because of an alleged illness. He cannot repeat long songs and discourses without the loss of many syllables and even entire sentences. He does not interpret severely classical composers and we

doubt if he ever heard a piece of even ever so small a classic caliber.

We are not willing to injure Tom's urbane and gentlemanly master, neither are we willing to disparage Tom's wonderful powers as a memorist but we utterly deny that he is endowed with the qualities of a musical genius. In all of Tom's performances—and we saw four—his fantasy did not take him beyond the bounds of his relationship to the tonic; to this he clung like a ship wrecked mariner to a spar—it was his tower of strength.[12]

This was only one of a plethora of outraged letters to the editor to *Dwight's Journal,* as the musically discerning customers vented their spleen. "Highfalutin,'" was one description of Oliver's style, "a tremendous olio of incomprehensible musical phrases, egotism and promises of the things which Tom was about to do."[13] Tom's performance consisted of nothing more than "the most commonplace pieces of the rub-a-dub tum tum diddle diddle order. I certainly did not expect he would be able to repeat it with any near approach to perfection," said one woman of the Audience Challenge, "but neither was I prepared for the utter failure which followed. Tom began with a faint semblance of the original music, then immediately fell into an incoherent fumbling among the keys and soon gave up altogether. And so the exhibition ended. I think you will pronounce Blind Tom a fine specimen of the richest Barnumesque."[14]

"I tried him with the Fugue in B flat no 21 out of the *Well Tempered Clavier* feeling perfectly certain that he could not possibly perform it after only one hearing," reported another. "Sure enough, he did fail. The subject he gave well enough and the response but when the third voice came, it was evidently chaos to Tom; only now and then a few notes of more intelligible connection would emerge from the general confusion."[15]

Far from hurting the show, the cries of humbug worked in Perry Oliver's favor, stirring up a welcome bit of controversy. Most of the audience—who only had a rudimentary appreciation of music—were witnessing something entirely different from what Mr. Weisel and his ilk reported. It had less to do with the music he played and more to do with Tom himself . Blind Tom was the show and the various items only served to showcase his extraordinary powers. "He did all they claimed for him. I am astounded. I cannot account for it, no one can, no one understands it," wrote a confounded St. Louis man.[16]

So if it was not musical virtuosity, which of Perry Oliver's wild claims did Tom fulfill so profoundly?

A GORGON WITH ANGEL'S WINGS

When not under the influence of sweet sounds his face is devoid of life and expression [went a review in *The Charleston Courier*]. We see this awkward and stupid negro led to the piano stool; he takes the seat, but the first touch on the keys shows us his soul is made for music. He sweeps his hands over the keys with the air of a master and then we behold the inspiration manifesting itself in his countenance and movement till interest changes to awe and we are dumb with astonishment. The melody penetrates his whole being. An ecstatic influence flows from the keys into his fingers and rolls like a tide through his veins, lighting up a fire in every nerve as it courses along. His head is thrown back; now it rests on one shoulder, now the other and again it falls on his breast. A light kindles the blank face and, as we gaze, wondering, the fashion of his countenance seems to change. It is absolutely beautiful. This divine ravishment increases every moment and, when he is thoroughly suffused with the inspiration of the melody, the muscles in his face twitch and his upper teeth are placed firmly upon his lower lip. A feeling of reverence steals over us as we behold this mysterious and sudden transformation.

While this review may possibly be a plant (*The Charleston Courier* published it two days before his actual concert in the city), it is by no means the only description of its kind. A cluster of letters and reviews also fixate on this mysterious transformation from beast to divinity. *The Atlantic Monthly*, after wallowing in descriptions of Tom's bestial barbarity, leaped to praise the harmony and perfection of his music. "The head fell farther back, the claws began to work, and the purest exponents of passion began to float through the room." "When I first saw Tom," reported another writer, "the door opened and a gentleman led forward a grinning idiotic Congo boy whom with some trouble he controlled. Tom appears more like an ape than a man. He bowed as if his head was coming off and while the gentleman was talking, kept grinning and rolling his eyes. He was led to the piano and took his seat. He threw his head back and commenced with all the ease, yet vim of a master."[17]

In these reports, Tom somehow shapeshifted from a jerky, fidgety, disjointed boy into a fluid, harmonious and focused "master" the moment his hands took command of the keyboard. The incessant squirming and rocking, the hesitant gait and blank open-mouthed stamp of "idiocy" vanished before the audience's very eyes. Oliver was right: whatever they had seen, whatever they had heard, nothing could prepare them for this transformation. This is what people remembered, told their friends about, crowded in to see, waxed lyrical over. His playing was a far cry from the great masters, but who cared? They had got what they came for: the Monster had become the Maestro, "a gorgon with angel's wings." "When the concert was over," wrote a Montgomery man, "I went to the stage and looked at Tom at close range. He had relapsed into his idiotic state and was swaying about, rolling his head from side to side, humming snatches of tunes and had to be led by the sleeve to keep him from straying off."[18]

In his book *An Anthropologist On Mars*, Oliver Sacks profiles Stephen Wiltshire, a British-born artist and autistic savant who, at the age of nineteen, erupted with extraordinary musical powers. In the course of Sacks's career in neurology, he had witnessed an astounding array of paradoxical brain conditions but was "startled" to watch Stephen sing Tom Jones's signature tune *It's Not Unusual*.

> He sang with great enthusiasm, swinging his hips, dancing, gesticulating, miming, clutching an imaginary microphone to his mouth, addressing himself in imagination to a vast arena . . . Stephen took on Jones' flamboyant physicality, adding to it the flavor of Stevie Wonder. He seemed completely at one with the music, completely possessed—and at this point there was none of the skewed neck posture that is habitual with him, none of the stiltedness, the ticcing, the aversion of gaze. His entire autistic persona, it seemed, had totally vanished, replaced by movements that were free, graceful, with emotional appropriateness and range. Very startled at this transformation, I wrote in large capitals in my notebook 'AUTISM DISAPPEARS.' But as soon as the music stopped, Stephen looked autistic once again.[19]

Was this also true of Tom? Did music offer him relief from the splintering effects of autism? Is that what fuelled his all-consuming determination to get to the piano? And did his relapse into the autistic state when forced to stop playing, trigger his bouts of anxiety?

Was music his sanctuary, his way of accessing a more integrated state of mind?

One hundred and twenty years would pass before questions like these could be asked; eighty years until "autism" was even diagnosed as a unique condition. In the nineteenth century, scientists divided "deficients" into various groups of ability: feebleminded, idiots, imbeciles, cretins and morons. These categories were then dovetailed into popular race hierachies to "prove" that the African was closer to the animal kingdom than the more highly evolved European. Race theories had Tom square, cut and stitched. Yet he seemed to possess a special something that made nonsense of them. How could this be an example of the lowest rung of humanity? A mind dredged of all intelligence and purity? African-American slaves may have had one answer but to a white mindset languishing at the self-appointed summit of the race hierarchy, nothing made sense.

Perry Oliver was not interested in solving the mystery but flogging it for all it was worth. And while his gift for the gab was instrumental in building up a head of steam, he did not achieve this success alone. While he was on stage loudly trumpeting Tom's glory, a genteel Englishman sold tickets by the door. But was this his only task?

It could never be admitted that the "Plantation Negro Boy" with his "one hour's instruction" was in fact traveling with his music tutor, and that teacher was largely responsible for *developing the show*. So while everyone who saw Blind Tom during these years was sure to remember the bombast of Perry Oliver, only a handful of insiders knew the name of William Henry Palmer.

LUDICROUSLY IMPOSSIBLE

If Perry Oliver genuinely believed that Tom was a "Heaven taught genius" when he negotiated the licensing deal with Bethune, by the time they played Savannah, Charleston, Mobile and Montgomery, he was painfully aware that Tom's repertoire and novelties fell well short of their potential. The show needed a good shake up and Oliver could not do it alone. Perhaps out of desperation, he secured a booking at the Spalding & Rogers Museum, the "educational wing" of an impressive circus complex. Here Tom's concerts were touted as "séances"—a small semantic shift that suggested that the great masters were channeling themselves into the body of the blind "witless" child. This they did four times a day, one hour apiece. Blind Tom, in short, was a circus sideshow act.

After Barnum had his way with them, "museums" were not simply repositories for natural, scientific and historical artifacts, but a uniquely nineteenth century euphemism for "freak show." It enabled showmen like Spalding & Rogers to exhibit their curiosities not in sinful sideshows but the learned environs of a "museum." Popular plays and variety acts could be viewed in the sanitary safety of a "Lecture Hall," while freaks were woven into "educational exhibits." And it was here—according to one unverifiable source—that Perry Oliver met a struggling magician-cum-musician named William Palmer, who himself was licking his wounds after a disastrous stage debut in New York. Whatever the circumstances of their meeting, Oliver immediately recognized that Palmer's background in music and illusion was ideally suited to Blind Tom's gifts and promptly enlisted his help.

While it is true that Blind Tom was taught, he also learnt astonishingly fast and could nail a polka or a waltz in an hour or so. "He would spin around the piano like a baboon mumbling to himself whilst Palmer played," remembered one insider, "and if he stopped Tom would rush headlong to the instrument and try to follow him as precisely as he had phrased. Two or three of such lessons sufficed and though he learned nothing accurately, nor played with any other expression than they had rendered, what he did was surprising, even to those who knew the process and the limitation."[20]

Palmer made a concerted effort to fulfill the promises Perry Oliver was feeding the public. The nine-year-old whose fingering was "unlike anything else before known"[21] churned out a smattering of light classics as best he could: Mendelssohn's *Spring Song*, Weber's *Last Waltz*, one of Beethoven's "so-called waltzes," a transcription from Liszt and, of course, something from Sigismond Thalberg, the Swiss piano virtuoso who had just completed a triumphant tour of the States. Palmer routinely altered the original scores to suit Tom's level of skill, prompting one irate listener to complain that Verdi's *Anvil Chorus* suffered from a dexterous twisting and dovetailing of so many strains that it was "both amusing and painful to those, like myself, who profess to know something about the originals."[22]

The classics thus covered, Palmer turned his attentions to a more popular selection of music: waltzes, polkas and a smattering of sentimental songs about Mother. In fifty years time, Tin Pan Alley would churn out a welter of bleary-eyed nostalgia songs with centralized, almost mechanized, regularity. But for now, music composition was less an industry and more a localized, *ad hoc* affair with hits created and transmitted by marching bands, blackfaced minstrels and the occasional child prodigy.

The name Eugene Baylor means little today, but one hundred and fifty years ago, the New Orleans pianist was enjoying a wave of popularity. It was no small feat for William Palmer to get Baylor to teach Tom his popular hit, the "famous" *Margrave Danse*. Tom's performance of it—sold to the public as if played from a single chance hearing —was as close to the horse's mouth as anyone was going to get.

Other teachers may have lacked Baylor's stature, but they certainly knew how to milk a sentimental song for all it was worth. Near the Tennessee line lived "a certain Major Maccionico who had a very great baritone voice. He taught Tom to sing *Rocked in the Cradle of the Deep* very much as he sang it. There was a tailor in Griffin, Georgia, by the name of Hamon whose tenor voice was fetching and he taught Tom two or three love ditties which Tom repeated in rich though guttural tones, yet in undoubted tenor."

Word for word, gesture for gesture, Blind Tom reproduced the soldier's quivering piety and the tailor's mawkish sufferance with utter sincerity—surely a sight more amusing than affecting—but mid-nineteenth century audiences lapped it up and *Rocked in the Cradle* was a fixture of Blind Tom's repertoire for decades to come. Music though was only half of the Blind Tom show and William Palmer was fully equipped to develop the novelties that were to dominate the second half of the program.

Like Blind Tom, William Palmer was a child prodigy. The son of an organist at Canterbury Cathedral, his gifts were cultivated by Franz Liszt who fast-tracked him into the Royal Academy of Music. But Palmer's musical career made a sharp and unexpected detour when the fourteen-year-old witnessed the astonishing feats of the French master illusionist, Jean Eugene Robert-Houdin. From that moment on, magic became Palmer's abiding passion and he devoted the next two and a half decades to emulating his idol, honoring him in his choice of stage name—Robert Heller—and adopting not only the signature tailcoat, top hat and cane but also a moustache, wig and heavy French accent for his 1858 American stage debut. The show ended in humiliating failure, the apprentice still unable to convincingly pull off Houdin's illusions—a crushing blow for the thirty-year-old desperate to gain a toehold in show business. But Palmer need not have fretted. In ten more years, "Robert Heller" would be hailed as "the greatest magician of his age," a droll and entertaining performer most famous for his rendition of Houdin's signature act—*Second Sight*.

Though it shared the same name, *Second Sight* the act had no connection with phenomenon chronicled by the slaves of Tom's youth. Far from communicating with the spirit world, this brand of magic was strictly for entertainment purposes, its success hinging on astute observation and a powerful memory. The magician (or mind reader) had to be able to absorb the details of every object in a room from a single glance. Once blindfolded, an assistant would present him with an item, which, after a few secret prompts, he then described in detail.[23]

When William Palmer met Perry Oliver in 1859, he was still grappling with the arduous demands of this complex act, but very quickly—and a tad enviously—recognized that young Tom's phenomenal memory was ideally suited to this form of "mind-reading."

Tom's early novelty acts bear all the hallmarks of *Second Sight*. The most perplexing of them involved Blind Tom smelling an object, then naming its color or identifying a person by the smell of their hand. "Flowers were handed to him of various hues of which he named the color after smelling," reported Mr. Weisel. "But that a blind idiot should have an idea of color is a thing ludicrously impossible." In keeping with Houdin's method, Perry Oliver could have slipped Tom a coded clue as handed him each flower. The question "what is the color?" signified, say, red while "can you name its color?" may have indicated that it was white.[24]

What is really "ludicrously impossible" is the notion that Tom could identify colors when he was off the stage, without a manager in sight. Oscar Jordan claimed that "Tom could feel a piece of cloth and tell the color, or smell the house and tell what was in it." And a Washington lady in the 1870's witnessed something similar during an informal evening with Tom at the Bethunes' home:

> I asked him the color of different objects held before him. To each of these queries he gave very correct replies and, regarding, apparently, with great intentness one of the ladies present, he slowly said, "I should say that her eyes are rather, rather blueish; her hair is

"Robert Heller"—the stage name of the struggling magician and musician. William Palmer was instrumental in developing Tom's stage act.

rather, rather brownish" and so on in a halting spasmodic manner. He continued to make invariably correct criticisms or most accurate guesses. If neither, then Tom must have been endowed with another sight as unerring and inscrutable as his musical comprehension.[25]

Even today it is difficult to explain how Tom knew the answer to the Washington lady's questions. Without more information, the scientists I have put this to cannot offer a definitive explanation. Maybe the Bethune family was playing a trick on her, they wonder. Maybe the entire experience was stage managed. But what if it wasn't? Then what?

Perhaps Tom had some vision, suggested one—certainly he could detect through his cataracts objects if they were silhouetted by a bright light, but features, colors, even proportions were said to be beyond his visual comprehension.

Maybe, then, he was a synaesthese. Many blind people develop synaesthesia—a condition where the boundaries of the senses are blurred and sensations that are otherwise experienced separately are joined together. Some people can hear music as color, while others can experience music as taste, scent or touch. This condition enables a blind person to have a relationship with the world of color; however—and this is the crux—the colors they see in their mind's eye do not correspond to the actual color of an object.[26]

Other blind people can "see" in the sense that they have attuned their ear to subtle variations in the acoustic landscape—echoes in a built-up area, crispness in a wide open expanse—and can quite easily describe objects in their midst. Tom certainly was capable of this. Eyewitnesses report that he could identify objects without touching them and knew if he was passing a tree or house while traveling on a train. But was he so sensitive to his environment that he could detect the wavelength of a color?

Whether Tom was hyper-sensory, cross-sensory, extra-sensory or very well stage-managed, the results were the same—he was extraordinarily adept at "mind reading." Impressed, magician William Palmer was inspired to push it further. The Audience Challenge, an act first initiated by the Bethunes, was reinvented. Instead of an audience member simply challenging him to reproduce their melody, Tom now sat beside the challenger and played secondo to a tune he had never heard before, then changed seats and played the primo.[27]

Palmer also developed one of Tom's most famous novelties: playing one song with his right hand, another with his left while singing a third—first with his hands to the piano, then with his back to the piano. This demanded a skill that magicians like Palmer and Houdin spent long hours perfecting: simultaneously following two or more trains of thought. "Nothing is more favorable in conjuring than to be able to think at the same time both what you are saying and what you are doing," noted The Great Houdin.

Blind Tom—again to Palmer's begrudging admiration—was able to execute this feat without any rigorous training. For this was an everyday state for Tom, his autistic mind routinely perceiving thoughts in detached, self-contained streams that were independent of each other. The great challenge for Tom, in fact, was precisely the opposite.

She Used to Wash My Face

AWAY FROM THE SPOTLIGHT, TOM WAS NEITHER BEAST NOR GENIUS BUT a singularly obsessive child who, when not immersed in sound, compulsively gamboled around on one leg, spoke only of the things that interested him and was mute to the things that did not. An indulged child, showered with more candy than love, with a volatile ego the size of the previous night's takings; a startlingly physical child who literally bounced off the walls of his plush hotel rooms; a stubbornly intractable child who steadfastly refused to do as he was told, forcing his master to beg, barter and flatter.

Mr. Weisel and his father witnessed first hand Oliver's tactics in his ongoing battle of wills with Tom. They had been invited to the hotel room to transcribe a composition Tom named in his manager's honor, *The Oliver Gallop,* and there came across the prodigy on the floor, kicking and laughing with his personal black servant. Oliver somehow had to get him behind the piano to play *The Oliver Gallop* one measure at a time.

Tom did not want to play that morning, that is he did not want to play what he was asked to play: he was peevish and fretful as a child. When asked to repeat The Oliver Gallop, so that we, his amanuensis, could write it, he said that he did not want his pieces written. "Why Tom!" said Oliver "you're going to have your pieces published. They'll go all over the world with your name on them, and everyone will play them and you'll be a great boy." "I don't want my pieces published and I don't want anyone else to play them," Tom said. Finally by threats and offers of candy he was induced to play it as often and in the manner we desire it. After we had completed our copy we sat down to play it. Tom was perfectly infuriated, tears coursed down his cheeks and he attempted to push me off the piano stool. "I don't want him to play my pieces," he said. Threats and candy again appeased his anger and he became as gentle as a lamb . . .

"That evening we presented the transcription to Mr. Oliver and played it for him. Tom again was very indignant. He said he didn't like me and that he wanted to go away out of this ole town. He cried to go and even candy and his musical box, with the everlasting Yankee Doodle in it, would not quiet him."[1]

Perry Oliver, William Palmer and the unnamed manservant—who, more than likely, bore the brunt of Tom's obstreperousness—learnt how to manage the child star's eccentricities and obsessions, but he himself remained an enigma. Beyond accounts that compared his gifts to the divine, his instinct to an animal or temperament to an infant, few clues exist to how he made sense of the world. Even the scientists who would exhaustively test his perfect pitch and astounding memory could not account for the anxieties and oddities of his everyday life. Thanks to contemporary research into the autistic imagination, the workings of Tom's capricious and highly original mind are now better understood.

"THE MOST WONDERFUL FEAT OF MEMORY I RECOLLECT"

Scores of people tell what is essentially the same story about Tom's phenomenal memory: he never forgot a thing. Mr. "C Sharp" had not seen Tom since he and his wife visited the Bethune home six years earlier. In the early 1860's, he chanced upon Tom and John Bethune on a train and to his infinite surprise, Tom greeted him with a "how'd'ye Mr. Sharp; how's Miss Fanny?" To which Sharp replied, "Why Tom, how do you know me so well?" "Oh I knows you, en Miss Fanny too. Don't you know when you were at our house as played dis tune?" and Tom whistled the very Miss Fannie had played him all those years ago.[2]

In 1860, Professor E. L. Ide of Frederick, Maryland, tested Tom with a little known German waltz to which he added some flourishes.

Twenty-one years later, on a return visit to the town, Tom played the piece note for note to the astonished professor. It was "the most wonderful feat of memory I recollect," pronounced one eyewitness.[3]

On another occasion, Lynchburg's Mr. E. D. Gallion asked Blind Tom when he had last performed there. "In 18-79, sir," replied Tom, in his halting manner. "So it was, so it was. It was in summer wasn't it?" suggested Gallion. "No sir. It was—in January—sir." "He's perfectly right," announced Mr. Gallion to the group, delighted with the result.[4]

Newspapers published snippets likes these in their droves. The questions may have varied but reaction remained the same: the tingle of surprise followed by the warm tones of flattery. For the questioner it was the ultimate ego boost—of the hundreds of thousands of people the famous Blind Tom had met throughout his career, he remembered "me." But any warm fuzzy feeling was misplaced. Tom did not just remember them, he remembered *everyone* with the same matter-of-fact disinterest. He was not pleased to see them or interested to know how they had been. Once he had promptly and honestly answered their questions, the conversation was over. Their meeting was just another dispassionate fact in his fact-filled brain. "He always spoke of himself in the third person," observed one of his managers. "'Tom wants to do so and so,' 'Tom is getting pretty hungry,' 'Don't you think its about time Tom went down the hall to see that piano?' It was the same impersonal interest in himself that made him rise when he had finished playing some great composition, and clap his hands uproariously. Others always applauded—He liked it too—Why should not he?"[5]

How different his involvement was from the personalized interest of those asking him the questions. Their recollection of events was blinkered by subjectivity, filtered by emotion and shaped by cultural norms. (Indeed, Tom may have disputed aspects of C Sharp's version of events. For a start, Tom did not speak in a broad Southern dialect, rarely asked questions and had a hesitant manner of address: "two or three words and a pause, two or three more and another pause and is never known to fail to tack a civil 'sir' at the end of his replies," *The North American* reported.) For people like Mr. Sharp, memories were intimately bound up with meaning, another episode in the narrative of their life and ultimately their identity. Whereas Tom's memory—which was independent of subjectivity, meaning and context—read more like a dictionary than a novel.

"She used to wash my face," is the response Tom once gave when introducing the daughter of the manager who had known him for twenty years.[5] Whether or not he liked this woman, whether she was kindly, rough, impatient or flirtatious was beyond his detection and concern. It was not a matter of poor language skills: quite the contrary, Tom had an extraordinary vocabulary. Missing from his conversation was the curiosity to glean intent, evaluate non-verbal body cues and figure out what was really going on. The result was a steadfast literalness that reduced complex issues to simple cause-and-effect explanations and somehow missed the point.

So when Perry Oliver—tongue firmly planted in his cheek—waxed lyrical about the dizzying heights of Tom's fame, the adoring public who marveled at his genius, Tom quite understandably took him at his word. He had no idea there was a darker, crueler side to the public's fascination in him. As far as he was concerned he was the "Wonder of the World," a musical genius, the marvelous curiosity of the age and he loved to be reminded of it.

The success of Oliver's little game highlights an important distinction that would elude Tom for all his days: the difference between the known and the unknown. "You cheat me! You cheat me!" he once bellowed to a young lady he was dueting with who, in order to test his memory, skipped a page of the score.[7] To him, dishonesty and deception were simply a matter of not playing to a set of clearly defined rules. For something to exist but not be known to him (like being called bestial and idiotic) was outside his comprehension. In this sense, he was the ultimate behavioralist, never questioning the nature of reality but accepting it just as presented to him, as if no other possibility existed. So while he was incensed by the young lady's minor infraction, he remained oblivious to the ever-greater deceptions that were to be instigated by his guardians and managers.

AN ISLAND

Tom was no stranger to expressing emotion, it was something he did in buckets. His challenge lay in recognizing the same emotions in other people and responding to them in a socially acceptable way. "Once in a small town his manager locked him in the hall as usual and Tom amused himself with the piano," recalled his manager's face-washing daughter. "When his manager returned he was surprised to find Tom holding a man down on the floor and almost choking him. The man was yelling out and Tom was delighted."[8] Tom's skewed reaction to other people's pain had been evident since early childhood but there was nothing cruel in his intent. He was simply unable to equate the sounds of other people's pain with the *sensation* of pain. He recognized these feelings in himself but not in others, hearing in their anguished and tormented cries only intense and exquisite tones.

For all his gifts of "second sight," Tom was unable to decipher unspoken messages that non-autistic people take for granted and had to be schooled in socially-appropriate responses, although this was met with mixed results: "To this day," reads the concert program, "any exclamation or expression indicative of pain gives him great pleasure; and though he will express sympathy for the sufferer, and prescribe remedies for his relief, he cannot restrain his expressions of pleasure."

In a word, Tom lacked empathy. Not only were a person's emotions lost in translation but so was their individual identity as Tom assumed that everyone's thoughts and feelings were just the same as his own—a singular notion in a society defined by race distinctions. But if fundamentals like this eluded him, how did he have any hope of comprehending the complex and secretive game slaves played with their masters? The lip service they paid to their Master's authority before slinking off into the woods to pray for their deliverance? How could he read that their ever-happy smiles were little more than a supplicant mask?

In Tom, Georgia's complex social hierarchy tumbled to the ground. Masters, mistresses, managers and slaves all possessed one mind: Tom's mind. But everyone else—black or white—was struck by the huge gulf that stood between them and him. It was a most intriguing paradox: within the all-encompassing homogeneity of Tom's world, "he stood apart," an island.

'I MIGHT FALL DOWN & KILL MYSELF'

A compulsive urge to move and mutter occupied Tom's every waking moment. "His fingers worked incessantly, his lips moved constantly in audible whisperings."[9] From the time he could walk, he was spinning and stomping, snatches of conversation unspooling verbatim. By the age of eight, if not playing piano, he was mumbling and tumbling on hands and heels. Audiences did not know whether to be shocked or amused by the wild leaps that accompanied each round of applause or what to make of his finely balanced poses. Phrenologist Orson Fowler, who met Blind Tom when he was sixteen, was stunned by his athleticism:

> One very singular exercise of his consists in standing on one foot, bending his body forward horizontally, and straightening the other leg out backward so that the foot is in line with his head. In this position he leaps around the room perhaps twenty times or more. His leaps are from a half yard to a yard-and-a-half in extent, and it almost makes one giddy to see him make these circuits, and at the same time apprehensive, lest his foot slip and he dash his head on the floor. In making these circuits he will go within six inches of the wall, but never hit it. He has various other methods of exercising his legs and hips, which must be seen to be appreciated.[10]

But why, Fowler surely must have asked himself. What impelled Tom to repeat the same spectacular motion over and over again? What drove him to adhere to this rigidly fixed pattern? Was it animal, physical, spiritual or racial? Or was it something quite beyond the nineteenth century imagination?

Cognitive psychologists today—who find in the computer endless analogies to the brain—would attribute this behavior to a weak information processing system. Autistic children, they say, experience sensory stimuli in disconnected streams that are independent of context and meaning (which explains why Tom could so easily master the magician's tricks of simultaneously following two or more trains of thought). A plethora of clinical experiments support this general hypothesis and the findings have coalesced into the Theory of Mind, a somewhat clinical description that underplays the terrifying bouts of anguish and torment associated with it.

"There was crying, blowing, clamouring and noises of the fishmonger, milkman, ragpickers, newsboys, dealers in popcorn—ear splitting noises, which were often drowned in the rumblings of the wagons and the cries of the street gamuns. All this shocked my aesthetic sense beyond expression," wrote one bewildered immigrant of his arrival in New York in 1846. If a sighted non-autistic person found the urban assault disorientating, then what would Tom—who neither forgot, differentiated or prioritized—make of the deluge of sensory information as he alighted the train at some of the South's larger cities: horseshoes and iron-tired wheels clopping and clanking on cobblestone streets; thunderous team-pulled drays; smells of horse urine, manure and harness oil; the confusion and scuffle of market day crowds. Go to pieces, perhaps? Splinter into fragments from the overload?

In these noisier times, special needs teachers have repeatedly recognized this fragmented identity in their autistic students' self-portraits—dismembered stick drawings: head, spine, legs and arms disconnected from one another, as if each limb was charged with a magnetic force field that repelled its connecting part. "Do you have to plug in your ears before you can make sense of what you are hearing? Do you have to find your legs before you can walk?" wrote one man of his childhood autism. "It wasn't enough to figure out just once how to keep track of my eyes and ears and hands and feet all at the same time, I had to find them over and over again. But I have found them again. The terror is never complete, and I'm never completely lost in the fog, and I always know that even if it takes forever, I will find the connections and put them back together again."[11]

These insights provide valuable clues about Tom. He walked with a quick, nervous step, was fretful and anxious, and his resentments were strong, even violent. He disliked cities and being in the midst of crowds, he was fearful of being overwhelmed by too many people. As Tom told two psychiatrists in 1865, the world was an unpredictable place:

DR. BLACKMAN:	Could you not get along by yourself?
BLIND TOM:	No sir, I could not get along at all.
DR. BLACKMAN	Why not?
BLIND TOM:	I might fall down and break my neck.
DR. GRAHAM:	If you could see could you not get along?
BLIND TOM:	I would not know which way to go.
DR. GRAHAM:	What would you do for a living if you were turned free in the city?
BLIND TOM:	Oh I would get sick.
DR. GRAHAM:	Get sick for being alone?

BLIND TOM:	O, I would catch cold . . .
DR. GRAHAM:	You are afraid all the time, are you?
BLIND TOM:	Yes sir. I don't want to be left by myself because I might fall down and kill myself. I might get lost. I could not see to get along.

Tom had no framework, no catalogue of experience, to guide him through new situations. Danger loomed around every corner, disaster courted every step, as if his prodigious memory and inexplicable "second sight" counted for nothing. Little wonder that he yearned to escape the overload and retreat into the certainty of performing the same elegant feat over and over again. Whether glued to the piano or executing gravity defying leaps, repetitive behavior provided him a safe harbor: not only did the grimaces and jerkiness disappear but the associated feelings of fragmentation did as well. Here he could revel, with effortless grace and ease, in a sense of containment and wholeness. As autistic savant Tito Rajarshri Mukhopadhyay so eloquently explains in one of his poems, "Spinning my body/Brings some sort of harmony to my thoughts. . . . The trouble is when I stop spinning/My body scatters/And it's so difficult to collect it together again."[12]

"THE 'A' IS WRONG"

Once Tom could escape the fracturing chaos of undifferentiated and constant change, a universe of endlessly subtle detail revealed itself to him. Powered by an almost superhuman capacity to concentrate on details most people would find inconsequential, he passed hours in absorbed rapture, his senses reveling in a fantastically intricate world of differentiated repetition: the crank of the butter churn, glint of sunshine in his eyes, the drip drip drip of water down a drainpipe, the clickety-clack of a train or warble of a bird. To the dying sound of a chord—the vibrational whisper between the sonic and the silent—his face would break out in a "score of nervous twitchings, which could not fail to show the intense delight that the chords gave his inmost soul."[13]

But this extreme sensitivity was also a source of distress. Mr. Weisel remembers his father randomly striking the strings of a cello in a hotel room. "Tom jumped up from his seat, clapped his hands to his ears, his face distorted and he cried: 'Oh please don't.'" Other reports tell of him frantically tearing at his hair, almost wild with displeasure, as he listened to a tonally-challenged schoolgirl shriek out a tune.[14] As Perry Oliver learnt to his peril, Tom would flatly refuse to play a piano that was even slightly out of tune. It was an obsession that intensified with age, Tom entering into pedantic and long-winded explanations of the whys and wherefores of piano tuning, as a reporter from *Ladies Home Journal* discovered in 1898:

> The day this writer called, the Negro pianist was expecting a tuner who would correct a faulty A on his concert grand. When I reached the house and pressed the button, the door was flung open by Blind Tom himself. My voice told him that I was not the tuner. With a childlike droop of disappointment he shut the door in my face.
>
> [His guardian] soon appeared. He suggested it might have a pacifying influence if I would hear Tom's explanation of the piano's shortcomings and promise to let the tuner know about them, so that he would promptly come to remedy them. This I accordingly did . . . . "The A is wrong" said Tom, pressing his finger on the note "and then this A is a little out too" sounding another two or three octaves above the first.

It was more than the ill-tuned note that affronted him. Tom was agitated because the note's imperfection transgressed the order of the octave. While concepts by and large eluded him, he was quite able to recognize patterns: that something could be similar, yet at the same time different. Middle A was similar yet different from upper A. But in strict adherence to this pattern, the note should be precisely just so and if it was not, the unity of Tom's fragile universe was literally in peril. When order was restored, then the world was his oyster and—as with the chord hovering on the cusp of silence—he could discover pleasure in things that few could even imagine.

For Tom, musical composition began with patterns. The order of the octave found on the piano could also be heard in the chug of the reaper, the song of a bird or patter of rain. It was then simply a matter of relaying this pattern—which Tom could discern to the nth degree—to the keys of the piano. Perhaps this is what he meant when he said he heard the wind and rain speak to him or the red bird teach him its song: they revealed to him the vibrational pattern intrinsic to their sound. In a world that could seem fragmented and incoherent, this limited and self-contained form of thought attachment was fertile grounds on which Tom's agile mind could begin to build its own systems of meaning: brilliant though rigidly narrow systems that did not necessarily coincide with general systems commonly accepted in the broader world.

"I'LL DO YOUR TOPLEY"

From the time he was young, Blind Tom showed a profound and highly idiosyncratic aptitude for language. The Bethune's cousin Oscar Jordan remembers that he "had the loveliest of visions, almost like poems but in his later years were loaded with peculiarities." A few of these "poems" have survived in the form of his *Vocal Compositions*, published when he was seventeen, and through pieces like *The Man Who Snatched The Cornet Out of His Hands* we can begin to fathom the mysterious gap between what made sense to Tom and what makes sense to the rest of us.

> Tell him to come up/I'll do your Topley/Don't be uneasy/Until I see you.
> Now he has gone up/Into his mason/Now you had hurt/Your Topley last night
> Now comes the tutti/Don't be in a hurry/Now I will have your/Band for to play me.
> One man had come up/And bought his cymbals/And snatched his cornet/Out of his hands.

At first glance, it is a nonsense although not an entire nonsense. The syntax holds, however simply, and the rhythm fits the eight line verse in 6/8 time. And while most individual lines make some kind of sense, the logic between one line and the next is less clear. Most intriguing is Tom's use of the words "Topley," "tutti" and "mason." "Tutti"—a musical term denoting "all together"—is used in an appropriate, though unconventional, way. "Mason" could be anything from a reference to the pianist William Mason, the secretive order, a tradesman, or even a phonics deviation of "mansion," leaving "Topley" as the only truly unfathomable word in Tom's private lexicon. This poem was based on an actual occurrence experienced by Tom and perhaps the meaning of "Topley" was forged by a random association that became forever fixed in his mind. "Sometimes, he used singular expressions,

"The thoughts expressed in these songs were suggested to the author by actual occurrences. The quaint form of the 'poems' furnish a striking illustration of Blind Tom's peculiar idiosyncrasies," reads the note beneath his bizarrely titled vocal compositions.

and asked unaccountable questions, as when he insisted that there was a lady in the audience playing on a fly," his manager told a Boston audience in 1866. "That happened several times, and once a lady humored him, and sent him a musical box as the fly. He was delighted with it, and kept it at his ear constantly." All testament to Tom's off-the-wall intelligence and original thinking.

Audiences who were captivated by the unexpected twists and turns of Tom's paradoxical mind seemed to suffer from a weak information processing system of their own, refusing to integrate his myriad of talents into a meaningful whole. As far as they were concerned Blind Tom had a single gift that spontaneously arose and would never change. But Tom encapsulated the American experience more than they could ever imagine. Like him, the country was teetering on the verge of disintegration, the Union of States poised to shatter into a collection of disparate pieces. In the propaganda wars between abolition and slavery, Tom was both an instrument and *cause celebre*, a cipher of the new explosive acoustic landscape and an enduring symbol of the old.

PART TWO

"FRANATICS"

Blind Tom in 1865.

- 9 -

Some Fellow Might
Steal Me

———◆———

THE WILLARD HOTEL, STANDING ON THE CORNER ON 14TH STREET
and Pennsylvania Avenue could, according to writer Nathaniel
Hawthorne, more justly be called the center of Washington than the
Capitol, White House or State Department. Just about everyone met
there. "You exchange nods with governors of sovereign States; you
elbow illustrious men, and tread on the toes of generals; you hear
statesmen and orators speaking in their familiar tones. You are
mixed up with office-seekers, wire-pullers, inventors, artists, poets,
clerks, diplomats, mail-contractors, railway-directors, until your
own identity is lost among them."[1]

Hawthorne could add to the mélange a child prodigy, a dilettante, a magician and a showman. For in May 1860, Perry Oliver
and eleven-year-old Blind Tom took up lodgings at the Willard and
here, in these fabled surrounds, William Palmer introduced them to
one of the hotel's best-loved residents, Henry Watterson.[2]

Son of a Tennessee Congressman, the pale skinny twenty-one-
year-old had spent half his life loafing about the Willard. It was for
many years his childhood home and the springboard to what was
proving to be a charmed youth. Officially in Washington to pursue
a career in journalism, Watterson's talent as an impresario made him
the darling of Washington society. Everyone loved Henry and none
more so than a bevy of Southern politicians' wives.

Watterson effortlessly bridged the world of politics and show
business. The previous year, he surprised even himself when *The*

New York Times employed him as their music critic. Admittedly a short-term arrangement, it was long enough for him to chance upon the magician "Robert Heller." Now both based in Washington, it was inevitable that they would meet again.

In the oak paneled halls of the Willard, William Palmer showcased his most promising student, Watterson's response outstripping anything he could have hoped for. "His crude, often grotesque, attempts to imitate whatever fell upon his ear, either vocally, or on the keyboard, were startling," Watterson wrote of this meeting almost a half century later. "Blind, deformed and black—as black even as Erebus—idiocy, the idiocy of a mysterious, perpetual frenzy, the sole companion of his waking visions and his dreams."[3] Here was a child who could conjure up the sybaritic presence of Senator Toombs, draw the song of the thrush from the piano then lapse into an endless round of one-footed leaps and spins. This was bigger than the pantomime witnessed daily on Capitol Hill, more arresting than a magician's sleight-of-hand or a virtuoso's masterful touch. Utterly intrigued, Watterson joined the tour party and, over the following months, chose the company of an "idiot" over the most influential minds of his time.

In stark contrast to the primordial chaos pouring from Tom, Perry Oliver was the master strategist, ever-monitoring the fault lines of American politics to predict the time and place of the next seismic shift. A hot-headed Southerner by instinct, it was perhaps the cordial atmosphere of the Willard that enabled him to ally himself with the son of a Southern Unionist and Stephen Douglas man—especially when that friend was as well-connected as Henry Watterson.

On the 9th of June in 1860, in a small private concert hall adjoining the hotel, Blind Tom made his Washington debut. About one hundred of Watterson's friends and acquaintances—including members of Japan's first trade delegation—listened as Oliver, in his high-falutin' style, explained how "music broke out on Tom like the small pox." While the prodigy's music was entertaining enough, it was his perplexing feats of memory that confounded all gathered. Only the Japanese trade delegation proved immune, looking on "with stolid indifference. It is pretty plain that they have no enjoyment of our music."[4]

Such trifles did not concern Oliver. Within days, word of Watterson's latest find reached the genteel drawing rooms of the Southern politicians' wives club. Miss Phillips and Miss Cohen—the daughter and niece of an Alabama Congressman—determined to see for themselves if the marvelous claims were true and invited the blind prodigy to a private soiree, testing his memory with a four-handed arrangement of Rossini's *Semiramide,* a task he passed with flying colors.

A musically-minded guest by the name of Harriet Lane was so impressed that a repeat performance was arranged at her place of residence. The niece and ward of James Buchanan, America's only bachelor president, Miss Lane by default was America's First Lady. During her time in the executive mansion, she had staged some of the most 'brilliant' music receptions of any administration. As ten-year-old Tom took his seat behind the elegant Chickering full grand piano, Perry Oliver could now boast the publicity coup of the year - although the historical significance of the moment may have eluded him. Tom was the first African-American performer to grace the White House.[5]

> At the invitation of Miss Lane, [wrote well-known Alabama socialite and senator's wife, Virginia Compton Clay] the Misses Phillips and Cohen took their places at the piano and performed a brilliant and intricate duet, during which Blind Tom's face twitched with what, it must be confessed, were horrible grimaces. He was evidently greatly excited by the music he was listening to, and was eager to reproduce it.[6]

It was here, in a duet with Tom, that one of the young ladies elided a page of the composition and cheated Tom, his display of drawn back indignation and anger a personal highlight for Virginia Clay. However, this is not the story that was reported. Rebecca Harding Davis's account in *The Atlantic Monthly* (presumably sourced from the hyperbolic Perry Oliver) enlarges both Tom's achievements and his failings. The limits of Tom's memory, it declared, were put to the test first with a thirteen-page then a twenty-page score. He triumphed in spectacular style but the following day collapsed, and was bedridden for days. After too prolonged an effort, Harding insisted, Tom's "whole bodily frame gives way, and a complete exhaustion of the brain follows, accompanied with epileptic spasms."

No reference to Tom's epilepsy has been noted before or since. It is a fiction invented by either by Oliver or Harding: a Dostoyevskyan flourish to help flesh out the stereotypical image of an idiot. In fact Tom's schedule was stepped up after the White House performance. Within days he was spotted with his manager at the House of Congress, the two soaking up the sectional vitriol.

CRUSHING INVECTIVES

Three weeks before Tom arrived in Washington, the South reeled with the news that an Illinois Congressman who denounced John Brown's abortive slave insurrection with words no stronger than "peculiar" and "absurd" was now the Republican's presidential nominee. As calamitous as Abraham Lincoln's election promised to be for the South, the prospect was becoming ever more likely, not because of overwhelming support for the so-called "Abolitionist candidate" but because of deep divisions in the Democratic Party.

That April, the Democrats convened in Charleston to elect their presidential candidate. Five days and fifty-seven ballots later there was no clear winner and the one man who consistently headed the pack—Illinois Senator Stephen A. Douglas—was reviled in the South for supporting Kansas' anti-slavery constitution. Already a group of Southern firebrands had bolted the conference in protest but even with their departure, Douglas still couldn't muster the numbers. Locked in a stalemate, the Democrats agreed to reconvene in Baltimore, thirty days later.

Such was the state of the union the day Blind Tom listened to the debate in the House of Congress. His stage performance of these speeches—delivered with such "accurate vocal inflections as to amuse and delight his audiences"—was for many the standout of his show, though nobody thought to leave any clues as to who he heard and what was said. However, the wife of one Virginia congressman, Sara Pryor, remembered the mood in the chamber:

> The nomination of Lincoln and Hamlin on a purely sectional platform aroused such excitement that the Senate and House of Representatives gave themselves entirely to speeches on the state of the country. Many of them appeared to be the high utterances of patriots, pleading with each other for forbearance. Others exhausted the vocabulary of coarse vituperation. "Nigger thief," "slave-driver" were not uncommon words. Others still, although less unrefined, were not less abusive. Newspapers no longer reported a speech as calm, convincing, logical, or eloquent. The terms now in use were: "a torrent of scathing denunciation," "withering sarcasm," "crushing invective," all the while the orator's eyes "blazing with scorn and indignation." Thoroughly alarmed, the women of Washington thronged the galleries of the House and the Senate-chamber. From morning until the hour of adjournment we would sit spellbound, as one after another drew the lurid picture of disunion and war.[7]

LEFT: *America's First Lady and niece of bachelor President James Buchanan, Harriet Lane, who invited Tom to perform at the White House.*
RIGHT: *Senator Stephen A. Douglas, the Democratic presidential candidate, who Tom imitated on stage after hearing him speak at a campaign rally in 1860.*

One week after his visit to Congress, Blind Tom was on stage repeating their crushing invectives and scathing denunciations to an audience howling with laughter. Reviews were euphoric. Overnight, Tom became the must-see show in town. And the time and place of this particular concert? Baltimore, June 18, 1860—the very night the Democratic convention opened.

Perry Oliver's sense of timing was anything but innocent. He had invested weeks planning this *coup*. Campbell's Minstrels may have been the convention's official entertainment but Oliver had worked the publicity machine overtime to snatch the limelight off the black-faced troupe and direct it squarely onto his eleven-year-old prodigy— "the true Ethiopian Minstrel." Oliver offered a show personally tailored to the politics of the day. The delegates who crowded into town for the heated showdown between Douglas and the Southern firebrands, cooled off in the evening, reveling in the slave child's dead-on impersonations of Washington's heavyweights.

The pattern was to continue as the election wore on. When Douglas hit the campaign trail later that year, Blind Tom and Perry Oliver were not far behind. In Lynchburg, Virginia, Tom joined a large and enthusiastic crowd to hear the "Little Giant," in his deep resonant voice, deliver an impassioned plea for unity and moderation, the thrust of his argument similar to a speech he delivered in Raleigh a few weeks later:

In 1850 the agitators of the North and the agitators of the South got us into similar trouble to the one now that threatens us. The Northern free soilers demanded the Wilmot Proviso prohibiting of slavery where the people wanted it. Yancey at the head of the fire-eaters of the South demanded that Congress should protect slavery wherever the people didn't want it. The issue then is precisely the issue now.[8]

Henry Watterson recalls how startled he was by Tom's graphic impression of "Judge" Douglas: an imitation that went beyond reproducing his silvery voice and agile tongue but somehow—almost impossibly—captured the gruff, physically emphatic countenance of the oddly-proportioned man. "Senator Douglas was very small," observed one journalist, "and there was a noticeable disproportion between the long trunk of his body and his short legs. His chest was broad and indicated great strength of lungs. . . . His mouth, nose, and chin were all large and clearly expressive of much boldness and power of will."[9]

Tom faithfully reproduced, not only the Little Giant's words and gesticulations, but the accompanying cries of the crowd.[10] If Douglas clapped a balled hand to his palm, so did Tom. If Douglas's open-handed appeal to the crowd was met with rousing cheers, so was Tom's. By all accounts his impression was instantly recognizable, even if a tad imprecise. "The *franatics* from the North and *franatics* from the South," he less than accurately intoned, and no one ever bothered to correct him because it always sent the audience into gales of laughter.[11]

But while Tom's popularity soared, the Democrats plumbed the depths of despair. Bolting was a time-honored tradition at Democrat conventions and, though technically split from the party, the Southern firebrands who bolted at Charleston marched up to Baltimore's Front Street Theater demanding to be readmitted. The matter was put to the vote and, before it even began, the convention became entrenched in another sectional deadlock, which dragged on for five grueling days.[12]

Given Perry Oliver's knack of being in the right place at the right time, it is hard to imagine that he and Blind Tom were anywhere else but in the packed gallery of the Front Street Theater, listening to the two factions slog it out. And after the concert each night, they would have been at the southern hotheads' midnight rallies where their charismatic, silver-tongued leader, William L. Yancey, would vent his considerable spleen.

I picture Tom standing beside his master, expression rapt, immersed in a volatile political soundscape. The feisty crowd chanting and hollering as "the grand orator and famed political stirrer" took center stage. Graceful, debonair, a man whose words rolled like "elegant majestic rivers winding over the flood plains,"[13] Yancey worked the crowd into such a frenzy that one opponent quipped: "The Southern Hotspurs are like the seventy ancient virgins in the siege of Ishmael—anxiously wondering when the ravishin' will begin."

Five days into the convention the ravishin' commenced. The majority decision to expel the Charleston bolters triggered a second bolt from most of the remaining Southerners.* The electoral consequences of dividing the Democratic vote was not lost on anyone: it was sure to clinch victory for the Republican's "Abolition candidate," trigger the secession of the rebel states and bring the nation to the brink of civil war.

The response from the Baltimore public verged on delirium. Ticket sales for Tom's concerts soared as tens of thousands crushed into the concert hall to glimpse his replay of this dramatic turn of history. A two-week season stretched into five. At the final show, Tom was presented with an elaborately carved rosewood grand piano, its silver plate bearing the inscription: "A tribute to genius, presented to Tom, the blind colored pianist by Messers Knabe & Co, Baltimore July 3rd 1860."

TROUBLE FROM ABOLITIONISTS

The season may have been a triumph both personally and politically for Oliver, who was itching for a good ding-dong with the Yankees, but it was not without its upsets and anxieties. On day three of the Democratic Convention, a dispatch reached *The Charleston Courier* via Augusta claiming that the blind Negro boy Tom had "suddenly and mysteriously disappeared from Mr. Oliver, abducted most likely by Abolitionists." Disturbing as this news was, it came as no surprise to many Southern readers.

Ever since the draconian Fugitive Slave Law made it a federal offence for a policeman *not* to arrest a runaway slave, bands of abolitionists had been taking the law into their own hands. They raided police stations and prisons and fought pitched battles with slave owners rather than see the runaways returned. Indeed, the very week of the

---

*Watterson's father, Henry Magee, was one of the few Southerners who did not join the second bolt and continued to campaign for Stephen A. Douglas.

Baltimore Convention, a Negro boy from Augusta was snatched by abolitionists while visiting Newark with his master.[14]

Such actions stirred up deep resentments in the South and abolitionists were simply "the best hated people ever known."[15] To men like Perry Oliver, they seemed to operate with impunity and a trip to a free state was literally a foray into enemy territory. Consequently in the twelve months he had managed Tom, Oliver had never exhibited him in a northern state. He was sorely tempted, one time even crossing into Indiana and arranging a concert in New Albany but, at the last moment, he lost his nerve and headed back south of the Mason Dixon.[16]

With Tom safe in the slave state of Maryland, abolitionist agitators need not concern Oliver—and yet they did. While Baltimore was ringing with Yancey's defiant cries, fears lingered amongst his supporters that the enemy was lurking in the Douglas camp. As reports of an abduction began to spread, the rumor took root: abolitionists had kidnapped Tom.

And why not? The moment seemed ripe. Home to twenty-five thousand Free Negroes, Baltimore reeked of a distinctly Yankee flavor, its sympathies unheard of in the rest of Dixie. Anti-slavery societies had long been part of the city's political landscape and the Underground Railway could depend on a number of safe houses to shelter a fugitive slave. So if, as the hotheads feared, abolitionists managed to get their hands on Tom, in no time he would be whisked off to the free state of Pennsylvania or beyond.

Three days passed before the rumor was confirmed as a hoax. The Newark abduction had somehow been confused with Tom. The prodigy may have been safe all along but his sense of safety would never be the same again. A doggedly literal child who accepted opinion as fact, possibilities as certainties, Tom began to suspect all strangers and worry that without his manager's protection "some fellow might steal me." It was a fear that would haunt Tom for all his life.

In January 1861—one week after Georgia seceded from the Union—Oliver decided to travel with Tom by steamer from Savannah to Manhattan where he planned to exhibit the boy. The decision was not as bizarre as may first seem, as many in the South hoped that the overwhelmingly Democratic metropolis would secede along with the South and become a "free city." If they did, Oliver and his marvel would be there to welcome them into the fold.

From his luxurious suite in the New York Hotel, the favorite resting place of powerful and wealthy Southerners, Oliver forged ahead with plans: an agent was appointed, the Hope Chapel engaged and a series of concerts scheduled. But the night after a successful private performance at the hotel, everything ground to an abrupt halt.[17] The steamer line servicing the New York/Savannah route was implicated in a gun running scandal. The (notoriously corrupt, Tammany Hall-ruled) New York Municipal Police raided a steamer as it pulled out of the docks, seizing five hundred muskets on consignment to Georgia's Adjutant General. The police attempted to impound the ship, but after severing the lines with an axe, the Georgians escaped, and with them, any hope of an alliance between New York and the Confederacy.[18]

The owner of the steamer line anticipated a reprisal from the police and so, evidently, did Perry Oliver. He immediately cancelled the concert and the following day returned to Savannah on the same embattled steamer line. This reaction was considered excessive by one Southern commentator who criticized his "unfounded apprehension of trouble from Abolitionists."[19] But Oliver was not taking any chances and kept Tom under close guard, wary that at any moment vengeful police might impound the steamer or abolitionists rise from the shadows and swoop down on his charge.

Perry Oliver was a man who either fancied himself as a cultural attaché for the Confederacy or was burdened with debt (including a hefty licensing fee which, Bethune would later allege, he did not fully honor) and after New York, he headed for the more lucrative pastures of Kentucky. Although it was a slave state, Oliver and Blind Tom were treading on shaky ground.

By now, the spring of 1861, seven Southern states had seceded from the Union. Kentucky had elected to join neither north nor south, remaining neutral. Strong pro-Unionist sympathies in the state presented risks that Oliver was prepared to take. For a time, all went well: houses were packed, reviews glowing and profits handsome—until, in far away North Carolina, state troops seized control of Fort Sumter. Overnight, another four Southern states seceded and Kentucky again refused to join them. Outraged by this disloyalty, Oliver pulled the plug on the bluegrass tour, giving a Covington reporter a taste of his fury: "Mr. Oliver came into our office the day after the fall of Sumter and called for his bills with a considerable display of temper. When asked why he did not continue his concerts as he had announced, said 'He is wanted down South,' and left Covington in high dudgeon with all

Yankeeism." Given Oliver's bombastic style and love of exaggeration, it is safe to assume he kept up the tirade all the way to the Kentucky line: Blind Tom securely lodged by his side, not missing a cursed word.[20]

Curiously—or perhaps not so curiously if Oliver was hoping to turn not only a buck but the loyalties of a state—Tom and his manager headed deeper into the storm. Like the border state of Kentucky, Missouri's loyalties were deeply divided and as Tom wrapped up a weeklong engagement in St. Louis, the city exploded into bloody violence. All that week, rumors of a Confederate conspiracy to seize control of the largest Federal arsenal in the West gripped the city. While this plot was foiled without incident, tension reached flashpoint on May 10, the night of Tom's final concert, when the ousted militiamen were marched through downtown St. Louis. Civilians hurled fruit, rocks, paving stones and insults at the Union soldiers leading the prisoners and in the confusion, the soldiers fired back, maiming and killing a score of people.

The screams and wails of a disbelieving crowd soon gave way to the blood-curdling howls of a mob on the rampage—sounds that must have reached Tom's ears. By this time he was either making his way home from his concert at the Mercantile Library Hall or already in his room at Everett House, both in the heart of St. Louis. The rioting continued well into the next day, Blind Tom holed up in his hotel listening as the city burned and the death toll climbed. By now, Tom was convinced that he was about to be taken away by strangers, stolen or abused. "Somebody might come along and shoot me," he insisted to a psychiatrist four years later.[21]

Tom's fragmented perception of reality equipped him with few psychological tools to cope with even the smallest disruptions to his routine, and his anxieties were ripe for manipulation. For the brutal fact was that Blind Tom had already been taken away from the people who loved and cared for him and carried off by a stranger. It was a pattern that would continue throughout his life as Tom was passed from one new manager to the next. Instead of allaying his fears of the unknown, his masters skillfully worked them to their advantage so that he anticipated the worst. Ultimately, it was Perry Oliver who defined the difference between the two strangers: one offered slavery, the other freedom, but in Tom's mind these associations were successfully reversed. The abolitionist was the predatory wolf while the profiteering master was hailed as the kindly shepherd and protector.

- 10 -

Thunder of War

To say that Blind Tom was the Confederacy's most high-profile black supporter implies he made a choice; that he, like fellow slave Harrison Berry, understood that this was one of a number of positions he could take and—whether through reason, fear or self-preservation—concluded that slavery was the best possible option for him and his people. Berry produced a thirty-page pamphlet defending slavery but such reflections were alien to Tom's hypersensitive, context-free world.[1] His delight in all things Confederate was driven more by destruction than deduction, and the day the church bells pealed out across the Georgian countryside, something irresistible began stirring. That day—January 19th, 1861—Georgia seceded from the Union. In every city, town and village, jubilant crowds spontaneously arose. Cannons fired, bonfires burned, banners unfurled and rousing patriotic speeches were met with chants and hollers. Up and down the main street of every county seat, military companies paraded, each stride marked by the beat of the drum and fife.

This wave of public excitement proved irresistible not only to twelve-year-old Tom, but thousands of Southern Unionists initially opposed to secession. Even reasoned men of science fell under its spell. "It was in the atmosphere," reflected biologist Henry La Conte, "we breathed it in the air; it reverberated from heart to heart; it was like a spiritual contagion—good or bad, who could say? But the final result was enthusiastic unanimity of sentiment throughout the South."[2]

Untouched by this "spiritual contagion," Georgia's half million slaves were powered by a very different vision: that of Moses leading his people out of Egypt and into the Promised Land. Hidden deep in the woods in the depths of night, huddled in circles, faces turned to the ground so that no one but God would hear, their prayer was for deliverance. Invisible, yet subversive—beyond the detection of their masters and mistresses who saw in their sunny smiles nothing but undying loyalty and unquestioned obedience—this covert double life left few traces. An oblique expression of it survives in folk characters like Br'er Rabbit, the renowned trickster who adopts a suppliant mask and, by way of guile, deception and role-playing, fools the wily Fox and achieves his end. But for Tom, the way of the trickster was meaningless. He had no hidden agendas—no concept of their existence—but instead accepted reality at its face value. Unable to detect a silent prayer or decipher the nuances of politics, he heard a single voice chime through the South: that of the Confederacy.

After the bloody violence in St. Louis, Tom and Oliver next surfaced in Richmond, Virginia—a city consumed in gaiety, frivolity and the certainty of victory, the summer air filled with the sound of tens of thousands of men enlisting, parading, gambling, dancing and outrageously flirting. *Zouave* drills followed *Tableau Vivants* followed officers' balls: all to the jaunty beat of the South's favorite song—*Dixie*.

Ever since a Louisiana company played a quickstep arrangement of the minstrel tune at President Davis's lavish inauguration in Montgomery, Dan Emmett's "hooray song" about a runaway slave's desire to return to his plantation home instantly became the theme song of the Confederacy. So complete was its identification with the rebel cause, New York pianist Richard Hoffman was forced to bury his latest composition, *Dixiana*, a rhapsodic reworking of what he considered to be a minstrel hit. Likewise, Blind Tom was expected to drop his beloved *Yankee Doodle*.

Perry Oliver must have gone through a lot of sugarplum persuading him to replace it with *Dixie*. Eventually a compromise deal was reached: Tom played the southern anthem alongside the northern one. His famous novelty act of standing with his back to the piano and playing two tunes simultaneously while singing another was adapted to become a seamless blend of *Yankee Doodle* and *Dixie*, "the two airs floating together in perfect time and tune."[3] First heard at a concert for the Savannah Soldiers' Independent Relief Society, the

Two of the many concerts Blind Tom performed in aid of the Confederate War effort.

TEMPERANCE HALL!

SECOND APPEARANCE OF

BLIND TOM!

The Celebrated PIANIST.

Saturday Eve'g Oct. 11.

CHANGE OF PROGRAMME!

FOR THE BENEFIT OF THE SOLDIERS!

☞ LET ALL ATTEND! ☜

Doors open at 7 o'clock. Performance to commence at 7½ o'clock.
Admission 50 cents; children and servants half price.
oct10

ATHENÆUM!

· · ·

THE CHARLESTON SUFFERERS!

BLIND TOM,

THE NEGRO BOY

PIANIST!

THE WONDER OF THE WORLD!!

WILL give Two of his MARVELLOUS and INIMITABLE Entertainments on

Tuesday and Wednesday Evenings, Dec. 17th and 18th,

In behalf of the Charleston Sufferers by the late disastrous fire.
DOORS OPEN 6½. Commence 7½.
Admission 50 cents; Children and Servants 25 cents.
P. H. OLIVER.
Dec 16 1861

act would become a fixture at the scores of benefit concerts he would play over the next four years.[4] And while never a patriotic rouser, it certainly was an uncannily apt reflection of the divided nation.

It is impossible to say how much money Tom's management donated to the Confederate cause: tens of thousands, certainly. At the outset of the war, Perry Oliver announced his plan to donate the entire proceeds of a major city tour to the war effort. "He thinks he can equip up to one hundred and fifty to two hundred men each week in this way, provided halls are provided free of charge and taxes are remitted," reported a Columbus newspaper.[5] Although this grand plan never materialized, funds from Blind Tom's concerts were channeled to all types of benevolent societies. In Atlanta, Oliver donated a night's takings to the Victims of the Charleston Fire—a devastating blaze commonly believed to be an attack by abolitionists.[6] In Alabama, Tom played for the families of Gainesville's soldiers. His benefit for the Hospital Association in Columbia, Tennessee inspired two gentlemen to donate a hundred dollars apiece.[7]

For those who find Tom's wholesale enlistment to the Confederate cause unpalatable, some comfort can be found in the likelihood that it was Oliver who made these choices for him and donated the money (after keeping a sizable portion for himself, purchasing a substantial home on Americus's most exclusive street). But even this rationale runs out of steam after July 21, 1861 when, at a nondescript junction thirty miles southwest of Washington, Confederate forces defeated an enemy vastly superior in size. Church bells tolled, drums sounded and the entire South whooped with news of the glorious victory at Manassas, certain it was a taste of things to come. "Heaven smiled upon our arms and the God of battle crowned our banner with laurels of glory," trumpeted *The Columbus Enquirer*. "Let every patriotic heart give thanks to the Lord of Hosts for the victory He has given His people on His own Holy Day, the blessed Sabbath."

To honor the victory, Tom composed what many consider his magnum opus: *The Battle of Manassas*. No one forced him to create it. Indeed, according to the notes on the sheet music—which is a direct transcript of Perry Oliver's stage introduction that Tom soon took to delivering himself—nobody even suggested the idea. He did it entirely of his own accord: a spontaneous expression of loyalty. Shortly after the battle occurred, the notes tell us, Oliver was in an accident that kept him bedridden in Nashville for several months. Tom was often in Oliver's room, listening as every little paragraph about the battle was dissected. He heard of fifteen thousand Rebels pitted against a compact column of fifty thousand Union soldiers ("What anxious hearts did watch that pyramid of smoke and dust! The enemy's columns like a huge anaconda, seeking to envelope us in its mighty folds and crush us to death"). Of the reinforcements that never arrived as General Beauregard's order somehow miscarried; of General Kirby Smith's eventual and triumphant appearance on the battlefield, his gallant troops dashing the charge with loud shouts and whoops; of the coach load of soldiers who heard the fighting and immediately quit the train, setting out over the countryside to strike the enemy's right flank like a thunderbolt; of Beauregard's rallying cry before he and his brave boys charged the eye of the battle's storm with a shout that seemed to shake the very earth. And of the enemy's retreat—first in good order, then in confusion—the cavalry bearing down on them as if the earth was opening behind them.

"If we consider the numbers engaged and the character of the contest, we may congratulate ourselves upon having won one of the most brilliant victories that any race or people have ever achieved," concluded one correspondent after delivering this near perfect narrative—a satisfying balance of adversity, suspense, will, tenacity, chance, valor and ultimate triumph; an intoxicating soundscape of musketry, cannons, trains, Rebel yells and horses. And after ten days of this crowing, scrutiny and speculation, Tom sat down at the piano and poured out his musical interpretation of events:

> In the first place [reads the sheet music notes] he will represent the Southern army leaving home to their favorite tune of *The Girl I Left Behind Me* which you will hear in the distance, growing louder and louder as they approach Manassas (the imitation of the drum and fife). He will represent the Grand Union Army leaving Washington City to the tune of *Dixie*. You will all recollect that their prisoners spoke of the fact that when the Grand Union Army left Washington, not only were their bands playing *Dixie*, but their men were also singing it.
>
> He will represent the eve of battle by a very soft sweet melody, then the clatter of arms and accoutrements, the war trumpet of Beauregard, which you will hear distinctly; and then McDowell's in the distance, like an echo at first. He will represent the firing of cannons to *Yankee Doodle*, *Marseilles Hymn* and the *Star Spangled Banner*, *Dixie* and the arrival of the train of cars containing General Kirby Smith's reinforcements; which you will all recollect was very valuable to General Beauregard upon that occasion after their arrival of which, the fighting will grow more severe and then retreat.

Southern audiences sat spellbound as Tom recreated *The Battle of Manassas*—Perry Oliver guiding them through each phase with a series of stage announcements: "The Eve of Battle," "The Reinforcements arrive under General Kirby Smith," "The Retreat." *The Athens Southern Banner* praised it "the finest battlepiece extant."[8] *The Fayetteville Observer* called it "picturesque and sublime—a true conception of unaided blind musical genius."[9] However not a single comment has been published by any of his black contemporaries—a silence that reverberates with accusations of treachery and betrayal. Given the context, one can understand the accusation that Tom was a fully-fledged Uncle Tom pliantly submitting to the will of white authority. Any hopes that he was a divine being bearing a message of hope had certainly been dashed by this point. Unlike the conjure men who drew on a force that undermined the omnipotence of white supremacy, unlike the trickster who exposed the hypocrisy and folly of the plantation hierarchy, Tom offered his enslaved brothers and sisters nothing but an endorsement of slavery.

WHAT MR. OLIVER READ TO TOM

The sheet music version of events may have the patina of history and authority but, once its claims are held up to scrutiny, its finish begins to look like less of a sheen and more of a whitewash—a clever publicity coup dreamed up by Perry Oliver.

The first anomaly is Oliver's contention that Tom heard a verbal account of a battle and transformed it into jaw-droppingly accurate soundscape of a battle. This runs contrary to everything we know about Tom's method of composing, in particular, and the artistry of autistic savants, in general. Savants do not interpret the world second hand, but instead, with barefaced directness, they create images, poetry and music in highly literal and mind boggling detail. Tom documented the sonic world around him as *he* heard it, not as somebody else did. Think of all the vital sensory data that would be lost once it was transposed to language! No words could accurately convey the sound of musketry and cannon and Tom would never be so imprecise to approximate another person's description of it. For him, was not a case of "What Mr. Oliver Read to Tom" but "What the Cannon and Musketry Told Tom."

Secondly, Oliver's timeframe does not add up. The actual battle took place in July 1861 and, according to the sheet music, no more than a month passed before Tom composed the piece. However it was not until April 18, 1862—nine months after Manassas but only two days after the fall of New Orleans—that any reference to it appears. A notice in

BLIND TOM.
THE INSPIRED MUSICIAN!
THE WONDER OF THE WORLD!
THE GREATEST MARVEL ON EARTH!
A Living Miracle!
Will give two of his inimitable Entertainments.
At Hibernian Hall,
THIS and TO-MORROW EVENING, APRIL 18th and 19th at 8 o'clock; Doors open at 7.
Also,
A MATINEE:
TO-MORROW, at 12 o'clock: Doors open at 11.
On each occasion TOM will perform his soul-stirring and thrilling Composition:
THE BATTLE OF MANASSAS.
April 18

The Battle of Manassas *premiered in Charleston, April 1862, ten days after Gottschalk's controversial performance in* L'Union *in St. Louis.*

The Charleston Mercury on that date announced that "Tom will perform his soul-stirring and thrilling composition: THE BATTLE OF MANAS-
SAS." After that, a concert did not pass without Tom reliving the South's
moment of glory. It was highly unlikely that Perry Oliver had been sitting on the piece like a mother hen waiting for the right moment to
launch it.

Thirdly, for a highly idiosyncratic mind who cared little for fashion, *The Battle of Manassas* very snugly fits into an existing genre: the
battle piece. For centuries, composers had been eulogizing military and
naval engagements with noisy, extravagant and jingoistic fanfare (they
were ideal for rousing finales). Indeed, in recent months another
Southerner had brought a Civil War twist to the genre, though not, to
Perry Oliver's apparent consternation, in praise of the Confederacy.
Louis Moreau Gottschalk—America's foremost piano virtuoso and
New Orleans' pride and joy—had turned his back on the South and
composed a powerful and heart-stirring battle piece, *L'Union:
Paraphrase de Concert.* Here, amid booming, clamorous descending
octaves, *Yankee Doodle* and *Hail Columbia* were woven together, cul-
minating in a silvery and dewy-eyed *Star Spangled Banner. L'Union*
premiered in late February 1862 on a New York stage draped with the
Stars and Stripes. However, Oliver most likely did not get wind of it
until Gottschalk performed it in politically divided St. Louis, days after
the Union victory at nearby Shiloh.[10] Instead of stirring up patriotic
passions, the virtuoso was heckled and abused by the local "Secesh"
crowd, and when faced with an equally divided crowd in Washington
many months later Gottschalk elected not to play it, lest the hall come
to blows and he "be the first one choked."[11]

Which begs the question, was *The Battle of Manassas*—which
burst onto the scene ten days after Gottschalk's St. Louis performance—Oliver's act of musical revenge? Did he plant the idea in Tom's
gullible mind, suggest to him a collage of patriotic pieces, reiterate
the narrative arc of the battle, then travel long distances so that Tom
could soak up the sounds of combat? For the rest of his career, *The
Battle of Manassas* branded Tom as a Confederate stooge and the
factually dubious introduction—which Tom delivered in Perry
Oliver's emphatic tones—reiterated the myth of spontaneous loyalty.
Yet like so much of his career, it was very likely stage managed by a
man who had so ably demonstrated his skillful publicity stunts in
Washington two years earlier. If anyone understood the synergy

between popular entertainment and political propaganda, it was the shrewd and grandiose former mayor.

But, as any songwriter can vouch, once a piece of music enters public consciousness, it takes on a life of its own. As the rebellion dragged on, Tom's wild and discordant echo of the battlefield—unfiltered by judgment or curiosity—became less a patriotic rouser and more a heart wrenching reminder of the tragedy that is war.

"SHE STOLE MY HARMONIES"

The Civil War invaded the senses, colonized the air and filled Southerners' ears with a "fiendish melody" from which no one on the front line could escape. "The clatter of military trappings, the rattle of heavy freight wagons and the measured tap of the drum constitute the music of the times," wrote a Richmond reporter in June 1861.[12]

In the battlefield, the decibel hell of war left soldiers grappling for comparisons. It rang louder and longer than the most violent thunderstorm, a cacophony of noise that beggared belief for the young recruits. But with each battle, their ears became more attuned to the voices of the big mouthed guns: the thunderous bellow of cannon, the sharp crack of musketry, the dry staccato of artillery fire, the whistle of a bullet whizzing by, the sudden silences broken by the shrieks of the wounded.

For soldiers too long in the battlefield, exhaustion played havoc with their senses. Confused, irritable and reactive, a mess of shattered nerves and battered cochlea, they hit the dirt at the slightest provocation. The snap of a twig cracked the air like a bullet, mosquitoes thundered in their battle weary ears, combat fire became indistinguishable from enemy fire. There were few cultural reference points through which soldiers and citizens could make sense of the aural assault, until they heard Blind Tom unspool the chaos of *The Battle of Manassas*.

"Thousands of soldiers heard him and many recounted these occasions, in wonder and amazement, in their diaries and journals," wrote Ella May Thornton, a white Georgia woman who dedicated many years in the 1950s to researching Blind Tom's life.[13] Perhaps as head of Atlanta's Public Library she had access to unpublished material or was privy to oral accounts because, despite my continuing efforts, these tales of wonder and amazement have yet to surface. However, the recollections of a number of schoolgirls have survived (Tom played at a lot of Female Academies during the rebellion), as have those of audience members after the war. All were uniformly struck by Tom's ability to reproduce the discharge of musketry and heavy guns, the trudge of soldiers and gallop of horses: not a sugar-coated, patriotic version of the battle but a dispassionately accurate depiction of the mayhem and chaos of war.

The impact of *The Battle of Manassas* on two Southern school-girls was so powerful that, fifty years on, both their daughters knew their tales. "Many times I have heard my mother tell of hearing Blind Tom in concert at Chattanooga," Rachel Peeble Rogers reported in 1942. "She well knew the sounds of war and many of its horrors and indelibly impressed upon her memory was the sounds of an army on the march, as they passed her house for days at a time. So what impressed her most about this Negro artist-genius was his faithful reproduction of the 'tramp tramp tramp' of marching men, the rumble of artillery field pieces and the hoof beats (all gaits) of the horses attached to the cavalry units—all of which was too perfect for enjoyment, but a miracle of performance. She thought this proved his genius more than anything else he did and she never saw a musician who could reproduce those sounds except Blind Tom."[14]

Katherine Pope Merritt's mother was a schoolgirl in Griffin when she first heard Tom play *The Battle of Manassas*. "The audience sat spellbound, and as the roar of the fiercely fought battle died away and the retreat sounded, they arose as one man, with the realization that they had listened to the rendition of a masterpiece."[15]

Impressive as these reports may be, they lie in stark contradiction to the experiences of many disappointed music researchers (myself included) who have unearthed the sheet music of this great Civil War "masterpiece," only to discover—once they sit down and wade through the routine thrumming of the drum motif and commonplace renditions of *Dixie, Yankee Doodle* and *The Star Spangled Banner*—that it fails to live up to its reputation. As music researcher Tom Stoddard concluded in 1970 after hearing a piano roll version of it: "There is little evidence of originality and the whole thing is singularly unimpressive. Without acting as Blind Tom's apologist, it is difficult to tell how much has been lost in the notating, transference and cutting of the piece."[16]

Although recent efforts by pianist John Davis have done much to redress the situation, I suspect Stoddard is right. Something *was* lost in translation and this perhaps offers some insight into Tom's crimson rage when Mr. Weisel attempted to transcribe *The Oliver*

Gallop. As Henry Watterson also witnessed, Tom guarded his melodies with the ferocity of a lion:

> I well remember in Atlanta where a party of us had him with us on and off for two or three months, a young lady one day sat down at the piano and began to play. Tom was at the dark end of the chamber, spinning upon his hands and heels, and mumbling to himself. He caught the sound of the instrument and stood for a moment still and upright. Then, like a wild animal he made a dash and swooped down upon her. Terrified, the poor girl shrieked and ran, whilst the rest of us held him writhing and trembling with what seemed to be rage. "She stole my harmonies," he cried over and over, "she stole my harmonies," and never again did he allow her to come near him. If she were even in the room he knew it and somehow became restive and angry.[17]

The mischievous Watterson was known to tease Tom by playing his compositions and, years later Tom would recall "Oh, yes; I like Mr. Wat-terson, ver-re well! But he would steal my homminies."[18] As infantile and irrational as Tom's behavior may appear, when it came to *The Battle of Manassas*, he had good reason to insist that the piece belonged wholly and solely to him: for the genius of the piece lay in Tom's powers of imitation.

The sum total of Tom's perfect pitch, hypersensitive clarity, elastic vocal chords, lack of inhibition and total immersion in the world of sound enabled him to re-create a "harum-scarum" battlefield like no other. As the Bethune's cousin Oscar Jordan noted, *The Battle of Manassas* was "never equaled unless played by Tom. He imitates all the instruments in the band, the firing of muskets, the boom of the cannon in perfect musical harmony on the piano, which no other man has ever done."[19] By contrast, the sheet music's instructions to *chu-chu-chu*, whistle like a train and simulate the cannon by pounding "with the flat of the hand, as many notes as possible, with as much force as possible" are so imprecise that one can understand Tom's outrage on hearing a layperson's feeble attempt to replicate his harmonies.

One of the best descriptions of *The Battle of Manassas* comes from a Boston man who captures the piece's clumsy imperfections, Tom's eccentric assimilation of Oliver's stage announcements and his utter abandonment in creating a soundscape of war:

He played with great gusto, announcing the various headings in a loud manner, which came very absurdly into the piece: The Northern troops marching to the tune of *The Girl I Left Behind Me*; the Southern Army coming up to the tune of *Dixie*. The eve of battle—a quiet passage. Trumpets calling. McDowell's march. Cannon sounding, amidst strains of *Yankee Doodle* and *The Marseilles Hymn*, *The Star-spangled Banner* and *Dixie*. Reenforcements for Beauregard. "Che! Che! Che!" went Tom's mouth, then a re-r-r-r for the whistle, and the same repeated; cannon banging all the while, in a delightfully noisy manner. "Retreat! Retreat! Retreat!" cried Tom, away flew the notes, and there was a general harum-scarum close.[20]

There is no question as to whether or not Blind Tom composed *The Battle of Manassas*. He did. What is in doubt are the circumstances leading to its composition. Exactly how much influence Perry Oliver brought to bear on the piece can never be known, although judging by his actions—a tour of the border states in early 1861, a spate of benefit concerts for the Confederate cause—it seems he considered Tom a tool to promote his political agenda. He had his own Promised Land in mind and Tom was taking him there.

In stark contrast, Tom operated on a gut level. This was widely observed at the time: one commentator even drew a parallel between the pianist and Confederate General Nathan Bedford Forrest, believing that he "felt the field as Blind Tom touches the keys of the piano." (Surely, the only occasion where the godfather of the Ku Klux Klan was compared with a black man.) But the inference is clear: like the illiterate Forrest, Tom let instinct be his guide. And while his radar may not have been attuned to the silent prayers of his people or political machinations of the day, he was nevertheless in communion with a spirit of sorts. This spirit knew nothing of enslavement and deliverance but like Thor, Mars and Ogoun—the Carribean's Lord of the Thunderbolt—encapsulated the powerful and destructive spirit of war.

Home Sweet Home

IN SEPTEMBER 1862, PRESIDENT LINCOLN ANNOUNCED THAT ON THE first day of the new year, slaves in Union controlled parts of the Confederacy would be emancipated.* Within weeks, Tom was back in Columbus under the direct control of General Bethune, cutting short the lucrative licensing agreement with Perry Oliver by a year.

General Bethune would later insist that Tom's early return was at the behest of his anxious parents who continued to live and work on the farm—a claim perfectly tailored to Yankee post-war sensibilities but less than convincing in the secessionist South.[1] Why, after all these years, would the patriarch suddenly concede to the wishes of his slaves when he knew what was best for everyone? Fear indeed may have prompted Tom's early return, but the disquiet was Bethune's. Following a series of reversals in the Confederate West, he was the one anxious about the future now that Lincoln's Emancipation Proclamation was re-writing the rules.

Not that he dared vocalize these doubts. On the face of it, Bethune's rock solid belief in the Confederacy seemed unshakable but, if the arc of his eldest son's military career is anything to go by, the eternal glory of the South was not the first thing on their minds.

---

*The Emancipation Proclamation did not apply to the three slave states that sided with the Union. Rather than risk losing their support, President Lincoln allowed slavery to continue in Kentucky, Maryland and Missouri.

"WILLING TO FIGHT BUT UNWILLING TO FALL"

Various documents have surfaced pinpointing John Bethune's whereabouts during the Civil War. When plotted on a map, one salient feature emerges: each step took him further away from the front line and closer to Blind Tom, the prize he had been eyeing for some time. Enlisting as a private in the Columbus Guards in the wake of Fort Sumter, John's unit was first deployed to the windswept beauty of Tybee Island. Ostensibly they were there to defend the Rebel-controlled Fort Pulaski, but in actuality did little beyond play cards, perfect their *Zouvre* drill (much to the delight of the young ladies of Savannah), supplement their ration of pickled pork with oysters and crabs and sidestep the drudgery of mess life with black manservants and cooks.

A year later, John was in the trenches of Yorktown surrounded by corpses from the previous day's battle. In the preceding months, he had marched hundreds of miles across Virginia, a footsore infantry man stooped beneath the weight of his equipment, while splendidly attired Virginian cavaliers flashed by him on horseback. A few days in the Yorktown trenches was enough to convince a swag of Columbus lads that they had had enough. "If you know where Uncle Tom is," wrote John's friend Thomas Michelle Carter to his mother, "somehow work out how some of us can get transferred into his company. There are nearly twenty men that would join him if we could."[2] "Uncle Tom" was Thomas Page Nelson, a lineal descendent of the founder of Yorktown who had cavalier credentials coming out his ears. He was organizing an independent cavalry company that offered relative safety and comfort. To become part of it, all John had to do was find himself a substitute—a simple enough matter when you had the cash and connections (John went further than this, securing a personal recommendation from Georgia's Governor Joe Brown). In June 1862, after a personal visit from "Uncle Tom," Thomas Carter, John and Joseph Bethune and a number of other "well-bred" Columbus gentlemen were transferred to the Nelson Rangers and fitted out with plumed hats, capes, sashes and freshly minted swords (double-edged with a cross hilt). Their first assignment, they were delighted to hear, was as General Kirby-Smith's personal escort company.[3]

The hero of Manassas, still hankering for more of "what the French call glory," was leading a small army into Kentucky, convinced that tens of thousands of loyal Confederates there would rally to the cause and enlist. It was neither the first nor the last time a campaign would hinge on this flawed assumption, and the ultimate failure of the "bluegrass bid" cast a long shadow of hindsight over its early triumphs: Kirby-Smith, flanked by the Nelson Rangers, parading into Lexington where they were hailed as deliverers.

For two glorious weeks in September of 1862, the cavaliers had a ball scouting the region, foraging for food and imposing on the local hospitality. "If it rains, we manage to get into a house and we live off the fat of the land," reported Thomas Carter. "If we were in camp we'd have to take all the rain and live off what the government gives us."[4] Thirty miles southwest of Lexington, across the Kentucky River, lay Harrodsburg, and here John first cast his envious eye over some of the finest saddlebred and thoroughbred horse studs in the country. Six weeks later, Kirby-Smith's hungry and ragged troops would limp back South, the frozen roads lined with smears of blood. But it was the elegant thoroughbreds pounding towards a bluegrass horizon that seared John Bethune's imagination. Within ten years he would be the owner of a stud in Harrodsburg, the blood of a Kentucky Derby champion running through its veins.

"I'm a dashing young Southerner, gallant and tall/I am willing to fight but unwilling to fall" went an infantry ditty that lampooned the pampered "buttermilk" cavalry. The barb was especially apt for John. After Kentucky, he parted company with the Nelson Rangers and as his former comrades headed off to Lynchburg, John signed on to Robinson's Cavalry, a unit of the Muscogee County State Guards responsible for patrolling the district in and around Columbus, Georgia.[5] Hundreds of miles from the front, the privations of war barely visible, John could now revel in the advantage afforded him by his gifted slave. He put Tom to work, entertaining officers and winning friends. One visitor—Charles Quintard, the well-known chaplain and surgeon of the Tennessee Army—noted that Tom was at first reluctant to perform for him because he had already spent four hours at the piano that day "for the amusement of some cavalrymen."[6]

Tom also led the dance music at Susan Bethune's wedding later that year. Chances are a sea of black faces stared through the doors and windows, scrutinizing the elaborate "twistifications" of the grand march. Outside in the yard, the servants were known to imitate these movements although not quite with the envy the planter class presumed. "Us slaves watched white folk's parties," one former slave woman remembered, "then we'd do it to, but we used to mock them, every step."[7] To the Virginia Reel, slave men patted juba and shouted. The waltz rapidly lost its decorous style while the slow and stately quadrille moved along in rapid shuffling steps, with hips swinging and shoulders jiggling. Although Charity "violently love to dance," no such description accompanies the account of Susan Bethune's wedding, though one can safely assume she and her family were there watching the festivities, peering through the window or preparing food in the kitchen, a world away from Tom.

Tom "was treated as such a pet that he scarcely knew him as his father," Mingo later complained to a Mississippi-born freeman, adding that his other children did not interest Bethune because there was "no money in them."[8] In 1854, fifty-year- old Charity gave birth to an "idiotic" daughter named Ellen—one of three or even four children born after the family's arrival at the Bethune farm.[9] Unlike Tom's uncertain entry into the world, Charity did not fear for Ellen's life—a telling indication of Bethune's benevolence—but this did little to soften the blow of losing the affections of her gifted son. Nor were they fooled by Tom's privileged position in the Bethune household. Fifty years later, Mingo's tidy summation was repeated almost word for word by Charity: Tom was taken away because "there was money in him"—clearly a well-worn phrase in their humble one-room cabin.[10]

A POOR DYING STRUGGLE

When Tom first returned to the Bethune fold, General Bethune appointed another stranger, Professor Loomis, to tutor and manage him. The arrangement proved less than ideal. After a short tour of Georgia and Alabama, Loomis resigned, the local press reporting of his "difficulties" with the truculent fifteen-year-old. Not privy to Perry Oliver's liberal use of threats, flattery and sugarplum, Loomis may well have been on the receiving end of a powerful blow. Even if it was only a blue-faced tantrum, no amount of money or persuasion could induce the man to withstand any more.[11]

Loomis's resignation was just one of many setbacks for Bethune. At first he had to contend with Confederate defeat, hyper-inflation and food shortages but as 1863 came to a close, a scarcity of supplies forced him to shut down his beloved newspaper and printing press. Far from weakening his resolve, he bounced back with

Sisyphean zeal. By the spring of 1864, he and Tom were touring through Mississippi and Alabama. The lawyer and newspaperman was now a traveling showman.

"If this be a poor dying struggle, Oh! Beautiful South, you are glamorous even in your death," lamented Frances Woolfolk Wallace. She was a Kentucky woman from a "hot" Southern family, who crossed paths with General Bethune and Blind Tom on May 19th in Tuskegee, Alabama. For two months, she had been traveling through Tennessee and Alabama in search of her husband—a captain in General Bragg's rebel army—and fifty miles short of the Georgia line took time out to savor a lifestyle she knew was doomed.

From the moment General Bethune and Blind Tom arrived on the morning stagecoach, Frances Wallace spent as much time as she could in their company. A singer and pianist herself, she was deeply impressed with Tom's musicianship: "He is certainly one of the greatest wonders of the day, indeed the greatest," she wrote of his concert that night. "He played the most difficult pieces, composed and arranged beautifully. After we returned home he came into our part of the hotel and we sang for him and he seemed pleased."[12]

The following day she dined with Bethune at a private soiree, where Tom delighted the group with performances on the violin and guitar. At one of these encounters, the conversation must have turned to Mrs. Wallace's harrowing flight from Union-controlled Kentucky and her journey through northern Tennessee, where she personally witnessed the carnage wrought by the Union Army under its new commander, General William Tecumseh Sherman. "Oh! What a scene of desolation and destruction," she grieved in her diary, "plantation after plantation destroyed, nothing left but the brick chimneys and the ruins—cotton strewn on the ground as far as the eye can see."[13]

It was a sorry tale Bethune was to hear again and again. At Lauderdale Springs—a once fashionable health resort in east Mississippi that was now a hospital for sick and wounded soldiers—Bethune came upon Brigadier General Mathew Ector and another general in the Army of Mississippi. In the previous weeks, Ector had lost most of his men and, cut off from the eastern front, was making his way back through Mississippi to rejoin the rest of French's Division.

In a letter to her son sixty years later, Eliza Smith, owner of the only piano in town, recalled how Blind Tom entertained the officers and their troops at her home. While she best remembered his imper-

Blind Tom at 15.

sonations of the congressmen in Washington, the ragged veterans were no doubt touched by his interpretations of two rebel favorites, *When This Cruel War Is Over* and *Home Sweet Home*. The two songs, both brimming with nostalgia and melancholy, could readily bring a tear to the eye of a soldier who faced the specter of death every day (as Mrs. Smith later learned, most of Ector's troops were soon to be dead "including the General whose name I can't remember"). *Cruel War* distressed soldiers so much that many officers banned it from camp, while the sentiments of *Home Sweet Home* were known to unite opposing armies.[14] Historian Bell Irvin Wiley tells of a spontaneous musical exchange that took place the night before a battle at Murfreesboro in early 1863 (where Ector, incidentally, led a command). The Northern band contributed *Yankee Doodle* and *Hail Colombia*, the Rebel band responding with favorites of their own. Then one of the bands struck up *Home Sweet Home*. "Immediately the other band joined in and, in a few moments the song was picked up by a multitude of voices from both camps. For the brief period the countryside reverberated with the notes of Payne's cherished song the animosities of war were lost in nostalgic reverie, and the fading away of the final notes found tears on the cheeks of scores of veterans who on the morrow were to walk into the maelstrom of battle."[15]

Unfortunately no soldier's account of Blind Tom's *Home Sweet Home* survives, although others have described it as a gem, emphasizing the strength of feeling behind Tom's performance. "After the delicious prelude," wrote one New Yorker, "he softly glides into the tenderly familiar *Home Sweet Home*."[16] "Of all productions in the current repertoire" wrote another, "none have finer or more difficult shades. Blind Tom proceeds, and were you to close your eyes, you could not tell but Thalberg himself was at the instrument, so perfect and so exquisite is the conception and the touch."[17]

Blind Tom struck a deep chord in his audience when he played *Home Sweet Home*—yet another paradox given his inability to "read" emotions. As a fourteen-year-old he could no more connect the sound of pain to its source than he could as a child, and here by a soldiers' makeshift hospital, he was unable to recognize battle fatigue in the veteran's agitated voices or agony in the cries of the sick and wounded. But behind the piano, Tom underwent a startling transformation, and I wonder if, along with his jerkiness and stereotypes, his emotional illiteracy also disappeared.

It was a characteristic Dr. David Viscott observed one hundred years later in Harriet, the Boston woman whose circumstances and symptoms were compellingly similar to Tom's. Behind the piano she too transformed: the "ungainly, awkward, inelegant lady" became "another person" with all the feeling and movement of a concert pianist. This transformation was more than physical. "Her ability to express feeling in music is in great contrast to the way she handles feelings in her life," Viscott surmised after a year's psychoanalysis. Only through music could she identify with another person's suffering or appropriately name emotions. Of *La Traviata*, for instance, she said, "Poor Violetta, her Alfredo, he's just not a nice man. He runs around a lot. Poor Violetta, she's got a bad cough. Right here in the chest. And she don't tell anyone about it. And, oh the pain, and she has such difficult things to sing with all that pain. It makes me so sad for Violetta."[18] What a contrast this was to the constricted, impassive and defensive behavior in Harriet's non-musical life, observed her flabbergasted doctor.

Given the profound change Tom experienced as he played the piano, his autism dissolving into nuanced flow, the fragments coalescing into a meaningful whole, was it also possible that the constricted, impassive and emotionally illiterate behavior of his non-musical life disappeared as well? Were the subtle shades of feeling Tom brought to *Home Sweet Home* his way of communicating his feelings to the world and sharing the feelings of others? Of experiencing empathy?

If he did, then it was momentary and contained in a vacuum and once it passed, the world fragmented again into disconnected parts. But the broader implications of the soldiers' melancholy could not have been lost on General Bethune. Keeping up morale in the insulated safety of Columbus was one thing, but touring through Alabama and Mississippi in the dying months of the war, Bethune was witness to a ragged and demoralized army reeling under a well-manned Federal assault and, at some point, the staunch patriot had to entertain the inevitability of defeat.

A SINGLE TEN-LINED SENTENCE

Ten days after his powwow with Mrs. Wallace, Bethune was back in Columbus. By now, northern Tennessee had fallen to the Union and General Sherman's army of 93,000 was pushing its way through the Appalachian Mountains. Knowing that Sherman would inflict the same punishment on Georgia that he had on Tennessee, pragmatism eclipsed principle and the southern stalwart entered into a legal agreement with Mingo and Charity over control of their son.

On the face of it, the gesture seemed to undermine the very cornerstone of Southern Civilization. According to Georgia law, Mingo and Charity were chattel and had no legal rights to assert over their son, a position that Bethune till now had openly endorsed. Tom had been installed in his house, then licensed out to a stranger without any consultation with, let alone approval of, his parents. Now, with Sherman on Georgia's doorstep, Bethune's sudden recognition of Mingo and Charity's legal rights must have seemed tantamount to surrender and surely undermined any satisfaction he felt in striking a fabulous deal.

But in a remarkable double-dodge worthy of the South's old nemesis Stephen A. Douglas, Bethune presented Mingo and Charity the illusion of compromise without conceding any of his power. This is the entire agreement between the lawyer and his illiterate and innumerate slaves:

> Georgia, Muscogee County—Indenture made the 30th May 1864 between Mingo Bethune and Charity, his wife on one part and James N. Bethune on the other, binding their son "Blind Tom" now sixteen years of age, the said J.N. Bethune to provide him with all the necessary subsistence and to instruct him in music and the said Charity and Mingo a good home, subsistence and $500 a year so long as he shall possess and control the service of the said Tom and to pay him $20 per month and 10% of his net proceeds.[19]

In a single ten-lined sentence, Tom was indentured to Bethune in exchange for a pittance.

Blinded by dollar signs, Charity and Mingo dutifully signed the agreement with an X. Compared to the loose change a slave could earn selling surplus vegetables or plying their trade, five hundred dollars a year was an enormous sum—a white overseer worked from sun-up to sunset for less.[20] However Tom's earning potential was at least one hundred times that amount, and far from heralding his entry into a free labor market, the contract merely perpetuated his servitude. As an attorney pointed out in a Cincinnati courtroom a year later, the terms of the indenture were unconscionable:

> One-tenth is reserved for the child and nine-tenths to the master. Let us take as an approximate value of the boy: the half interest for three years is worth $20,000 gold; the whole interest then, is $40,000 in gold—that's $13,333 per year. So Tom's value for a five year period is $66,666 gold. Of that sum, Tom would get his 10% and $20 per month—in all $7,866; his parents get $500 per year—in all $2500—leaving the net receipts of the operation in the hands of the master—$52,300 in gold.[21]

Money, however, was not Mingo and Charity's only reason for signing. Bethune would later insist that Tom's parents feared he might be taken by fraud or force and were "anxious that he should be under the protection and guardianship of some person in whom they might confide."[22] The likelihood of this occurring was very real—yet for all the paranoia about abolitionists, the culprits were far more likely to be con men and swindlers. The conjoined twins Millie and Christina were kidnapped as young children by an exhibitor, who eventually sold them to a slave speculator who in turn, sold them to a Philadelphia showman. Even when their hapless master eventually won them back, he continued to be swindled as one poor judgment of character followed the next. A similar tale dogged the early life of Blind Boone, a black Missouri-born pianist who came to prominence after the Civil War. Kidnapped as a teenager by another fraudulent exhibitor, he was gambled away in a card game then stolen back before finally being rescued by his stepfather.

While Mingo and Charity dwelt on these uncertainties, Bethune knew that force and fraud were not the only ways of losing Tom: there was always good old American competition. In a free and open market, Tom's emancipated parents could simply be made a better offer. Already, in the spring of 1863, an enterprising black showman by the name of Tabbs Gross had approached Bethune, traveling across three states and two enemy lines to negotiate the deal.

BARNUM OF THE AFRICAN RACE

Even the most begrudging Cincinnati newspapers were quick to point out that thirty-five-year-old Tabbs Gross was a remarkable businessman. Born a slave in Kentucky, he somehow convinced his master's son to lend him the money to purchase his own freedom. He then moved to Cincinnati where he educated himself and turned his mind to show business. With only a discarded panorama of *Uncle Tom's Cabin* to his name, he traveled to London and staged a production of the play, a venture which generated him "a handsome amount of money" and earned him the title "Barnum of the African Race."

Buoyed by this success, Gross hit upon the idea of managing Blind Tom and resolved to cross the divided nation to meet with Bethune. Unable to secure travel papers from the military authorities in Nashville, he continued regardless, undaunted by the very real risk of being kidnapped and re-enslaved, or arrested and executed as a Yankee spy (the Rebel army refused to take any black Union prisoners alive).

Gross arrived in Macon in April 1863 and met with General Bethune. Surprisingly Bethune was prepared to do business with the former slave, agreeing to sell Tom and his family for the sum of $20,000 in gold plus a half-share in the boy for five years—an outrageous sum compared to the $500 annuity he was paying Tom's parents and one that was far beyond Gross's means. There the negotiations ended, Gross returning to Cincinnati by way of West Virginia.[23]

A man who loved a challenge, the more Gross achieved, the more he was prepared to risk and, having got this far, would he really let this one go? Bethune hedged his bets that he wouldn't. And who would Gross be negotiating with next time: Bethune or Tom's emancipated parents? It may have taken Bethune some time to accept the inevitability of a Confederate defeat but the penny finally dropped after Frances Wallace assured him that, just like Tennessee, Sherman would make Georgia howl. And, as the Union General broke through the Appalachian Mountains into the state, Bethune stepped down from his pedestal and entered into a legal agreement with his slaves.

But what did it really matter? He now had an asset that, in time, would prove more valuable than land or cotton, and would enable him to play out his cavalier dreams as if defeat or emancipation had never really happened.

- 12 -

Fiah Up De Engines!

———•———

"THE STORES AND EVERYTHING JUST FLEW OPEN. THE STREET WAS FULL of tobacco and everything you can imagine, and among the rest about fifty barrels of whiskey. The soldiers and citizens, negros and everyone got drunk. It was the awfulest time I ever seen," wrote a young Iowan infantry man as he watched Union troops exact their revenge on the fallen city of Atlanta.[1] The thousands of terror-stricken refugees who poured into Columbus during September of 1864 had even more hellish tales: Yankee soldiers rounding up planters *en masse* and imprisoning them or inviting the slaves they had just liberated to tie their masters to the whipping post and humiliate them.[2] The Yankees were out for retribution and, as Bethune absorbed these tales, he began to suspect that the invaders would be every bit as brutal in victory as they were in war.

The family hatched a plan to escape to Europe. They would head south to Louisiana, then east into Florida, catch the first blockade runner to Havana, where they would board a ship for Europe. The four girls—Mary, Susan, Cherry and Fannie—set off first. General Bethune elected to stay behind to protect his property from vandals, he later told his grandson.[3] However, judging by his actions, the property he had in mind was not the farm but Blind Tom. A series of letters John and General Bethune penned to the Confederate Secretary of State in late 1864 reveals that Bethune was anxious to secure a passport for Tom: official documentation that would establish his legal claim on Tom and satisfy England's staunch anti-slavery legislation.

"Tom needs to visit Europe before he grows too old," read one letter, "his value as a Prodigy consists to a great extent in his Extreme youth . . . It would be cruel to permit such talent as his to die out for want of opportunities which alone can be given him in Europe."[4] Not half as cruel as the Yankees nabbing Tom, imprisoning Bethune and leaving the family penniless. The requests were forwarded to an already overwhelmed War Department and ignored. Bethune vainly waited in Columbus for a reply.

A curious turn of events then came John Bethune's way. Recently appointed a military judge, he was hardly in a position to take a "walking furlough" and join his father in Europe, no matter how badly he wanted too. But in January of 1865, John and four Confederate officers from unrelated units (including the brother of Susan Bethune's Louisiana-born husband) set off to Mandeville, a luxurious resort town just across the lake from New Orleans. As tantalizing as the gambling houses and dance halls may have been, it was an odd place for a Confederate officer to be, for Mandeville was miles away from the front line and awash with Union troops. Whatever informed John's behavior—whether it was folly or scheme—by January 16th he was a prisoner-of-war *en route* to a military prison in New Orleans. When he was paroled exactly two months later, it was under the strict condition that he would "leave the United States, go to some foreign country and not return during the war," an outcome so convenient, I cannot but wonder if it was a roundabout way of deserting.[5] Not daring to test his parole and return to Columbus, John headed straight for Florida. His father, who may or may not have been aware of developments, waited in Columbus until he could wait no more.

THAT WELCOME DAY

April 16, 1865. Lee's army had surrendered at Appomattox a week earlier. Sherman was battling Johnson's beleaguered army in the Carolinas and another advocate of Total War, twenty-eight-year-old Union cavalryman General James Harrison Wilson, attacked the last great manufacturing powerhouse of the Confederacy: Columbus. Women and children ran through the streets like people deranged. The roads leading out of the city were choked with wagons as the invaders systematically began to destroy anything of value.[6]

A local historian reported that Blind Tom heard Wilson's Army cannonading Columbus and the next day sat down to reproduce the sounds and fury of the conflict.[7] A tidy image if not for the fact that, by the next day, Tom and his one-legged, sixty-two-year-old master were on the road bound for Florida. Bethune, who limped badly crossing uneven surfaces and struggled to get in and out of wagons unassisted, knew that the journey was dangerous. If a wheel broke or they became bogged in the mud, if the Yankees held him at gunpoint and separated him from Tom, he had few resources to fall back on.

The crippled Scottish autocrat and the blind African youth were just two of tens of thousands of people in motion: a white population fleeing an invading army, grieving the death of their great Southern civilization. Yet along the same roads strewn with the carcasses of hogs and cattle, by fields trammeled to the ground, burnt and stripped of vegetation, beside scorched and violated plantation homes, another dream was realized: a moment of Biblical proportions akin to Moses leading his people out of Egypt and into the Promised Land. After a hundred years of hoping and praying, God had extended His mercy upon the Children of Africa and delivered them from bondage. With an intensity rarely heard outside the "hush harbors" and cabins, freed slaves shouted and prayed with "an eloquence that would move a stone." "Near every cross road and plantation, old men and women and young children would receive us with shouts of joy, exclaiming 'Glory be to de Lord! Bress de Lord! The Day of Jubilee is come! Dis nigger is off to glory!,'" reported one Union soldier.[8] The first urge for many freed slaves was to rove. "Many took to the highways and byways and walked around and roamed, aimlessly for days!" one former slave remembered, some in search of family, some simply to discover a formerly forbidden world.[9]

Traveling at a snail's pace on the same gouged and rutted byways were General Bethune and Blind Tom, although their journey was anything but aimless. Desperate to avoid the scrutiny of Union soldiers, Bethune most likely stuck to the back lanes, but nowhere could he dodge the thousands savoring their newly found freedom. On a conceptual level, Tom had a limited understanding of events but his highly-tuned senses must have told him the air was now ringing to a different tune: the thunder of war had morphed into the delirium of liberty. At night, it pealed out even louder as emancipated slaves gathered in circles around campfires and "joined in a kind of hymn 'bressin' de Lord,' their finely modulated voices chiming in one solemn chorus."

It is difficult to know the impact of this euphoria on Tom but—as always—there are clues. Twenty years after the war, there was a popular revival in plantation melodies and Tom's managers cashed in on the fad, publishing four of his songs which all, to varying degrees, exhibit a familiarity with the mythic resonance between the Children of Israel and the slaves of the American South. One, in particular, seems to be about the Day of Jubilee and interpreted literally, *That Welcome Day* may describe the events of April 17, 1865:

> I met my mother in the morning
> Talking about that welcome day,
> I met my mother in the morning
> Talking about that day.

The night Wilson's Raiders stormed Columbus, few slaves would have slept, instead passing the night in frenzied prayer, although Mingo and Charity's joy was dampened by Bethune's plan to "carry off" Tom to Europe (as Mingo confided to the Mississippi freeman, "it was something that he did not like but could not help").[10] No matter how early Tom left for Florida, his parents were there to bid him goodbye and perhaps impress on him the historical importance of this welcome day.

The song's chorus depicts a literal and detached picture of what he must have encountered on the road:

> Zion's children coming along, coming along, coming along,
> Zion's children coming along
> Talking about that day.

Another clue comes from a 1934 article by the daughter of a Georgia planter, Gretna Green, who encountered Blind Tom about six weeks after surrender in the elegant drawing room of a fine plantation home:

> While the white men conversed, Tom rocked back and forth on the bench near the door. He kept up a kind of *sotto voce* soliloquy saying "Phew! phew! Fiah up de engine!" to the great amusement of his young listeners both white and black. After a while his master interrupted this peculiar monologue by remarking "Tom, suppose you fire up your engine now."[11]

"Fire up the engines" is an expression bound up with the age of steam. A wood-fuel fire could build up a head of steam powerful enough to send a twenty ton locomotive hurtling down a track. The term also had a metaphorical dimension. "*O, keep the fire burning while your soul's fired up*," were the words to a spiritual that Columbus-born slave Mary Gladdy sang as a girl.[12] George Carter, a freed slave from Savannah, used the phrase to describe the music of fevered jubilation that followed emancipation.

> Soon as the Yankees came I ran away from Cap'n Potter and went wid another nigger. . . . I'se put tuh firin' de enjin gain. I done met Gen'l Bragg in Macon t'roo Dr. Arnold. I play fuh him on muh cane whistle. De Gen'l sho' libs good music . . . I wuz still firin' de enjin w'en Sherman come.[13]

For Tom, who loved trains nearly as much as he loved music, the cry "fiah up de engine" was irresistible. Some months would have passed since he had actually heard a train. Union soldiers had systematically ripped up tracks and destroyed bridges while fuel was in desperately short supply. While precious few trains were "firing up" in Georgia that week, there were plenty of jubilant souls. "Fiah up de engines," which Tom enunciated with a black Southern accent, seems unique in his lexicon to this particular period (none of the many people who later encountered Tom on trains recall him hollering it out). Admittedly the leads are speculative but not wildly so, and Tom may have latched onto this expression during his weeks on the road, perhaps so impressed by one freedman's efforts at "firin' de enjin," that he adopted the catchphrase as his own.

NO MORE GENERALS

General Bethune and Blind Tom set off to Florida by way of Oglethorpe—a small town sixty miles southwest of Macon (where Wilson's Raiders were now headed). It was a logical choice but if Bethune had known of the Federal Army's interest in a military prison twenty miles south of Oglethorpe, he may well have chosen another route.

Andersonville was infamous amongst Union soldiers: in the fourteen months of its existence, thirteen thousand of its forty-five thousand Federal prisoners had died from malnutrition, disease, poor sanitation, overcrowding and exposure to the elements. Such was the

North's outrage that the camp's commander was the only person executed for war crimes after the Civil War.

Unbeknownst to Bethune, the day he arrived in Oglethorpe, Wilson had ordered a detail of riders from the Ohio Seventh Cavalry to travel south and destroy the prison. By chance, a local woman named Rebecca Latimer Felton encountered the advance regiment of this detail shortly after they left Macon and watched them take "all they care to have and trample down crops before they slipped away."[14]

The cavalrymen hurtled further south, determined to reach Andersonville the following day. At the same time Tom and Bethune lumbered into Oglethorpe from the west. After two days, they were only sixty-five miles from home, their slow progress hampered by a torrential downpour that turned the already deplorable roads into bogs. In poor spirits, Bethune sought shelter in a nearby plantation house owned—according to the family's version of events—by a kindly widow. After a good meal the two slept soundly, but the rejuvenating effects of their rest were dashed when they discovered the entire bottom floor had been taken over by Wilson's cavalrymen— only this time they were neither foraging nor racing to Andersonville but seeking refuge. Sometime in the intervening twenty-four hours, the boys from the Ohio Seventh had learned of Johnson's surrender.

Forty years on, one of the horsemen, Mr. D. Boon, recounted the moment in a letter to *The New York Sun*.[15] "We had arrived in Oglethorpe only a few miles from our destination, when we met a band of handsome young officers in gray carrying the flag of truce, who directed us to suspend further operations. It was General Sherman's orders these Confederates were delivering to us, and there was nothing to do but immediately suspend operations."

If these boys had just heard of the surrender, Bethune most likely had just learned of it too—most probably from the very men who had plundered and destroyed Columbus the previous week. Bethune seems to have made some effort to press on with his journey but the officer-in-charge barred them from leaving the house until further orders arrived. Tom and Bethune were effectively under house arrest: a heart-stopping moment for the General whose flight was predicated on the fear that the Yankees would impound Tom and arrest him for aiding the Confederacy. But far from panicking, Bethune responded with cordial hospitality and good ole Southern charm, as Mr. Boon's recollection of the day reveals:

We had nothing to do and a dozen or so of the Seventh Cavalry were entertained at a house near town. After some conversation concerning the war, the master of the plantation said he had a black musical prodigy, a blind boy whom he would like us to see and hear before we departed. After accepting his cordial invitation, quite a number of us sat for hours and listened to all the airs belonging to the South, as well as every tune we could hum or whistle from *Annie Laurie* to *Yankee Doodle,* which the blind Negro boy repeated on the piano.

However as revealed in *The Story of Blind Tom*—a children's book based on anecdotes supplied by Susan Bethune's son—Bethune's genial hospitality was calculated. And right now his main problem was not courting the Yankees, who were proving more pliable than anticipated, but containing Tom's fury towards them:

Tom was angry. He wanted to get to Florida. The General thought Tom might have a temper tantrum if he and Tom couldn't leave soon. The General knew that this would be one of the worst things that could happen . . . "I have a plan which may get us out of here," the General told Tom. "You must obey me. Do not say a word to these men except to answer them politely. Our family is depending on us."

The General was talking to one of the Union soldiers the next day. "Gentlemen, there is a fine piano in the music room. Would you like to have Tom entertain you this evening?" The soldiers began to laugh. "Can he play the piano?" asked one of the men. "Let's hear him try," called out another.

After supper, the soldiers moved into the large music room, expecting to see something like a minstrel show. There was loud talk and laughter. The moment Tom struck the first chord, the laughter stopped. There was complete silence. It seemed as though Tom was coaxing the music from the piano with his fingers but with no effort. The Union soldiers were amazed.

It had been a long time since the soldiers had heard beautiful music. For months they had seen nothing but bitterness, hatred and the ugliness of war. They dropped their rough words (and) began to remember their loved ones at home. Forgot for a while they were engaged in a war and these people were their enemies.

Bethune, it seems, told them of his wish to take Tom to Europe and, malleable as putty, the Ohio Seventh played straight into his hands. "Men," announced one of the officers, "let's give this boy safe transportation away from here. This boy is too talented to be harmed. Nothing must happen to him." The next day, the Union officers issued Bethune with papers requesting safe passage for the two.

The stuff of family legend: in spite of the Confederacy's humiliating defeat, Bethune is triumphant. The South may be whipped but not this old warhorse. Cut away the bombast, however, and what remains is no longer a man of high principle but one who, in the absence of strength and power, is forced to use role-playing, cunning and wit to succeed. Almost overnight, Bethune found himself in a situation akin to the slave's favorite trickster—Br'er Rabbit—and learned to survive without the protection of power and privilege.

Somewhere around this point General Bethune shrewdly dropped his beloved moniker and became "Mr." Bethune, priming Tom with a catalogue of stock answers should he, once more, be grilled by the Yankees. Answers not unlike the ones Tom gave Dr. Graham three months later:

DR. GRAHAM:	You like Mr. Bethune, don't you.
TOM:	Yes sir. The army is disbanded now. I am a free man because the army is disbanded. We've quit fighting.
DR. GRAHAM:	You never fought anybody?
TOM:	No sir.
DR. GRAHAM:	How came you to get free through this war?
TOM:	Well because Mr. Bethune told me to call him that name, and now I call him that, and the army is disbanded, and there are no more Generals.
DR. GRAHAM:	There are no more slaves. Did he say that too?
TOM:	The army is disbanded.

Tom and Bethune continued their slow journey south—at some point ditching their horse and wagon for a stagecoach—and somehow maintaining a degree of sartorial splendor. Gretna Greene remembers the two arriving at a plantation home close to the Florida state line, Tom "neatly dressed in white trousers and a blue jacket trimmed with brass buttons." helped the distinguished old gentleman descend the stagecoach. "He limped badly and had to lean upon the arm of the boy as they made their way towards the house."

Gretna Greene at first assumed that Tom was Bethune's valet until she discovered him in the drawing room with the other gentlemen. This was remarkable in itself, but nothing compared to events that followed. At Bethune's suggestion, Tom entertained the party with a rendition of *Rocked in the Cradle Deep* and, as he launched into the chorus, one of her relatives, a young lady, attempted to join in. "Tom stopped singing at once and turned his forbidding countenance towards her. 'Hash' he cried, 'I want to sing myself.' The young lady 'hashed.'"[16]

Gretna Greene was astonished. No servant ever spoke to a white person like this. And as the night wore on, she began to fathom Tom's unique place in the plantation hierarchy. After dinner, for instance, he made a beeline for the piano, his hands still reeking with grease. "My cousin intercepted him and demanded that he wash his hands. At that Tom turned his back and refused to play anything at all." The children's demands rapidly turned to pleas but still Tom would not budge. Finally, they sought out General Bethune whose quiet, non-confrontational approach—firm with a hint of flattery—produced results. "'Come Tom,' he said, 'you must wash your hands. The ladies want you to fire up your engine.' Tom consented to his master's request and after cleansing his hands, returned to the piano for another long session."[17]

Bethune may have seemed in control but, even in this remote corner of Georgia untouched by war, he was still wary that Union soldiers might separate him from Tom and grilled his host about the troop movements in the area. "He seemed greatly relieved when told we had seen no soldiers."

In time, Bethune's fears came to be couched in the language of heroics. Far from a crushing blow, these testing times were remembered with great fondness. What could have been one of the lowest points of his life became an adventure: two outlaws on the seas of sedition, their catchphrase "fiah up de engines" encapsulating their dauntless courage, ingenuity and—according Bethune's grandson — friendship. "Between my Grandfather and Tom, a deep affection and mutual respect was born when they were wandering around Georgia together dodging Union soldiers," recalled Norbonne Robinson. "The General would never let Tom be imposed upon and Tom always responded promptly and gladly to the General's orders and requests."

In fact, the Yankees had little to no interest either in arresting Bethune or taking Tom from him. As soldiers repeatedly informed the emancipated slaves they came upon, they were fighting to restore the Union, not to free the slaves. The Federal army's often brutal attempts to ditch the hordes that followed them very quickly taught the slaves that Sherman had no intention of leading them to the Promised Land. The Cincinnati boys in the Seventh Cavalry, in particular, held little sympathy for the abolitionist cause—although it would be many months before Mr. Bethune could fully appreciate that, for a significant number of Ohioans, abolitionists were "the best hated people" too.

Bethune was reunited with his eldest son and daughters in Florida sometime in May although—much to Tom's continued frustration—they never completed their mission and escaped as planned to Europe. Blockade runners were now charging extortion rates. This, and the amnesty President Andrew Johnson offered all prisoners of war, may have been enough to convince Bethune that it was safe to return to Columbus. For Tom, who cared nothing for politics, the abandonment of a plan he considered undeviating and fixed was incomprehensible. If Bethune faced a tantrum when the Union officer obstructed them in Oglethorpe, he needed to reach deep into his bag of tricks to placate Tom, enraged and disorientated by this cataclysmic change. One doubts, in this instance, Tom "responded promptly and gladly to the General's orders and requests;" Bethune himself admitted that when Tom was "infuriated" he was "as intractable as the winds."[18]

"Europe in the spring" seems to have become a new catchphrase for Tom. That September, a newspaper article spoke of Tom's "great desire to go to Europe in the spring."[19] Even after he toured the continent in the winter of 1866/67, he was still unable to speak of Europe without associating it with spring. Twelve years later, his response to a question about how he was treated in Europe was: "very well, I long to go back this spring."[20] Right up until his last days, Tom "often spoke of his desire to go to Europe," a telling indication of how this nagging lack of resolution—this rupture to the order of the universe—vexed him for the rest of his life.[21]

Despite Tom's truculence, General Bethune's will ultimately ruled the day. They returned home to Columbus. But it was a brief visit, just long enough to have the indenture agreement endorsed by the newly formed Freedman's Bureau and for father and son to team up with second son Joseph, W.L. Anderson—a former comrade of John's who stuck with the Columbus Guards all the way to Appomattox, perhaps not "well bred" enough to join the Nelson Rangers—and General W.P. (Pinkie) Howard, a music professor and old family friend. By late June, the party of six was on its way north intent on conquering the Yankee stage.

Three short months after the collapse of the Confederacy, it was business as usual for the Blind Tom Concert Company, an extraordinary accomplishment given the Yankee-imposed controls curtailing the movements of southerners. General Bethune evidently had someone behind the scenes, pulling strings, securing passes, enabling him to rise like a phoenix from the ashes and restore his lost fortune.

- 13 -

Yankee Justice

———————•———————

IN JULY 1865, "HIS EXCELLENCY, THE PRESIDENT OF THE UNITED STATES" received a letter concerning "a Boy who lives in the State of Georgia known as Blind Tom . . . I think this boy would be of great service to us just now in relieving the want of the four million Bondsmen made free by the Government. Now I see a chance to raise a few hundred thousand dollars to buy clothes for the women and children who are now by the thousands in our Freedmen's camps. This Boy is one of our race and should be doing something for the public good."[1]

This letter appears to be penned by an educated African-American, perhaps overcompensating for his humble start with the "His Excellency" *faux pas*. (Mr. President, surely.) One gets the sense from this letter that the author had personally witnessed the disease ridden destitution in the freedmen's camps that had sprung up across the South—thousands of freed slaves squatting in abandoned army bases, rife with smallpox and pneumonia, their only help coming from abolition-inspired benevolent societies.[2] He may also have seen how a small band of Quakers were toiling to transform a hellhole like Kentucky's Fort Nelson into a self-sufficient black community, or drawn inspiration from the fleeting success of Mississippi's Camp Cornith, a rambling shanty town of fifteen hundred that became a close-to-independent community with schools, hospitals and hundreds of acres under cultivation.*

*Under the order of General Sherman, the camp was abandoned in March 1864 and relocated to Memphis, 93 miles away, but the momentum was lost and efforts towards a new camp came to nothing.

So were these the values of the man who hoped to recruit fifteen-year-old Blind Tom to the freedmen's cause—self-help, cooperation and education? Or was he an arch pragmatist, capitalizing on the humanitarian disaster to further his own show business ambitions? What was driving the man who, only two weeks earlier, had courted General Bethune's favor and helped members of the Blind Tom Concert Company cross Union lines?

CINCINNATTI NEGRO VS GEORGIA PLANTER

Two years after his meeting with General Bethune, Tabbs Gross had not given up on Blind Tom. The new emancipated age had barely begun before he was bankrolled and off to Georgia where he intended to meet with Bethune and close the deal. And close it he did—acquiring, in principle, a half interest in Tom's management for the sum of $20,000. A $1,000 down payment was made and a second installment of $4,000 was scheduled for Nashville, two weeks hence.

But the second installment was never paid. Something about Bethune's behavior roused Tabbs Gross's suspicions and he refused to hand over the money until they reached Louisville. But in Louisville, it was Bethune's turn to decline. Gross upped payment to $5,000 but Bethune was adamant: Tom was staying with him. Why? Because Tom desired it so? Or perhaps after tallying the receipts from three sellout concerts in Nashville, $20,000 seemed too cheap by half. It is possible too that Bethune never had any intention of honoring the contract, seeing Gross as the most expedient way North. Whatever changed his mind, it was a matter Bethune considered devoid of legal consequence. Emancipation fever may have raised the hopes of black folk throughout the country but, in July 1865, they were still politically disenfranchised with few legal rights. Dredd Scott still the order of the day, the Blind Tom Concert Company moved on, beyond the war ravaged South to go where Perry Oliver had longed to go but dared not tread— New Albany, Indiana—and reap the financial benefits.

However, surrender was the last thing on Gross's mind. He pursued Bethune to New Albany and took his case to the city's probate judge who—without even clapping eyes on Tom—issued Gross with a writ of *habeas corpus* and a letter of guardianship. Tabbs Gross then made a beeline for the hotel to claim what he believed was his, but General Bethune was one step ahead of him. Five years may have passed since Blind Tom fled the city with Perry Oliver but the message had not changed: a stranger was after him, intent on carrying him off.

As circumstance would have it, Blind Tom's next concert appearance was in Gross's hometown of Cincinnati and the morning of the first performance, he and a local attorney—the well known abolitionist William Martin Dickson—served Bethune with a writ of *habeas corpus*, this time for illegally restraining Tom of his liberty. Unlike the New Albany writ that focused on the breach of contract, this bid challenged the legality of Bethune's claim on Tom. Before a court of law, Bethune had to establish that he was Tom's guardian, while the prosecution was out to prove that Blind Tom was his indentured servant.[3]

"ARE YOU A STRANGER?"

The writ served, Tom—accompanied by W.P. Howard—was taken to the Sheriff's office where he was to remain until the preliminary hearing that afternoon. News flashed through the city and by lunchtime hundreds of curious townsfolk, including a reporter for *The Cincinnati Herald,* converged on the building, eager to catch a glimpse of the curious creature:

> When we entered the Sheriff's office, we found [Tom] seated, eating his dinner, which he did with a considerable display of appetite and a liberal use of his fingers. After he finished his dinner he retired to one corner of the apartment and, heedless of the crowd looking on, engaged in amusing himself in a manner peculiar to himself. He seemed to be in a curious state of exhilaration. Sometimes he would perch himself on one leg and hop around in a circle, crooning to himself as he hopped. Sometimes he thrummed the air with his fingers, with the liveliest energy, and then would break into a sort of rude walk-round. His features were constantly agitated by some apparently joyful thought or inspiration. Sometimes he would rub his hands together with unmistakable ecstasy. At the request of Mr Howard, he sang a verse from *Rock Me to Sleep Mother*, his chin quivering with excitement and occasionally a thrill seemed to ripple over him from head to foot . . . When introduced to a gentleman, his first question is "Are you a stranger?", to which he generally receives an affirmative reply.

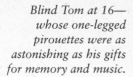

*Blind Tom at 16—
whose one-legged
pirouettes were as
astonishing as his gifts
for memory and music.*

Thoroughly entertained, the citizens of Cincinnati then followed him into the Probate Court. Tom spent the first part of the preliminary hearing in a state of considerable apprehension and repeatedly asked W.P. Howard, "what are you going to do now?" But as the hearing wore on, he soon forgot all but himself. "His wealth of extravagant smiles returned and his eyes rolled exultantly in their orbits. He would frequently stretch himself back in his chair and indulge in a low, prolonged chuckle, rattling his finger over his thigh or tapping himself with dazzling rapidity on the chin or breast. A strange, silly, divinely gifted creature, truly."[4]

Publicity like this was priceless and, thanks to a judge who allowed the prodigy to honor his concert engagements, Blind Tom filled Mozart Hall eight nights running (netting a good $4,000 in the process). The boys from the Ohio Seventh, who had returned home just that week, could not believe their eyes: the black prodigy who had played for them only a few months earlier in the plantation house in Oglethorpe was now the toast of the town. "His imitations on the piano of music boxes, banjos, locomotives and a Scottish fiddle are very clever," wrote *The Cincinnati Daily Commercial*. "The tuning of a Scottish fiddle threw the audience into violent fits of laughter. His vocal imitations of a runaway train are extravagantly eccentric. His notion of letting the brakes on and off and the deafening rumble of the train, could only emanate from his own curiously organized brain."[5]

Only one section of the community elected to stay away. *The Colored Cincinnatian* asked its readers to boycott the show to protest the theater's segregated seating arrangements. But their campaign was about more than the profanity and filth of the topmost gallery. Solidarity ran deep amongst Cincinnati's Free Negros and the community stood by Tabbs Gross, whose court battle with Bethune was seen as yet another episode in an ongoing crusade for equality and justice. A history of mob violence, police brutality and the necessity for self-help had long convinced them that they were stronger together than alone.

CAN THE COURT SUSTAIN SUCH A CONTRACT?

Cincinnati was a town as divided as the river it sat on—the Ohio marking the unofficial border between the slave states and free—and for decades the city's two and a half thousand freemen had been pummeled and nurtured by these opposing forces. The city's leaders, with strong blood links to the South, had passed some of the most draconian black codes of any free state and endorsed the excesses of the racist police force. At the same time, Quaker Levi Coffin had helped over a thousand fugitive slaves cross the Ohio while nearby Oberlin College had opened its doors to African-American students. So a custody battle between a Cincinnati Negro and Georgian Planter over a celebrity ex-slave stirred a great deal of passion in the city. Its outcome would be a measure of the shifting balance of power, an indication of what to expect in this America's brave new post-emancipation world. And both the prosecution and defense knew it—the knowledge of the possible consequences charged every tactic, informed every word.

Take, for instance, Tabbs Gross's attorney, William Martin Dickson. He was not just any old abolitionist lawyer with the requisite clientele of fugitive slaves and disgruntled freemen, but a member of President Lincoln's inner circle and had helped frame the Emancipation Proclamation. Dickson's wife was Mrs. Lincoln's first cousin and the Lincolns had stayed with them during a visit to Cincinnati in the 1850's. Perhaps most significantly, Dickson was the erstwhile commander of the Black Brigade of Cincinnati, a work unit that three years earlier had deliberately styled itself as a military unit and helped paved the way for black enlistment into Union

ranks. What had begun as an exercise in the abuse of police power—
all able-bodied black men rounded up at gunpoint, herded into town
and impressed into service—had, under Dickson's leadership,
become an enduring symbol of black pride. "Men of the Black
Brigade," rallied their captain at the flag presentation ceremony,
"assert your manhood. Slavery will soon die; this slaveholder's rebellion will shortly and miserably perish." Deeply empowered by this
experience was a man in Regiment One, Company C—Tabbs Gross.[6]
After six weeks of building reinforcements on the banks of the Ohio
River after his stint with the work brigade, he was in enemy territory, on his way to negotiate with General Bethune.

It would not have taken Bethune long to appreciate that William
Dickson was a powerfully connected Republican and a hero amongst
to the city's freemen, while he himself was an alien in a foreign land.
Now in the witness stand on the first day of the hearing, Attorney
Dickson before him, bombarding him with questions about his loyalty to the flag and constitution, the thought must have crossed
Bethune's mind that the Yankees had finally cornered him. To punish
him for his sins against the Union, his prodigy would be delivered into
the hands of the ideological enemy, the abolitionist, while he would
be banished to military-occupied Georgia and forced to eke out a living amid its charred ruins. This was Yankee justice.

The feeling of doom only intensified when the judge appointed
two psychiatrists to determine if Tom was even capable of choosing
a guardian. So far the defense's most powerful weapon was Tom,
who had been loudly insisting that he wanted to stay with Bethune.
Dr Graham's report to the court now defused that device: Tom's
judgment was impaired, Dr. Graham informed the court the following day, his reasoning powers were defective, his resentments were
strong, possibly prone to violence. And his tendency to judge a person purely on whether or not they treated him kindly, Dr. Graham
concluded, was too narrow a criteria on which to base an informed
decision.[7]

The prosecutor Dickson then turned his attentions to the indenture agreement. Did Mingo and Charity understand the difference
between their $500 per year and Bethune's 90% slice of the net prof-
its? Were they aware that they could realize many thousands of dollars, buy a home and educate their children, Dickson asked WP
Howard during his cross-examination? Based on Bethune's own

income projections, out of $20,000 gross earnings the indenture entitled Blind Tom to little over $1,500 a year, his parents $500, leaving Bethune with over $10,000 in gold. "Can the court sustain such a contract?"[7] Perhaps not, but was it enough to persuade the court to award Gross custody of Tom? Either way, General Bethune wasn't taking any chances.

As soon as the midday recess was announced, Bethune headed straight down to the Adjutant General's Office where he placed his hand on the Bible and promised to faithfully support, protect and defend the Constitution of the United States and abide by all acts of Congress and presidential proclamations, including the proposed amendment to give black men the vote. Faced with losing his cash cow, the Southern stalwart enlisted his pragmatic heart to the Union.

A PIMP & A RACKETEER

Bethune's lapse of faith did not necessarily spell victory for William Dickson. Right from day one when Judge Woodruff interrupted him and irritably asked whether it was really necessary to go into a detailed account of Bethune's secessionist past, Dickson knew on which side of the river the judge metaphorically stood.[9]

The medical examination also backfired. Although Dr. Graham's opinion was precisely what Dickson wanted to hear, it neither swayed the judge nor the rest of Cincinnati (the transcripts of the interview made front page news), who were overwhelmingly struck by the image of a simpleton terrified by the prospect of being torn from his kindly former master, a father figure he had known virtually all his life.

TOM:	(*looking round agitated*) Mr. Gross is trying to carry me off.
DR. BLACKMAN:	No he isn't.
TOM:	Where is he now?
DR. BLACKMAN:	He is not here.
GENERAL BETHUNE:	Tom, tell them whatever they ask you—don't be afraid . . .
DR. GRAHAM:	Suppose they were to tell you that you were free? What would you do?
TOM:	I would just go to Mr. Bethune.

DR. GRAHAM:	He would take care of you, would he?
TOM:	Yes he takes care of me. Oh, he's a good man, sure . . .
DR. GRAHAM:	You like Mr. Bethune, don't you.
TOM:	Yes sir. The army is disbanded now. I am a free man because the army is disbanded. We've quit fighting.[10]

The defense tabled a court record showing that in 1860, Gross had been convicted of keeping a house of ill fame. A great outrage, countered Dickson's camp, alluding that the charge had been trumped up by a corrupt police force. But Dickson's riposte was immediately quashed by the judge. Who was he to falsify a court record, he thundered.[11]

Tabbs Gross's military service in Kentucky was then held up to scrutiny. He had been amongst the first batch of recruitment officers in the state to begin signing black soldiers up to the Union Army. Such was the animosity towards these agents that six were lynched by white mobs while Gross was thrown into jail under order of the Governor of Kentucky.* However the defense's star witness, General E. Powell presented Gross—not as a Union Army hero—but a bounty-scalper who impressed unsuspecting slaves into service then shipped them off to states that paid him a sizable bounty.

Dickson did his best to present the real reason behind Gross's incarceration. But details of the policy differences between the President and Kentucky Governor lacked the punch of General Powell's emphatic words: Gross took "runaway colored persons from Kentucky and sold them to Massachusetts." By day's end, Tabbs Gross was branded a pimp and racketeer.

But the day was not without it triumphs for William Dickson, who perhaps relished the gasp that rippled through the courtroom, as he called upon a black witness to mount the stand and testify against a white man. Isaac Turner, a "crudely-spoken" Mississippi born freeman who had worked alongside Gross in the Black Brigade, told the court his curious tale. In the euphoric wave of emancipation, he traveled to Georgia on business of his own and,

---

*Although Kentucky was exempt from the Emancipation Proclamation, Lincoln's decision to allow black recruitment effectively put an end to slavery there. Male slaves only had to sign up to the Union army to secure their freedom.

by chance, visited the Bethune farm where he met with Mingo and Charity.

Immediately General Bethune smelt a rat, becoming flushed and irate as Turner recounted the details of his meeting with Tom's parents. "What kind of freedom was it if I have to have a pass," Mingo asked Turner after being told he could not leave the farm without his master's written permission. Mingo was not entirely sure if slaves were really free, "he had heard it said but also heard that the Legislature would put them all in bondage again"—hardly the words of a man whose master had voluntarily set him free. (Earlier Bethune had insisted it was he, rather than the federal government, who emancipated his slaves).

Their conversation soon turned to Blind Tom. Mingo complained about his lack of authority over his son; that he did not fully understand the contract he had signed with an X. Turner told him not to place the boy in anyone's hands. He was a wonder that the Saxon race had yet to turn out and, if they brought him to the North themselves, Mingo would be considered a powerful man and Charity a powerful woman for producing such a son. To this, Mingo asked Tuner not to speak of the matter "lest something might happen."

By now Bethune was so vexed that he dismissed his attorney and began his own cross-examination, accusing Turner of traveling to Columbus at Gross's behest with the express intention of luring Mingo and Charity north. Turner made strenuous denials, insisting he was on his way to Alabama in search of family. But was this simply too much of a coincidence? Would Gross really have made a bid for Blind Tom without any consultation with his parents?

It was a question Tabbs Gross never got to answer. He barely had time to announce his desire to take Tom to Cincinnati and "adopt the boy as my own son" before his examination was over. By now Dickson was nursing doubts of his own. Tom was no orphan and Gross knew exactly where his parents lived. He may have sent Isaac Turner to sound them out, but he personally had not consulted with them, opting instead to negotiate with Bethune. For a custody battle to take place without Mingo and Charity's knowledge—let alone involvement—was unforgivable. How could Dickson, a committed abolitionist and social reformer, now be party to a claim that denied Tom's parents their basic moral rights?

Dickson rose for his summation. His task was to somehow having persuade the court that Blind Tom was Tabbs Gross' rightful custody – but how could he do this, when he could barely convince himself:

> The struggle between Gross and Bethune is a struggle as to who could make the most out of the boy. His and his parent's interests were not considered. I felt this when Mr. Gross first came to me and felt it may be considered by the court an insuperable objection to delivering the boy to him. I so stated it to him and asked if he were willing that I should ask the Court, in that event, to give this wonderful being to some good man who would have the interest of the boy, solely, in view. He at once gave his consent. . . . Assuming that your Honor will not give this boy to Gross; to whom will you give him?

Dickson then offered up an answer: Levi Coffin, the hallowed Cincinnati Quaker and unofficial president of the Underground Railway. "I would have this guardian go to Georgia, see to these aged parents, gather together the broken fragments of his family and bring them to some place where they would be well cared for and educated. Then let the boy sing for the benefit of himself and his family."[12]

But Dickson's utopian vision failed to make an impression and Judge Woodruff's ruling in Bethune's favor came as a surprise to few. The depths of his sympathies were clear when he described Bethune as "a venerable man, of unusual intelligence and kindness of heart." In contrast, he dismissed Gross as little more than a "stranger" in "questionable moral shape, his eye merely on pecuniary advantage."[13]

Tabbs Gross must have left the court wondering how much had really changed. Slavery may have been dead but the white power base was alive and kicking. By virtue of his race, he was branded an alien and a traitor while Bethune was welcomed open armed into the fold. For Bethune, it was a revelation. Far from the abolitionist ogre ruling the north, robbing him of his God given rights, he discovered that—even in the free state of Ohio—the high-minded rantings of a puritanical abolitionist held no more sway over the population than they did in the South.

POSTSCRIPT

A local history of Columbus alleges that, after the court case, Tabbs Gross and an "unidentified white Yankee" traveled to Columbus to persuade Mingo to break his contract with General Bethune. "Twelve thousand dollars in specie was offered to him and the money exhibited." But, the historian was proud to report, loyalty ruled the day. Blind Tom went back on the road and Mingo and Charity went back to the farm. Another twenty years would pass before their loyalties would be tested again.[14]

An equally unsubstantiated story claims that Tabbs Gross followed Blind Tom to England two years later and unsuccessfully put his case to the English courts.[15] But in fact Tabbs Gross's failed bid for Blind Tom put an end to his show business ambitions. In 1867, he moved to Little Rock, Arkansas and, in a curious parallel with General Bethune, became both a lawyer and newspaperman, publishing the state's first black-owned newspaper, *The Freeman*. Until his death from tuberculosis thirteen years later, he played an active role in the state branch of the Republican Party, stirring up the rank and file with his controversial and maverick views.[16]

PART THREE

CLANGOROUS AGONIES

Blind Tom in his early twenties.

- 14 -

The Great Musical Mystery

"HE STANDS FIVE FEET, SEVEN INCHES HIGH, WEIGHS NEARLY ONE HUNDRED
and fifty pounds and is one of the most compactly built, vigorous and
healthy persons we have ever met," wrote the phrenologist Orson
Fowler of sixteen-year-old Tom. "His legs are splendidly developed
and as hard as those of any gymnast. He has broad square shoulders,
a full chest, a well-knit frame throughout and is as sound and healthy
as a human can be."[1] On stage, Tom's boundless vitality was electric. In
an age of Thunder Virtuosity, where a generation of pianists—the
acolytes of Franz Liszt—lifted their hands high, tossed back their
manes and pounded the keyboard in a hail of trills and a rumble of
chords, snapping strings and cracking hammers, sweeping up the
piano in a blaze of arpeggios and down in a fanfare of octaves, Tom
had moves that would blow them off the stage.

If Louis Moreau Gottschalk (who had just fled the country in a
wave of scandal) had turned American audiences on to bravura
excess with his white gloved comedy of high manners and monster
pianos that dwarfed the standard concert grands; if the young repub-
lic deferentially bowed to the European mastery of Sigismond
Thalberg, his velvet fingers polishing the keys with lightning fast
arpeggios; then "grotesque," "uncouth" and "primitive" Blind Tom
was thunder virtuosity's pariah. Though he would match Gottschalk
in fame and outdraw critically acclaimed pianists like Richard
Hoffman and William Mason, the musical establishment snubbed
him, but they could not ignore him.

In the twelve months following the war, Blind Tom took the
north by storm, as managers John Bethune and W.P. Howard staged

concerts in cities across the former enemy's territory. (General Bethune had bowed out of the tour after Cincinnati). Such was Philadelphia's "wild enthusiasm" for Tom, that a one week engagement stretched to four. New York, Boston, Albany, Pittsburgh, Louisville and Cleveland also came to know of Blind Tom, his lithographed portraits plastered across each city, his name in every newspaper. Part high-minded piano recital, part Barnum-styled curiosity show, the American stage had never seen anything like Blind Tom.

"He was led in by a showman, placed in the middle of the platform and left to himself," reported the acclaimed writer, Horace E. Scudder of a performance in Boston's Tremont Temple. Tom made a bow, then in a high pitched, monotonous voice began to recite a speech and speak of himself in the third person, "as if he were the showman, and the real showman, leaning against the piano, and looking on, was Tom."[2] He spoke of "this boy Tom as a mere creature of music," who was "ignorant of the Almighty's reason for choosing the piano as the instrument which he was to play," and wondered why "a being of the lowest scale of humanity should have so much genius."[3] He warned that the musical marvel was liable to take twists and turns that not even he could predict, "such is the capricious, impulsive and entirely unregulated nature of Tom's mind."[4] The introduction over, he dropped the showman's persona, resumed his "strange, eager, restless manner," sat down at the piano and played an air from the opera *Lucrezia Borgia*.[5]

"Our Negro prodigy has an amusing habit of applauding himself," disdained one critic. "No sooner has he struck his last chord than he takes to clapping with all his might and with a hearty earnestness leaving no doubt of his sincerity."[6] Solid, agile and unbelievably powerful, a fly ball in full cryptic flight, northern audiences could not take their eyes off him. As W.P. Howard shared with them details of his peculiarities, Tom would mill about the other end of the stage, playing with his fingers and trumpeting strange sounds through his nose. "He would suddenly clap his fingers to his ears, as if some sound offended him, and again feel the ends of his fingers in a wondering kind of way, as if he thought the music was still on the tips, and could be rubbed off."[7]

Nothing, it seemed, could upstage Tom. "As the new tune begins," wrote an intrigued scientist of the Audience Challenge, "Tom

Louis Moreau Gottschalk, America's premiere thunder virtuoso.

takes some ludicrous posture, expressive of listening, but soon lowers his body and raises one leg, so that both are perfectly horizontal representing the letter T. He moves upon that improvised axis like a pirouette dancer but indefinitely. The long gyrations are interrupted by spells of motionless listening, with or without changes to the posture, or ornamented with spasmodic movements of the hands. This is his studying posture."[8]

All of this before he struck a note. When he did, audiences recoiled at his rawness, warmed to his honesty. "He seems to be under a mesmeric influence, and is sometimes so excited and agitated as to tremble from head to toe as if suffering from intense pain," noted a reporter.[9] The scientist agreed: "When he sends certain clangorous agonies, his shoulder blades bear down directly on the keys and his whole frame vibrates with the instrument."[10]

"His playing was rude in general, but quite effective by a sort of wild pathos which he threw into it," added Horace E. Scudder. "He liked noise in his music, and imitative sounds. When he sang, there was something unearthly in his voice, as if he were some strange animal singing, I only dimly guessed what."[11] "As the piece progressed," furthered another audience member, "he seemed to become more and more absorbed, and utterly isolated from the outer world. Sometimes he played with immense force, but at others his touch was exceedingly delicate; and when he played thus softly, he stooped over the instrument with his ear bent down to it, as if he were listening intently to some distant strain of music, and feared to lose a single note. Then he would throw his head back, and look as though he were invoking some invisible spirit in the ceiling."[12]

Yankee audiences came in their droves, paying anywhere between twenty-five cents and a dollar for the pleasure. Fathoming the great musical mystery of the age was a highly lucrative affair.

MEN OF MIND

"Rough and uncouth as he appears, he has the power to draw around him the elite of the city," observed *The Philadelphia Enquirer*. "Men of intellect, men of mind, all go to see Tom—not to witness his antics, not to listen to his limitations, but to be astonished, confounded and amazed at the effects he produces on the piano."[13]

Heading the pack of the great and good was Dr. Edward Seguin, a psychiatrist at New York University who challenged the idea that idiocy was untreatable and had developed a program that enabled the mentally disabled to acquire some degree of independence. (When he migrated to the United States in 1848, no facilities—either public or private—existed for the care of retarded children. By the time he died in 1880, he had helped organized eleven.) For years, Seguin had been cataloging symptoms into groups and no form interested him more than the condition he was to call "idiotic genius."[14]

"Blind Tom is another example of isolation of the mind (superficial idiocy)," he concluded in his landmark study, *Idiocy and its Treatment by Physiological Method*. It was an assessment that resonates in Leo Kanner's first description of autism eighty years later: the individual withdrawing from the fabric of life into the self. For Seguin, diagnosis was just the first phase of the process. Next came treatment and his case study speculated on how Tom might benefit from his educational program:

> Tom is evidently improving in his mind since he was thrown into company. Now the question arises—if he can be elevated above his idiotic condition, will he lose the acuteness of his musical sense, exchanging his artistic genius against an even more general common sense?[15]

It was a question that John Bethune was not prepared to explore. Public education, women's suffrage and uplifting the dispossessed may be the order of the day in the academies of Boston and New York but, in the South, the ideas espoused by Seguin were as dangerous and subversive as abolitionism. (Indeed it was not lost on John that most of the people who advocated the education of idiots were abolitionists).

The Bethunes' response to the reformist zeal of this Yankee do-gooder was made clear in the biography in the 1868 concert program. Although they systematically refuted the perception that Tom was an "idiot," educating him was strictly off the agenda. "He never has been able to distinguish one alphabetical letter from another. Even could the boy see with a partial dimness, it would be almost criminal to enlighten him on a subject, which, in his case, would be totally useless."

This was patently false. Tom could not see letters but he was quite able to distinguish one from another, as evidenced by a novelty item developed by W.P. Howard. "He called for a gentleman to hold up some object," wrote Horace Scudder. "I held up my watch; the man struck the notes in a peculiar way, and Tom spelled it correctly."[16] "An opera glass was held up and the letters of these two words were struck upon the piano," reported another confounded witness, "Tom caught them at once and spelled 'opera glass.' The same was done with the world 'watch,' 'umbrella' and 'walking cane.' Nobody has been able to explain exactly how this was done."[17]

The explanation, in fact, was deceptively simple. Tom had long been familiar with the notes of the octave. W.P. Howard seems to have built on this, assigning to each piano key a letter of the alphabet. When somebody held up a hat, W.P. Howard would hit the corresponding keys and Tom would then name spell H-A-T.

Tom's comprehension of written English went further than this. At the concert Scudder attended, audience members were invited to call out words, which Tom then spelled phonetically, calling each letter out loudly.[18] At some point, W.P. Howard must have grounded Tom in the principles of phonetics, an elaborate system of rules and exceptions that the prodigy took to like a duck to water. "He always spells a word according to the sound that is carried to his ear," recalled Mark Twain. "And he is an enthusiast in orthography. When you give him a word, he shouts it out—puts all his soul into it. He says, 'O, r-a-n-g, orang, g-e-r, ger, oranger, t-a-n-g, tang, orangger tang.' But the feeble dictionary makes a mere kitten of him."[19] Within no time, Tom was attacking words like Aurora Borealis, Chunnenuggee, curiosity, Opelika and physiology: "'f-i-l, fil, l-i, li, o-z, oz, fillioz, z-y, filliozzy, g-y, filliozogy.' 'Hieroglyphic' was a wander amongst the h's and g's and l's and y's and x's."[20]

For decades this act delighted Tom's audience and—by extension—his management. As wildly as they applauded, one salient point was consistently overlooked: W.P. Howard had taught Tom to spell. The blind youth had acquired a level of literacy that few emancipated slaves could match. No wonder Edward Seguin rounded off the assessment with the comment, "Colonel Bethune's kind and gentlemanly manners cannot keep off the remark that he likely makes more by Tom than Tom would by him."

"BY NO MEANS IDIOTIC"

Reading bumps was a peculiarly nineteenth century preoccupation and, while never accepted by mainstream academia, Phrenology and the brain organs of Tune and Time were part of the nineteenth century lexicon. According to phrenologist Orson Fowler, who examined Blind Tom in 1866, Tom's were exceedingly well developed. Aside from the recommendation that "when Tom dies his skull be preserved as a scientific curiosity," his examination of Tom imbues him with a rare dignity and humanity:

> He is by no means idiotic in any organ or faculty and those who tend him and know all about him make no such claim. He is odd, full of queer antics . . . His ways are his own and are somewhat eccentric. His reasoning powers have not been cultivated . . . His mind seems to centralize in one direction . . . The head shows great moral development, more than ordinary kindliness of disposition and a full degree of the social faculties. Looked at then from all standpoints it must be confessed that Tom is a remarkable person; but he is quite far from being an idiot as others have claimed.[21]

However, the conclusions of lesser men who worshiped at the temple of Science lacked the same rigor and objectivity. With the publication of Darwin's *The Origin of Species* in 1858, new buzzwords entered popular consciousness and the search for the "missing link" led many directly to Blind Tom. "As I looked at him I confess to have been more than half-converted to Darwin's theory," one amateur mused. "His shambling figure is the personification of ungainliness; while the constant rolling of his sightless eyes and idiotic leer of his enormous mouth seem to be closely allied to the peculiarities of a baboon. We wonder if it is merely the natural result of the long degradation of his race, or if only a few generations back his ancestors really were the *gnodrumana genus*."

But something about Blind Tom drew even those locked into racist stereotypes to philosophical, even mystical, conclusions. The amateur scientist who had begun so contemptuously, wrapped up his assessment of Tom on a reverential note: "I cannot understand how anyone, however sceptical he may have been before, can disbelieve, after attending Tom's concerts, that we have something in our natures better, purer, higher, than mere intellect."[22] "What is intellect and what is idiocy?" asked another man, who in his previous paragraph dismissed Tom as a "barbarous African." "Where is the narrow dividing line that separates the philosopher from the fool?"[23]

The seamless shift from the evolutionary to the arcane was part and parcel of late nineteenth century popular culture, white America's flirtation with the supernatural by no means ending with the Age of Reason. In this stolidly Victorian era, people experimented with Ouija boards, table turning, parlor séances and spectral materializations in an effort to communicate with the dead. And through the esoteric prisms of Spiritualism and Theosophy, Blind Tom was also appraised anew.

"To me it is as clear a case of mediumship as I ever saw," declared the eminent Spiritualist, Warren Chase, who saw in Tom's awkward gestures and rolling eyes evidence that he was "under influence"—communicating with the dead and channeling spirits.[24] By pure "psychic sympathy," furthered a Theosophist, Blind Tom's overwhelming love for harmony and music put him *en rapport* with the consciousnesses of the great composers. "Think if we could get that kind of rapport with the Masters of Wisdom, what couldn't we do? Just through his love of music, of the magic of sounds, he was able to bless himself and make heaven for others."[25]

For all Tom's supposed psychic sympathy with the dead masters, he was pointedly excluded from the company of the living masters. To them, he was little more that a musical parrot.

THE CROWNED HEADS OF EUROPE

With Louis Moreau Gottschalk's flight from the country, the title of America's premiere Thunder Virtuoso was open to for the taking. While Richard Hoffman and William Mason may have been feted by opinion brokers at *Dwight's Musical Journal*, it was Blind Tom who was the household name. An unlikely contender, he was fast becoming the country's most famous pianist—so what was stopping him from becoming its finest too?

The idea of Blind Tom filling Gottschalk's pampered shoes appalled many critics. "He is not a great pianist and can never be one because he lacks intelligence; he has a quick perception of the sensuous charm of a melody, but no comprehension of the meaning of a musical composition," opined one New York critic.[26] However at least one man believed he had the makings of a first-class pianist, and that was his stage manager and tutor, W.P. Howard.

"A good natured, lazy man, with one of his waist buttons gone," W.P. Howard came to the Blind Tom Concert Company with no previous experience in show business. And no burning ambition either, telling the Cincinnati court that he accepted the $200-a-month job because his "financial affairs had collapsed with the Confederacy" and he did not care to starve. However the music professor and long-time friend of General Bethune did seem to know something about a higher order of music and was determined to expose Tom to it. With the American concert stage still in its infancy in 1866, that meant only one thing: Europe. So in the company of W.P. Howard and John Bethune, Tom set off for the great cultural Mecca, arriving not in his long-awaited spring but midsummer.

"He played before the crowned heads of Europe" is a sentence repeatedly used by the American press to encapsulate Tom's achievements here, and certainly he drew audiences in London large enough to crowd the great room of St. James' Hall,[27] performed at a private soiree at the Queen's concert room in Hanover Square,[28] played a knockout three week run at the Egyptian Halls (a London venue dedicated to freak shows and curiosities) and caused a minor sensation wherever he appeared in Britain and northern Europe. However, I am stumped as to the identity of these alleged monarchs. There is no record of a performance before Queen Victoria or her son the Prince of Wales, and the 1868 concert program—which delights in name dropping—offers no further details.

Perhaps the clue lies in the rather particular expression "crowned head." For if any such head turned to hear Tom play, it seems to have been Emperor Napoleon III, whose grandfather Napoleon Bonaparte so famously crowned himself. (Tom's management per-

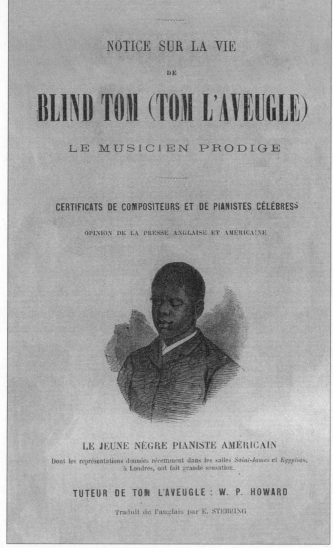

Le Musicien Prodige—the cover to the French concert program.

haps opted not to mention him, as his name was still an anathema in the United States after openly supporting the Confederacy). While I have no hard evidence of any imperial performance, a good number of people from his court did see Blind Tom, most notably the wife (and niece) of the Austrian Ambassador to Paris, Princess Pauline de Metternich, an influential socialite, fashion queen and confidante of the empress.

"Vraiment merveilleux," was the conclusion she and her friend, the opera composer Daniel Auber, reached after seeing Tom's show. Indeed, once W.P. Howard learned that Monsieur Auber was amongst them, he invited him up on stage to challenge Tom:

> We all urged him, for the curiosity of the thing, to play something of his new opera, which no one as yet had heard, therefore no one could have known it [recounted the princess's American friend, Lillie Moulton]. Auber mounted the platform, amid the enthusiastic applause of the audience, and performed his solo. Then Blind Tom sat down and played it after him so accurately, with the same staccato, old-fashioned touch of Auber that no one could have told whether Auber was still at the piano. Auber returned and bowed to the wildly excited public and to us. He said, "This is my first appearance as a pianist, and my last."

What impressed the group from Napoleon's court was not just Tom's imitation of Auber's music—and, as it transpired, that of Prince Metternich's, who could not resist rattling off one of his own fiery waltzes—but Tom's inexplicable sense of their mannerisms and gestures. The mystery that only deepened when they visited the artist's room after the show "and found poor Tom banging his head against the wall like the idiot he was. Auber remarked, *C'est humiliant pour nous autres"* [It is humiliating for us all].[29]

Perhaps Daniel Auber was the "musical celebrity of the old world" who presented Blind Tom with "a very handsome silver mounted crystal flute," a gift that was to become Tom's most prized possession[30] and a moment for W.P. Howard that made all the indignities of a show business career worthwhile.

"THE MOST PERFECT ORIGINALITY"

The mantle of traveling showman did not rest easily on the music professor whose previous career in an Atlanta ladies' academy was the epitome of respectability. Determined to purge the show of its vestiges of charlatanism, W.P. Howard had been busy collecting testimonies that affirmed the integrity of his claims. Already seventeen Philadelphian music professors had subjected Tom to numerous tests—had him identify up to twenty notes struck randomly and simultaneously; repeat after a single hearing any piece, either written or impromptu; and perform difficult compositions by Thalberg,

Gottschalk and Verdi—and concluded he was "among the most wonderful phenomena recorded in musical history."[31]

W.P. Howard would soon add a few more strings to his bow. In Europe, he secured testimonies from Charles Hallé—an avid Beethovenist and now head of the Royal College of Music—and Ignaz Moscheles, an old-school virtuoso, beloved as the most "noble and respected a figure as music had to show." While Hallé was impressed by Tom's discerning ear and Moscheles found him a "singular and inexplicable phenomenon," both stopped short at declaring Tom a prodigy with the potential to become a great pianist.[32]

For a youth obsessed with music, who for the past ten years had practiced up to twelve hours a day, one would—quite frankly—expect a little better. Was he not on par with, at least, one of the middling salon pianists whom the public had taken to heart? What did they have that Tom was missing?

Artistry, according to Norwegian violinist Olé Bull. Although he considered Blind Tom to be "a marvelous freak of nature," his musical feats were imitation and imitation only.[33] Tuition, was Professor Jay Watson's answer. After testing the prodigy, the well-known New York musician and composer concluded that if Tom wanted to play complex pieces with strange harmonic progressions, then he needed to be taught. "Good old 'Dame Nature'" is not so prolific in forming great musicians as many sanguine people seem to think," Watson reflected in the *Musical Messenger*, "but of all the musical prodigies whom I have met (and they are not a few) Blind Tom has certainly disappointed me the least."

W.P. Howard fully appreciated the implications of Watson's words. If he wanted testimonies that proclaimed Tom a great pianist, then the prodigy needed to stop touring, direct his energies away from novelties and tricks and immerse himself in study. Failing that, the high-minded music professor, in collusion with John Bethune, was forced to do what any half-decent showman would do. He simply made up a few testimonies. "History affords no parallel to Blind Tom," wrote a good but anonymous friend of *The Dundee Advertiser*. "Tom is as genuine an artist as either Thalberg, Hallé or Madame Goddard."[34] "Tom's execution is unsurpassed by the best professional performers of the day," echoed a man only known as "John Law." By interspersing these fake testimonials amongst the genuine praise in the concert program, a type of osmosis took place and the effusive sentiments of one seeped into the more guarded other.

A SMALL-BANG DOWNWARD ARPEGGIO

A contributor to *The Musical Independent* who first saw Tom as a five-year-old, again at fifteen, then immediately after his stint in Europe, was delighted to announce he had "added some very important pieces to his repertory and his playing had gained exceedingly in taste and artistic finish." His repertoire now included "three sonatas of Beethoven, fugues by Bach, Liszt's magnificent transcription of *The Wedding March*, Chopin's funeral march, a half a dozen difficult fantasias by Thalberg and a very large number of pieces by Ascher, Goria, Liszt, Gottschalk, Heller, Chopin."[35]

The predominance of Sigismond Thalberg in Tom's repertoire reflected America's high regard for the Swiss virtuoso and one-time rival to Liszt. The first of the European masters to perform in the States, the operatic fantasies that were the mainstay of his 1858 sellout tour were the same ones that Tom now played. Highly pianistic and difficult to play, these works abounded in trills, *leggierissimo* octaves, filigree scales, rapid, broken-up, arpeggiated figurations, before wrapping up with a small-bang downward arpeggio—all of which had earned Thalberg the moniker *Old Arpeggio*.[36]

Tom learned these and other pieces of digital gymnastics from Europe's most celebrated teachers: Hallé, Moscheles and the one time toast of Paris, Stephen Heller, now an impoverished recluse battling depression. "I had an impression as if I had seen [a monkey at the Jardin des Plantes] suddenly descend from the bar where he had been swinging by his tail, and sit down to play Beethoven," he wrote to his friend Charles Hallé. Nonetheless Heller was intrigued. "I tried his memory. He floundered, and even put something of his own, in such a way as to lead me to think that he knows more than he seems to do, but he still remembered enough to surprise me. It is evident that his aptitude is extraordinary."[37]

As Heller was to discover, Blind Tom could learn a complex classical piece entirely by ear in the space of an afternoon. After playing the entire composition, the teacher broke the piece down into complete phrases that were repeated two or three times. "Tom stood tense throughout, all his being focused on the music," remembered Eugenie

Abbott, a young American woman who taught him Liszt's transcription of Schubert's *Die Forelle* around this time. "When he had heard a certain amount he indicated by words and sounds that he wanted to play. Then he would sit at the piano, playing what I had done. He instantly recognized any wrong note and would shake his head, uttering disapproving sounds and motion for me to play again. Anything he got pleased him greatly; but what he did not get annoyed him. When he felt satisfied, he would go on, doing another portion in the same way. Thus we went on for four hours of absolute concentration. I do not think he ever wavered from the subject in hand. This I think would have been impossible by someone having his full mental faculties. At the end of this period, he knew the composition and played it very acceptably."[38]

Two months later Eugenie Abbott heard Tom perform *Die Forelle* at a concert and felt as though she was almost listening to her own performance. It was this trait, some insisted, that disqualified Tom—indeed his entire race—from the ranks of legitimate artists. "I cannot regard Tom as an artist, but as a clever imitator of a power for which the Negro race—*atavis editi simil*—have at all times been remarkable," wrote Otto Spahr, expressing attitudes that were typical of the day. "The colored poet Phillis Wheatley is a poet very much as Blind Tom is a musician, her verses being the merest echo of the common jingle of her day," furthered a commentator in *The North American Review*. "A fatal facility of imitation stands in the way of this interesting race."

Did this prejudice color the critic's assessment of Tom? Was the "musical parrot" charge merely a way of negating his artistry? Stephen Heller was not the only person to acknowledge that Tom's imitations often included "something of his own." However there is no denying that Tom was extraordinarily adept at imitating. He could easily copy the styles of the masters but would he ever develop a distinctive one of his own?

Such questions W.P. Howard was no longer interested in answering. His finances restored, he could now retire from show business and return to a life of respectable obscurity. John Bethune cared not a penny about elitist sensibilities. Tom was his ticket to the good life. While his Southern brothers struggled to feed themselves, the Bethunes were in clover, their indentured servant the toast of the North, his name bandied about in scientific academies, esoteric lodges, saloons and streets. Less than two years ago, they were penniless. Now they stood ready to join the South's most rarified elite.

- 15 -

Heavenly Tones

—————◆—————

JOHN BETHUNE'S STINT AS A FOOT SOLDIER WAS NOT WITHOUT ITS JOYS, even during his long soggy march through Virginia in 1862. After bivouacking night after night without tents in the rain, he entered the fabled land of Fauquier County and there he saw perfection. It was not the gentle rolling hills, sparkling rivers and villages brimming with old-world charm that moved him, but the sight of floating plumes, flashing sabers and elegant steeds. Home to the Confederacy's two most prestigious cavalry units, Fauquier County was a byword for impeccable horsemanship, chivalry and valor. They were the apple of every Southern belle's eye, the envy of every man.[1]

Flush with cash after Blind Tom's tour of Europe—$100,000 according to one unsubstantiated source—John Bethune was now in an ideal position to appreciate style over substance, illusion over truth and the power of believing one's own fictions.[2] For a mere $16,000 cash, he and his father purchased a 420-acre farm, two miles outside of the picture perfect town of Warrenton—an old-time manor with stately locusts, fruit laden orchards, crumbling stone walls and neighbors that included Confederate Generals Pemberton, Huger, Lomax, Davis, Fitzhugh, and both General Lees.

Overnight, the Bethunes became part of Virginia's cavalier elite. In no time General Bethune was vice-president of the Warrenton Riding Club organizing horse shows, foxhunts, steeplechases and elaborately costumed medieval gymkhanas, where the golden age of chivalry was faithfully simulated without the remotest hint of irony.[3]

It was a toss-up as to which was the greatest self-deception: the idea that the Bethune's ancestral homeland, the remote and rustic Isle of Skye, was a cradle of cavalier stock or that their wealth and status had nothing to do with the brilliance of a lowly slave.

A KITTEN PLAYING THROUGH FALLING LEAVES

At the end of his concert season in May, Tom would be brought to the farm for his summer vacation, [remembered General Bethune's grandson, Norbonne Robinson].

> My parents lived in Washington and practically every summer of my childhood was spent on that Virginia farm. It was my grandfather's rule that Tom's vacation was his own. After a long concert tour, he should have plenty of rest.
>
> Tom would amuse himself every day by turning handsprings on the lawn or going through a form of exercise peculiar to himself. The gyrations he performed on stage were but a toned down sample of what he would do in the yard at the farm. Somersaults, handsprings, cartwheels and every other form of gymnastics were a daily occurrence. Through it all Tom was like a kitten playing through the falling leaves . . .
>
> Once, wheat was being cut on Grandpa's Virginia farm, I drove Tom out to the field in a buggy and followed the reaper. Delighted with the rhythmic sound of the machine Tom came back to the house, sat down at the piano, composed a piece called The Reaper and dedicated it to me. How it would sound now, I don't know but at the time I thought it was fine.[4]

Norbonne Robinson's memoirs offer a rare insight into Tom's off-stage life between 1868 and 1874. Free to roam the farm without fear of strangers, Tom—now in his early twenties—passed his days with people he considered his friends. And without doubt, Norbonne was his friend, their relationship unencumbered by money and founded on a mutual commitment to fun. Less straightforward was Tom's relationship with the adult members of the Bethune family. In an effort to maintain the traditional pecking order, the Bethune sisters would call upon Tom to churn the butter or fetch a pitcher of water from the spring (tasks that he clearly enjoyed—the spring, in particular, was a favorite place). They offered him "warm friendship" but expected back "devotion."

A rare porrait of Blind Tom and General Bethune, taken some time after Bethune had him declared non compos mentis.

To the sisters, Tom was more than a servant but not quite family and certainly not the financial powerhouse of the clan. He lived in a shed roof annex attached to the main house, a plain but comfortably furnished room of about twelve feet square. Next door in the main house lived Bethune's youngest daughter Fanny, her brother James, his wife and young family. Beyond this house was a comfortable cottage especially built for General Bethune. Of the three living quarters, Tom's was by far the most basic, although no expense had been spared on the Steinway grand that physically overwhelmed his compact quarters.[5] It was a strange and incongruous sight to see him playing the magnificent concert grand, hour after hour to no one but himself, commented a well-known Washington lady (who may have been James's young bride, Narcissa).[6]

Far from incongruous, at moments like these Tom was fully connected to himself, his music and the natural world. Unconstrained by the demands of his stage show, liberated from strictures of the hotel room and plugged into the vibrations of the living world—the cool earth and steady tinkle of the woodland spring—he joyously bounced from garden to piano to garden again. Norbonne remembers sessions that that went on long into the night. "My own choice out of Tom's great repertoire would be Franz Liszt's arrangement of Schuman's *Erl King*. I still retain memories of lying in bed on summer nights at the farm and hearing Tom play it. Those familiar with it know it calls for a good left hand. Tom had a forearm and fist that would be respected by Jack Dempsey or Joe Louis, plus fingers soft and delicate as those of a baby girl. To the listener, there was no thought of Tom's fingers coming in contact with the piano. The music simply arose in heavenly tones."[7]

As well as exploring other people's music, Tom created his own, drawing inspiration from the natural world. "Blind Tom's own compositions and improvisations were astonishingly interesting and often very beautiful," commented one of his music tutors who was lucky enough to hear them. "They indicated a desire to make new musical combinations [and were] very original. He would play for hours at a time, occasionally one of the great masterpieces, and then going off into his interesting improvisations."[8] Apart from *When This Cruel War Is Over*, none of these interpretations and improvisations were written down but dissipated into the air, returning to the ether from which he drew them.

The Washington lady remembered him giving an "exquisite" private performance one full-mooned August night and in the rapturous silence that followed, she noticed him rise from piano and slip out into the rose garden. "Knowing that Tom's inspiration was upon him," they followed him outside:

> We could plainly see, dancing in and out among the rose trees, a dark grotesque figure, leaping from bush to bush in perfect ecstasy and abandon, pausing for an instant, as if perforce to penetrate the mystery of blue and of stars, then hopping wildly about as if satisfied with what had been revealed to him and to him alone.
>
> We waited for his next move. . . . [He] tumbled into the room: he did not walk nor run, but simply was there, all in a heap, a confused mass of head, hands and feet, [and] only having partly regained his perpendicular, he announced: "I will now tell you—what—what that stars—have—said to me." Seating himself at the piano, with a prelude of most exquisite chords, he suddenly burst into such brilliant, such wildly gay, at one moment, and at the next such heart-breaking melodies as never heard below the stars.[9]

"He was a sensitive robust sounding board for any kind of noise, musical or otherwise, and experienced actual ecstasy when a sound passed through him," recalled Norbonne. Is that what Tom was experiencing in the rose garden? An ecstatic trance? Perhaps he had slipped into an altered state of consciousness that was intense, euphoric and paradoxical, a strange brew of adrenalin and endorphins, high tension and relaxation so often associated with mysticism and shamanism.[10] "The sound will drown me," is how filmmaker Maya Deren described the moments leading up to her possession in Haitian Voudou rite. "At such moments one does not move to the sound, one is the movement of the sound, created and borne by it, hence, nothing is difficult."[11]

Throughout history, irrespective of faith or tradition, mystics have been known to fast, dance, shout, sit, breathe, chant and twirl with the intention of transcending the dualism of everyday life and perceiving the continuum of life. Was this the ecstasy that powered Tom's wild improvisations that, at times, strayed from the harmonic into dark, discordant territory? "The wild weird strains from his crystal flute murdered sleep in the most shameless manner," wrote the Washington lady of one frenzied midnight marathon. "Indescribable strains . . . notes rising into a shriek of agony . . . then melting away into a wail as soft and full of sorrow as that of Orpheus for his lost Eurydice."[12]

In the great scientific flowering of the nineteenth century, rationality equaled progress and irrationality was equated with savagery. So the notion that Blind Tom may have been in dialogue with the stars was preposterous. Altered states like an ecstatic trance had no place in a civilized society. Indeed to observant scientists, busy cataloguing and, in some instances, reducing the mysteries of nature, the schizophrenic in the grip of paranoid delusion and the wild-eyed trance of a shaman seemed to share a number of symptoms—a detached identity, delirium, visions and voices—and were consequently lumped into the same category: insanity. So too with Blind Tom. While no one who knew him genuinely believed him to be insane, the power of inductive logic enabled an alarmingly short line to be drawn from incommunicable ecstasy to insanity.

Charity claimed that when Bethune carried off her son at the end of the war, she never saw or heard from him again. Although they longed for word of him, they did not know where he was, how he spent his time, or even the whereabouts of the Bethunes' new residence in Virginia. It was a situation that brought much grief to Mingo, who would die in 1873, his great desire to see or hear from his son unfulfilled.[13]

Bethune may have prided himself as a man of chivalry and virtue, but he seems to have anticipated that Tom's parents had neither the education nor the resources to assert their rights as Tom's natural guardians. So when Tom's five-year indentureship came to an end on July 25, 1869, he and John began searching for a legal framework that would permanently keep Tom in the family's "protection." Whether it was father or son who hit on the solution, it certainly took the two of them to exploit their powerful connections and secure the result. In early 1870, Thomas Bethune—without being examined by a physician or the permission of his parents, with no witnesses to testify to his insanity, indeed without any of the safe-guards specified by law—was adjudged *non compos mentis* by the Virginia Probate Court of Fauquier County. The lunatic was then committed to the keep of John G. Bethune.[14]

In fact, Tom seemed to have outgrown aspects of his childhood autism. Certainly his social graces were no more refined—he still slammed doors in the face of advancing journalists with an ungra-cious "I d-d-don't want to s-s-see anybody;" or abruptly informed chatty admirers, "Well now you have talked long enough, good-bye!"[15] But those who knew him well were privy to moments of sly wit and surprisingly subtle nuance—characteristics rarely associated with autism.[16]

Norbonne Robinson recalled a day when an unwelcome visitor showed up at the farm and Tom greeted him by extending his left hand. "You must use your right hand in shaking hands," the visitor told him. "I can shake hands just as well on this side," he retorted, much to the amusement of the rest of the family. Another time, he was talking with a bunch of Bethune grandchildren, amongst them a twelve-year-old who liked to call himself "Big Jim Bethune." "This is little Jimmie, isn't it," Tom jibed as he ran his fingers over Jim's face. "No," replied Jim. "It's Big Jimmie." "Ah," came back Tom, "Little Jimmie has been drinking this morning."[17]

When it came to women it was easier to insist that Tom's affec-tions for them were either doglike and devotional, or better still, non-existent. W.P. Howard would tell audiences that Tom had "no love for anything but music, and no capability of attaching himself to anyone."[18] While every manager from Perry Oliver on insisted that he had "an aversion for females," a rumor that took root after the ten-year-old tackled a young lady to the ground when she began playing one of his compositions.[19] However, these claims do not stand up to scrutiny. In the nineteenth century, the piano was bound up with femininity and women made up a sizable proportion of Tom's teachers, audience challengers and fans. "By request of the lady, he seated himself and played [the *Signal March*] to the admiration of all the young ladies gathered around," reported one Southern newspaper in 1865.[20]

One source hints that Tom may have developed a crush on at least one of the white girls who flocked around him. During his medical examination, Dr. Blackman asked him what he dreamt about last night. "I called Miss Tarbell last night," sixteen-year-old Tom replied. "Who is Miss Tarbell?" Blackman enquired. Tom rolled his eyes, twisted his hands and howled, "Who-ee, who-ee, who-ee; b-hoo, b-hoo, b-hoo-ee!" He then—the report continued—"went off into a series of gyrations and genuflections that would puzzle a gymnast to describe and which Dr Blackman, muscular as he is, said would soon break him down."[21]

Any interest Tom may have shown in Miss Tarbell would have been swiftly quashed by his managers and indeed, as he grew older it seems that Tom was instructed to keep away from women. Cousin Lizzie Bethune remembers Tom being "shy of the woman folk" when he visited their house in the 1870s—an explanation that conveniently sidestepped a potential explosive situation. Frankly, it would be more astonishing if Tom were somehow devoid of any sexual or romantic desires. Like hunger, sexuality is pre-conceptual and pre-verbal and just as fundamental a drive among autistic people as anyone. Certainly socially appropriate behavior can be an issue, the private nature of self-pleasure not always an obvious consideration to the autistic mind. Tom, it seems, was instructed to tone down his pelvic thrusts and gyrations on stage, though what else he was schooled in is a matter of speculation. Like most young men his age, he probably had a keen interest in sex and may even, at some point, have wistfully longed to find a life partner. But for Tom, entering into and maintaining intimate personal relationships was an unfathomable mystery. Unless it was facts about a composer or the finer details of piano tuning, Tom never had much to say; one stagehand complained that he "never explained anything."[22] It was only behind a piano that his constrictiveness disappeared and the full palette of emotions poured from him: joy, sadness, longing, hope.

This casts an interesting light on a nightly summertime ritual on the Warrenton farm. "In the parlor was an old-fashioned Steinway Grand belonging to maiden Aunt Fanny," reported Norbonne. "She could have been a concert pianist if she could overcome her innate shyness and play to someone outside the family. In the evening Aunt Fanny and Tom would sit down at her piano and play a few duets. The duets seemed to whet Tom's appetite for he would wander back to his own room and play for hours."

There is more to a duet than meets the eye. It is a wordless game of phrasing and response. Moments are lingered on, teased out, seized upon, snatched and reclaimed—a playful balance of dominance and surrender. Little jokes, gentle provocations can be lobbed in, twists and turns that—judging by the high incidence of husband and wife duet teams—offer plenty of scope for flirtation. Indeed, a number of piano duets, such as Schubert's *Fantasie in F minor*, are said to aid and abet love and courtship, the piece's painful sighs and deep water calmness demanding that the two players intertwine and breathe as one. While we have no clues as to Tom and Fanny's favorites, the physical act of playing together every day, entering that special space so beloved by musicians, was possibly the most intimate relationship either had with a member of the opposite sex. Without uttering a single word, in full view of the entire Bethune family, Tom and Fanny may have been having quite some conversation.

THE PROFESSOR

"Once in a while, one of my aunts would pretend she was going to whip me," recalled Norbonne. "I would whimper and effect fright. Tom would hover like a hen over a chick, protesting and begging that I not be whipped. Finally my aunt would relent and tell Tom that because he asked it, she would let me off."

Even as an adult, other people's games of pretense were puzzles that Tom could never solve—a feature that psychologists would argue is a hallmark of autism, pretense presupposing a capacity to "mentalize" or separate the idea of an object from its physical state—to imagine, say, that a box was a pirate ship, child's play basically. However, while Tom struggled to understand other people's games, he had a firm grasp on his own. Every time he walked on stage and consciously adopted the persona of Senator Stephen Douglas, the Washington Congressmen or Uncle Charlie from Warm Springs, was he not engaging in a form of pretense?

As Tom grew older, role-playing became a daily feature of his off-stage life. "He would hold long audible conversations with numerous figures that to the rest of the world seemed like non-existent characters of his own invention," reported Norbonne. One day John Bethune overheard him conversing with a new character and asked him who he was. "His name is Arthur Smokeson and he's not such a very good cook at that," was Tom's cryptic reply.

Dr. Smokeson became a fixture at Warrenton. While not much of a cook, he was an exacting music teacher and formed the basis of a game Tom regularly played with Norbonne and "one of my aunts" (Fanny, perhaps?). "Catching me and Tom somewhere around the place, assiduously engaged in doing nothing," continued Norbonne, "my aunt would suggest it was time for a singing lesson. Whereupon Tom would walk out of the back gate and disappear behind the tool shed and return as Dr. Smokeson. He would accompany me as I sang, and tell me to sing more loudly or softly according to his whim."

The Washington lady was tempted to believe in a "dual state of existence" after she saw Tom embody the character of a music teacher known as Mrs. Flaherty. As this character, Tom would, on the dot of eleven o'clock every morning, appear in the parlor, greet them, fill them in on the considerable suffering and wants of the Flaherty family, before putting the Bethune sisters through their musical paces. Then, as suddenly as she arrived, Mrs. Flaherty would bid her farewell. Hard on the heel of her departure, "The Professor" (as Tom wished to be addressed) would tumble into the room with his usual leaps and gymnastics and in his sharp jerky manner mention that he just seen Mrs. Flaherty driving over the hill. Has she been here? This was the ladies' cue to deliver a detailed account of the lesson, The Professor plying them with all sorts of questions. Every day, this performance was repeated verbatim and "had any one present addressed him out of time or place, great would have been his indignation. While Mrs. Flaherty, no one dared mention Tom or the Professor and vice versa, and no smile or suggestion of improbability was tolerated."[23]

So was this imitation or invention? Or was it a way for Tom to step outside his monosyllabic, emotionally constricted mantle and engage with other people? Was this an indication that his social development was proceeding well?

"I AIN'T GOING"

"A regular row occurred twice a week when George the Handyman gave Tom his bath," recounted Norbonne. "Sometimes Tom would arm a one-man rebellion and flatly refuse to let George touch him. 'His hands are too rough,' he would protest. The sound of Grandpa thumping down the hallway would soften his mood. 'Thomas, what is this foolishness? Go in there and let George give you your bath.' "[24]

No one, except John Bethune, knew how to manage bullheaded Tom better than the old General. By all accounts, he did it with great kindness, humor and patience. But this may have been as much for his sake as Tom's. As long as he gushed with benevolent paternalism, Bethune could pretend that the decision to send Tom back on the road for yet another exhaustive tour season was in Tom's best interest instead of his own.

If Tom had his way, he would never leave the Virginia farm. It was General and John Bethune's design that he did and, as the summer came to a close, the wills of the two parties were set on a collision course. But just as George bore the brunt of Tom's resistance to cleanliness, this battle was fought by someone further down the chain of command: Thomas Warhurst, the new manager of the Blind Tom Concert Company.

Once a member of the family happened to mention to Tom that Mr. Warhurst was coming down the following week. Tom announced to the family repeatedly over the next few days, that he would never leave the farm again for as long as he lived. From then on Mr. Warhurst would just turn up. He planned to have his midday meal at the farm and take Tom away on an evening train. . . . [But] at the sound of Mr. Warhurst's buggy, Tom would race out the back gate and down to the spring—his favorite spot.

I was once sent to get him and he was pacing up and down, occasionally doing his T exercise. "Tom," I called, "Mr. Warhurst wants to see you." "Goddamn Mr. Warhurst," yelled Tom. "Tell him to go to hell! I ain't coming up there." And so Mr. Warhurst came to Tom.

Tom met Warhurst's cheerful greeting with a surly growl. But he knew the great genius was nothing more than a Grade A, blown in the bottle, undiluted ham. So when Tom vowed, with a crescendo of profanity, that he was never going back on the stage, he replied: "Well that's a pity Tom. In the New York office we have hundreds of letters from all over the country asking when you are going to play again. So-and-so and so-and-so had been asking about you. . . . Do you remember the night on so-and-so where the crowd was so big we had to open the doors and windows so people could hear standing outside."

On and on he went, gradually calming Tom down until finally he became enthusiastic. By the time he had his dinner, he would be raring to go. As he got into the carriage to drive to the railroad station, Tom would be mentally miles away, on tour, playing before enthusiastic audiences. His goodbyes to us would be polite and absent minded.

So was this manipulation or a decision reached by Tom? Not wishing to injure his family's good name, Norbonne elects the latter, drawing a picture of warm hearted, good-natured benevolence, as if Tom was a boy reluctant to return to boarding school. "Cajolery and flattery were included in the infallible formula," he recalled, quietly ignoring the other half of the formula—the threats.

In years to come a tour manager by the name of A.H. Gott would recall the tactics used by John Bethune's future wife to pull Tom into line. On one occasion Tom broke a piano pedal during a performance, stormed off stage, punched an assistant in the face and refused to continue the concert unless he was given a new piano. "Well, that's too bad but all right," Mrs. Bethune uttered in grieved tone, "we'll pack up and go home and not travel any more, ever. It'll be pretty lonesome home, but nobody will want to hear you play anywhere, ever again, now that you have disappointed them, and nobody will care for Tom any more." In five minutes Tom was begging to go back "and he never played better in his life than he did the rest of the program."[25]

Emotional blackmail—the withdrawal of affections—had a galvanizing affect on Tom. He may have shunned people's mindless twitter and endless questions but, like any good diva, he craved their love and adoration: a life without the buzz of applause and the roar of laughter was no life at all. After anxiously contemplating a world without love, he was then offered the solution: go back on tour, on stage and play. And Tom—unable to detect the hollow praise, feigned sincerity, overblown horror and sham sorrow—swallowed the bait, hook, line and sinker. Norbonne may balk at the word, but if this practice was calculating, devious and inspired by self-interest, then this was manipulation. The affections of the Bethune family came with conditions.

Perpetual Motion

———◆———

THE VAST RIBBON OF STEEL THAT OPENED UP THE WEST AND LINKED THE country from coast to coast created untold riches for a lucky few schooled in enterprise and the abuse of power. While the Bethunes' fortune paled in comparison to the robber barons of the Gilded Age, they too owed their success to a few shady deals and those thousands of miles of track across desert, prairie and mountain range that enabled them to bring Blind Tom to once isolated regions in record time. By 1874, Tom had traveled the length and breadth of the United States and Canada so many times that his managers could confidently claim that he had probably been "seen by more people than any one living being," having played almost every town of any size plus a whole lot smaller in between.

Tom loved train travel and was enraptured by the rhythmic click of the wheels and howl of the whistle. Another euphoric moment for him was his first step onto the platform. The solid earth under his feet was greeted with an ecstatic dance and he would frequently reach down and pat the ground with his hands. It was perhaps at one such moment of exhilaration that the heavyweight champion and "Boston Strongboy" John L. Sullivan came across Tom. The legendary boxer watched him leap with unrestrained grace, power and dexterity around the railroad junction and confided to Tom's manager that, despite thirty knockout punches under his belt, he would not care to tangle with him.[1]

In January 1869, Mark Twain was on a lecture tour every bit as grueling as Blind Tom's when he encountered the prodigy immersed in the rhythm and chug of the locomotive. At once Twain dashed off his impressions to his editor at the *San Francisco Alta*, which were later reworked into his weekly column:

> A burly negro man on the opposite side of the car began to sway his body violently forward and back, and mimic with his mouth the hiss and clatter of the train, in the most savagely excited way. Every time he came forward I was sure he was going to brain himself on the seat-back in front of him, and every time he reversed I was as certain he was going to throw a back-somersault over his own seat. What a wild state he was in! Clattering, hissing, whistling, blowing off gauge cocks, ringing his bell, thundering over bridges with a row and a racket like everything was going to pieces, whooping through tunnels, running over cows—Heavens! I thought, will this devil never run his viewless express off the track and give us a rest? No, sir. For three dreadful hours he kept it up—and you may know by that what muscles and what wind he had . . . . Instead of lying down at night to die of exhaustion, [this tortured brute] was to sit behind a grand piano and bewitch a multitude![2]

Fifteen years after their first meeting, Twain's fascination with Blind Tom had not abated. He never missed an opportunity to see the blind star, one time attending his concerts three nights in a row. Twain's book editor recalled a meeting in 1885 at which Tom was the primary topic. "Tom used to soliloquize about himself and his music, and Mark's memory was full of his quaint sayings, of which Mark poured out in a stream to me."[3]

"It must be well stayed, stayed well, stayed up well or it will not stand," was Tom's opinion on the difficulties of piano tuning, as expressed to Mr. S.R. Smith during a conversation on a train in the early 1880s. By now, Tom's howls of unity with the locomotive, while no less exact, had been tempered to a murmur but Mr. Smith, a school teacher from Uniontown, Pennsylvania, was more astonished by Tom's ability to know exactly where he was at all times: "crossing a river," "backing up to Brownsville."[4] Many years earlier, another man writing under the pseudonym Mr. "C Sharp" met Tom on a train in Georgia and noted the same phenomenon. "As we dashed along at perhaps thirty miles an hour he could always tell whether we were passing woods or open fields, houses, cuts, embankments, bridges, or almost anything else," Sharp recalled. "I remember we entered a small village on the railroad and when I asked Tom what

For eighteen years Blind Tom toured North America with manager Thomas Warhurt.

was outside, he promptly replied, 'A heap of houses.'"[5]

If Tom knew the rest of the railroad network like he knew these corners of Georgia and Pennsylvania, then the continent unspooled before him like a songline, the buzz of industry and progress increasing in volume as the century marched on. Inside the carriage, Mr. Smith was impressed by the progress in Tom. Eager to dispel the constant allusions to Tom as half-civilized or bestial, the black school teacher sensed the presence of a great untapped potential. "I firmly believe if he had a chance to learn he could converse on the topics of the day," he concluded. "Think for a minute! He only goes from hotel room to hall and from hall to hotel room, then to the cars. He has no chance to learn. It's a mystery to me that he knows as much as he does."[6]

AN INTERLOCKING SYSTEM OF FAÇADE & ATTACHMENT

Mr. Smith's summation was more accurate than he would ever have hoped it to be. Joseph Eubanks began working in the ticket office with the Blind Tom Concert Company in 1869 and traveled with Tom for eleven years. After falling afoul of General Bethune in 1885, he drew a damning picture of Tom's life on the road. "Blind Tom was kept closely confined in his room wherever he was and shut off from all communication with others, excepting his music teacher and the agents who brought him on stage to play. His meals were brought to his room and he was taught to shun all communication with strangers and made to believe his fellow men were enemies and desiring to do him injury."[7]

Other reports are consistent with Eubanks's claim. From the railway station, Tom was whisked off to a hotel—albeit the best the town had to offer (though sometimes this wasn't much)—and was not seen again until he left for the concert. At the popular "fest" town of Dubuque, Iowa, famed for its winter balls and spring horse racing season, he stayed at Key City House across the hallway from *The Chicago Tribune's* fashion editor, who was alerted to his presence when his strange hisses began to echo through the entire floor. "One looks at him with feelings of awe that anything so uncouth could create such perfect harmony," she wrote of his one-legged jumps. "He was conscious of my presence, but perfectly indifferent to it, a servant brought in his dinner—he eats in his room. He still continued the singular contortions of his body but his practiced hands manipulated the food."[8]

This routine continued for decades, although Tom's spiraling weight took the edge off his more spectacular pirouettes. Clad in woolen stockings, trousers and a blue flannel undershirt, he would swing like an elephant or slowly hop about the hotel room.[9] As his girth grew even wider, he would balance over a bed end and bounce his head rapidly against the mattress, all the time whispering to himself random snatches of conversations heard along the way: a baby at a railway depot crying "yah yah yah," the mother soothing, "poor thing, poor little baby, there there there," and an irascible old man muttering in between, "There it goes again. Oh kill that brat."[10] Or a recitation of all known facts about various composers: "Wagner. Yes. Wagner. Mr. Wagner. Richard Wagner. Wagner. Mr. Wagner is dead. Yes. He is dead. Dead. His last opera. Yes. His last opera. His last opera was *Parsifal. Parsifal.* His last opera."[11]

In the confinement of his hotel room, the space to accommodate Tom's boundless energy was in short supply, although the fuel to power it certainly was not. Food had long been used as a negotiating tool, a sure-fire way to reconcile him to the will of his managers. Not surprisingly, by the time Tom was in his mid-twenties, mealtime had evolved into a convoluted ritual. "He would always insist that the sugar bowl should be full to the brim," recollected his manager's daughter. "Unless it was full, Tom would storm and refuse to eat anything. Then when he had finished his meal, he would steal the sugar and hide it." Strangely for the man who loved butter churning, butter was his anathema. "He would smell everything on the tray," remembered a stagehand, "and if he detected the presence of some rogue butter, he would shout and cry until it was removed, not only from the tray but from the room and it seemed impossible to deceive him about its whereabouts."

Once everything met his approval, the eating commenced. "Sometimes he ate with his fingers but more often with his mouth directly in the dishes like an animal. He ate meat first when he wished, his vegetables first when he desired or his dessert first if that seemed best."[12] If, as some people contend, table manners are a mark of civilization, then this was savagery pure and simple, proof to some—if any more be needed—of his primitive urges and brute intellect. "It was an instinct to be gratified as swiftly as both hands could convey to his mouth the food, which was swallowed with the avidity of a starving savage beast, and at the conclusion of each exhibition of gluttony, the leaping and dancing invariably followed, accompanied with the protruding of the exaggerated eyeballs," recalled a Washington lady.[13] Any attempt to clean him was resisted with wholehearted ferocity—a rare concession granted to his manager's daughter who was allowed to wash his face.

Inevitably, some moments spilled over into violence. At a high-toned hotel in St. Louis, Tom played his beloved twenty-two keyed flute long into the wee hours. Eventually, a guest complained and Joseph Eubanks was sent in to silence him. But, as he entered the darkened room, Tom seized him and flung him through the door. Another time he took a dislike to a Louisville music teacher, knocked him off his stool and threw him out of the room. Joseph Eubanks, again in the firing line, was pummeled for trying to protect the teacher.[14]

Tom's strength and ferocity—plus a deep-rooted fear of being carried off by strangers—also worked in the management's favor.

They could leave him unsupervised in his hotel room or, on concert days, alone with the piano in the hall. "He will permit no one in his room when his master is absent," reported the fashion editor. "If anyone enters, Tom advances in a threatening manner, and the intruder is only too glad to retreat."[15] In one instance, his manger returned to the concert hall and found Tom holding a man down on the floor and almost choking him. The man was yelling out and Tom, who could never mask his pleasure at other people's pain, was delighted.[16]

In the hours leading up to his concert, Tom was dressed in a suit—an interlocking system of façade and attachments—especially tailored to accommodate his intense dislike of constrictive clothing. Cuffs were buttoned onto the sleeves of his jacket. The broad white shirt was a dickey, while the bosom insert was attached to the waistcoat and fastened at the back. "These were put on just before he left the room and taken off the minute he returned."[17] The next day it was more of the same: hotel room to hall and back again, sometimes twice a day. After the weeklong engagement was over, Tom was taken to the railroad cars and then to the next town.

HIS MEMORY'S DISPOSAL

From 1868 to 1884, the Blind Tom Concert Company was managed by show business veteran Thomas Warhurst. Under his stewardship, touring had never been more profitable and, after the first few tour seasons, John Bethune was able to spend less time on the road with Tom and more time spending the money Tom had made for him.

Thomas Warhurst had cut his show business teeth touring circuses, minstrel shows and variety acts (including a stint with the up and coming magician "Robert Heller") and brought a wealth of experience to the Blind Tom Concert Company. Well versed in the pitfalls of popular entertainment, he created a show that not only catered to the widest possible audience, but was lean and portable. Overheads were minimal and returns were high.

During W.P. Howard's brief reign, Tom basically played according to whim, drawing from a repertoire that, according to a special notice in his concert program, was vast:

Blind Tom can only play what he hears or improvises. Until about two years ago a list of pieces that Tom had heard was kept, numbering nearly 2,000. Unfortunately this catalogue was lost. Since that period he has heard perhaps 3,000 pieces, and his repertoire now numbers upwards of 5,000, entirely at his memory's disposal. From this extensive store Tom will introduce selections from Beethoven, Bach, Mendelssohn, Chopin, Thalberg, Gottschalk, and others; and also give his marvelous and amusing Imitations, Recitations, Anecdotes, &c., &c.

Even during Warhurst's time, the implication was that Blind Tom would seize upon a random selection of these pieces and therein lay the night's concerts. However, only a fraction of the fabled 5,000 pieces were ever heard. Night after night, year after year, decade after decade the same show was trotted out—a bizarre marriage of the solo piano recital and the variety show—that drew on a carefully balanced mix of classical pieces, popular hits, novelties, laughs and audience participation.

In an age when froth was supplied by the Salonist, panache by the Virtuosos, poetry by Romantics and substance by the Classicists, the "Blind Negro Boy" had all the corners covered. By its gravitas, pride of place belonged to Beethoven, usually *Sonata Pathetique* or *Moonlight*. Next was a virtuoso piece that Franz Liszt had a hand in composing or re-working—a transcription from the *Rigoletto* opera, Mendelssohn's *Wedding Song* or Schumann's *Erl King*. This was followed by a heavily arpeggiated Thalberg fantasia and a rich sentimental dose of Gottschalk—*The Last Hope, Home Sweet Home* or *The Old Hundred*. An operatic potpourri or two came next, generally *Lurline* or *Il Travatore*, then a popular march, invariably Pease's *Delta Kappa Epsilon* and always, but always, *The Battle of Manassas*.

Next came the vocal selections: Major Maccionico's baritone lived on in *Rocked in the Cradle Deep*, followed by one or two plantation melodies, mostly *Them Golden Slippers* and perhaps one of Tom's "absurdly incoherent songs of his own." Then came the novelties: the Audience Challenge; playing two tunes while singing a third—*Tramp Tramp Tramp, The Fishers Hornpipe* and *Yankee Doodle* (although this later evolved into a series of improvisations based on audience selections). The imitations judiciously followed: the Scottish fiddle, bagpipes, church organ, guitar and banjo, railroad train, musical box and Douglas's speech, before the evening

A promotional brochure for a Blind Tom concert at New York's Mechanic Hall.
Tom's show changed surprisingly little over the decades.

ended with a display of spelling, the words "hat," "gloves," "hand-kerchief," and "umbrella" arising with predictable monotony.[18]

Not surprisingly, after Tom's third or fourth appearance in a major city, the critics'—and the public's—enthusiasm began to wane. The "good and highly appreciative" Chicago audience in 1869 was, by 1871, only "fair sized," his show deemed "less novel." By 1875, Chicago audiences knew exactly what to expect. "All this is quite familiar to most concert goers, so that he has quite a limited number of curiosity seekers to draw upon."[19] Responsibility for this musical holding pattern was laid squarely at Tom's feet: "His musical genius is not one of growth."[20]

One doubts whether this conclusion would be applied to popular comedian Billy Barry, whose entire career hinged around a single gag, to say nothing of luminaries like Gottschalk, Thalberg and the volcanic Russian virtuoso, Anton Rubinstein, whose grueling U.S. tours locked them into remarkably narrow repertoires. "May Heaven preserve us from such slavery!" moaned Rubinstein after performing 215 concerts in 239 days. "Under such conditions there is no chance for art—one simply grows into an automaton, performing mechanical works." "I seem like an uncontrollable machine and play machine-like," wrote an exhausted Gottschalk, who was known to perform 109 concerts in 120 days. Blind Tom—who regularly played up to 35 concerts a month—kept up a similar pace for nine months a year, year in, year out.

If Tom ever complained about the grind—the two-horse towns where the only hotel was infested with bedbugs and the only kitchen was closed, the penny pinching venue owners who refused turn on the heating, the second-rate pianos, late trains and missed connections—there is no record of it. And surprisingly, there is little evidence of much unevenness to his performances, the good night/bad night syndrome that afflicts most touring musicians. In 1882, *The Arkansas Gazette* grumbled that he whipped through Mendelssohn's *Wedding Song* too fast then fixated on the "crunch-a-crunch" sound of the train too long, while the *Sedalia Daily Democrat* complained that his Stephen Douglas imitation sounded more like "the bray of a donkey than the dulcet strains of an Aeolian"—but these criticisms are rare.[21] Tom's reviews are remarkably consistent. Routine and differentiated repetition came easily to him and no matter how many times he performed the same show, it never grew stale to him, his considerable onstage charm winning over audiences night after night. "He is like a curious compound of imbecility and talent," wrote one critic. "The whole care of entertaining the audience fell entirely on Tom and the concert was not in the least dull or even monotonous. In fact, there was an entire naturalness of exhibition, where whatever was done was performed with ease and facility—with none of the restraint and formality of an ordinary concert."[22]

However, the show could remain the same only if Tom was in perpetual motion, pushing the limits of the railroad network, rolling up to culture starved towns of the West where he was easily the biggest name in town, a beacon of quality music, who could effortlessly outplay their best musicians. In St. Joseph, Missouri, Tom once exposed the town's music professor as a fraud after playing *The Maiden's Prayer*—a piece the professor claimed to be his own composition—note for note, in better style than the professor ever had. "The excitement ran high for several days and so, we will add, did the professor."[23] Occasionally Thomas Warhurst was forced to snatch a complicated piece of sheet music before the contender had a chance to upstage Tom, as he did in Boone, Iowa. And in Philadelphia, Mme Anna Amalie Tutein somehow managed to slip through the net, challenging Tom with Beethoven's *Third Concerto in C Minor.* However, the management worked this to their advantage, inviting her to teach him it and other virtuoso pieces for the extravagant sum of five dollars a day.[24]

Even several amateurs came close to outplaying him. An old Swiss cabinetmaker wrapped up his challenge with a yodeling chorus—a split pitched falsetto that defied Tom. "Vainly did he twist his neck and turn and wriggle his body but the obstinate tone would not warble." It was infuriating to Tom, but the audience loved every sidesplitting minute of it.[25] Another time a challenger opened with a few routine chords, ran his hands out to each end of the keyboard, dawdled a bit of tremolo, then bent over and struck the middle note with his nose. Tom repeated the first part without issue then hesitated. Puzzled, he started again, but again was stumped. Then, with lightning rapidity, he started from the top, shot his head down and banged the middle note with his nose.[26] The applause was so deafening that the nosedive became the surprise twist of many Audience Challenges to come. In Janesville, Wisconsin, the audience was baffled when a stagehand struck a discordant note in the middle of Professor Titcomb's challenge. But how they applauded when, at the precisely the same point in the music, Tom reproduced it by striking it with his nose. "He impressed me then as being the most wonderful man in the world," remembered Carrie Jacobs-Bond, herself a child prodigy, who forty years later would be one of the best selling songwriters in the country.[27]

"ONE OF US"

While Blind Tom was plugging away on the road, John Bethune was either in Warrenton with his prize bulls or Harrodsburg with his prize racehorses. Occasionally he was persuaded to join a long tour, just in case his puffery and blarney was needed to snap Tom out of a mood. However, there was one tour that John needed no convincing to join. Although Blind Tom had scoured the rest of the country many times over by 1877, the tour company had barely touched the south during all twelve years of Reconstruction. But as the last of the Federal troops packed their bags for home, John Bethune decided it was time to embark on an extensive tour of the South, with himself on stage directing the show.

"Tom will draw wherever he appears in the South," predicted Nashville's *Daily American*. "He was 'one of us' during the late unpleasantness and his return brings to mind many agreeable memories."[28] Indeed it did. In Augusta, Georgia, Tom's rendition of the old-fashioned plantation hymn *Moses in Egypt* brought the house down, while his staccato delivery of *Lord I'm Almost Surrounded* conjured up warm memories of the slaves' syncopated songs in the cotton field—a nostalgic return to a time when life, for white folks, seemed kinder. But no matter how many halls Tom filled "until corsets were a superficial luxury," or how constant the laughter, or warm the applause, the tour did not generate a single mention in the black press.[29]

In February 1879, in his hometown of Columbus, fifteen hundred people crowded into the Springer Opera House and wildly applauded Tom's performance of Beethoven's *Twenty-first Sonata* and Listz's *Hungarian Rhapsody*. In the gallery sat Charity, who had not seen or heard from her son since he was carried off at the end of the war. Now in his presence for the first time in fourteen years, she was sidelined once again. John Bethune did not call on her to grace the stage; that honor went to Blind Tom's first music teacher, Professor Chase, who tested Tom with his most recent composition *The Happy Maiden's Gallop*.[30]

It was a bittersweet moment for Charity. Of course, she was intensely proud of her thirty-year-old son but also felt snubbed and disappointed that many of her children and grandchildren were not able to share the moment. Elnora Walker, the daughter of Tom's brother Lewis, remembers staying at home that night as her family could not afford the price of a ticket. Lewis earned fifty cents a day as a livery worker at the Palace Stables, her Uncle Dee was a janitor, while her aunts cooked and washed white people's laundry.[31] As a girl, Elnora helped her mother with the laundry from a local hotel. "Soon as we came home from school we ironed sheets and pillowcases and tablecloths. We lived in a shotgun house on East 17th, hauling bath water in a tub from the outdoor faucet and heating it for baths on the wood stove. We had to drag that tin tub in the house every night."[32]

"My father's people were as close as they could be," she continued, "you just had to tell me you was kin to my father and you was close to my family." So if Charity was still receiving the $500 payment—as General Bethune later insisted she was—the entire family would have benefited. But clearly there was nothing to share—not even a swag of complimentary tickets to the show. With Tom securely in the Bethunes' grasp, the annuity seems to have dried up, if it had ever been paid at all. Of the twenty thousand dollars the Blind Tom Concert Company was netting each year—the equivalent of at least five million dollars by today's standards—Charity's family saw none of it.

In stark contrast, Cousin Lizzie Bethune's daughter, Julia, remembers receiving complimentary first row seats when Blind Tom played the Texan town of Navasota. "Cousin John Bethune announced that Tom would play a piece which was played for him years ago by a lady in the audience; and after his playing, Father arose and verified the fact."[33]

MISSOURI RAGTIME

Blind Tom played St. Louis at least three times in his career: in 1860, 1880 and 1890—the last date, three years before ragtime exploded into popular consciousness. A few short blocks from his hotel room was St. Louis's tenderloin district, where scores of itinerant black pianists worked the saloons, pool halls, gambling dens, dance halls and brothels, their jaunty "rinky-tink" style ringing through the air. It was a sound that Blind Tom would have found new, yet in some ways familiar. Many of these tunes were essentially marches set to a syncopated beat—something that the black drum and fife bands in Columbus had long flirted with. The sound also had a sympathy with the jangle of the banjo, which Tom had already translated to the keyboard. But these pianists were taking it one step further, creating a polyrhythmic sound that displaced the accentuated bass rhythm against the right hand and hit the beat on the second and third.

Even if lip service to that virtue called respectability prevented a seasoned entertainer like Thomas Warhurst from taking Tom on a tour of the Tenderloin, a trip to the docks on the Mississippi would have been just as musically enlightening. Here, the levee apron rang with the chant of work songs as roustabouts and stevedores lugged and unloaded cargo, shouting out the first moaning measures of the levee blues.

This was the St. Louis known to the pianist John William Boone —or Blind Boone as he was professionally known—an early exponent of ragtime who also played the popular classics, sentimental ballads, descriptive pieces and plantation melodies that were Tom's home turf. In fact, Blind Boone would later promote himself as "the only known rival to Blind Tom," after putting it to the test one winter's night in Columbia, Missouri.

*Blind Tom vs Blind Boone. The legendary Audience Challenge
between the two pianists established fifeen-year-old Boone's reputation
as the "only known rival to Blind Tom."*

The son of an emancipated slave, Blind Boone lost his sight as an infant after a bout of brain fever. By five, his prodigious musical talent had revealed itself and, by twelve, his tin whistle band had become a familiar sight on the streets of his hometown of Warrensburg. There, he caught the eye of a gambler who lured him away with stories of Blind Tom's wealth and fame. Exploited and abused, gambled away in a card game and kidnapped back again, he learnt a hard but valuable lesson about the hazards of bad management.

Finally he was rescued by his stepfather and sent to the St. Louis School for the Blind but there he was banned from the whites-only music room and forced to weave brooms. He soon ran away, disappearing into streets that were ringing with piano and banjo ragtime. By the time Blind Tom toured Missouri in 1880, fifteen-year-old Boone was a fine pianist, able to play difficult pieces entirely by ear and cocky enough to believe he was ready to take the old dog on.

The challenge was arranged in Columbia. The old Garth Hall was packed with black folk on one side and white folk on the other, their loyalties divided between the contender and the champ. That night, Blind Tom opened with the *Missouri Gallop*, adding a few variations of his own. He followed it up with *The Battle of Manassas* and few other "star renditions." Two local musicians first challenged him and Tom easily trumped them both but, by now, the audience was crying out for Boone. The contender was "discovered" in the wings and led to the piano and opened with the light and breezy *Butterfly Gallop* with his own variations. Blind Tom equaled the challenge, flamboyant variations and all, then answered back with his *Delta Kappa March*, his tribute to Pease's old standard. Blind Boone, who also possessed an encyclopedic memory and extremely sensitive digits, reproduced the march without difficulty. But before the applause had subsided, Boone cut in with Blind Tom's *Missouri Gallop*, variations and all. At this, the champ was thrown into a state of great nervous excitement, agitated by the upstart stealing his thunder. By now, the entire audience was squarely behind the hometown hero. "Well, it brought down the house!" remembered one of Blind Boone's managers. " 'Give him a chance,' the people shouted, 'and he can be as great as Tom!' " As the crowds pushed forward to shake Boone's hand, Blind Tom was led from the stage, whisked from the building and taken from Columbia the next day.

This incident largely established Boone's reputation in the region. He began touring the Midwest, his concerts so closely modelled on Blind Tom's that they featured *The Battle of Manassas,* an Audience Challenge, imitations of several instruments on the keyboard, and a left hand/right hand rendition of *The Fisher's Hornpipe* and *Yankee Doodle.* Unlike Tom however, Boone was firmly in control of his finances. An early tour netted over $18,000, which he and his manager paraded in a king size carpetbag through Warrensburg all the way to the bank. Within ten years, he would build himself a substantial family home plus another for his mother, as well as indulging his taste for diamonds and fancy jewelry.[34]

Blind Tom, who was far more famous than Boone, earned significantly more than that—between twenty and twenty-five thousand dollars a year for all eleven years Joseph Eubanks toured with him. Even as his popularity waned, the profits were still impressive. One season in California in the mid-1870s was said to have generated $40,000. A month-long tour of Virginia in 1884 reportedly took over $5,000, most of which was profit.[35] Blind Tom indeed was "a great money maker" and most of it was squandered on John Bethune's racing stable in Harrodsburg, while Tom—to quote Joseph Eubanks—"never received a cent."[36]

The Things Revealed

"I DON'T THINK TOM WAS ENTIRELY BLIND," RUMINATED HIS TOUR manager, A.H. Gott, "On several occasions I remember his calling my attention to objects which he could not have known about without seeing them."[1] Stagehand Frank Davis put Tom's unassisted rambles through the empty concert hall down to his phenomenal memory but was stumped to how he knew it had "stopped raining" or was "beginning to snow." A woman was stunned to watch Tom rise and walk directly to the piano in her drawing room, even though it had not been touched in his presence.[2] Another woman was "paralyzed" after an Audience Challenge, when Tom played—exactly as she did—a two-handed piece with his left hand and his right hand behind his back. "I was so frightened at this uncanny climax I left at once. And to this day, I am wondering why Blind Tom put his hand behind him!"[3]

Despite Tom's acute sensitivity to the subtlest shifts in the sensory environment, he was less aware of the one concept that defined him: race. Norbonne Robinson "cannot recall Tom's relationship to other Negroes. In fact I doubt that Tom knew any distinction between the two races. From infancy he stood apart." But is Norbonne, once again, being diplomatic? Stagehand Frank Davis recalled a rather uncomfortable exchange that took place one winter's day in Boston:

Tom turned into a bootblack's stand on Howard Street to have his shoes shined. While he sat, muttering, in the chair, the bootblack, a Negro, was gleefully recounting to another bootblack the story of a quarrel. "En he says t' me" he said, "Go on, yo' niggah." Instantly there was an interruption. Blind Tom leaned forward and said, in his

"I'll play the number as the lady should have played it,"
was Tom's response to a white Alabama lady's musical efforts.

soft, hesitating, stammering voice, "Are you—are you a nigger?" The bootblack looked at the towering, jet black, blind man and grinned. "I expect I am," he replied. Ponderously Tom climbed down from the chair, one shoe shiny, the other untouched, "Tom ain't goin' to have his shoes shined by no nigger," he said definitely. And although he did, he did at a different shop and he didn't know the bootblack's color.

Odds are the story was met with guffaws and belly laughs as it made the rounds at the theater: a black man who didn't know he was black! However, on closer inspection, it neither proves nor disproves the issue raised by Norbonne Robinson.

Certainly Tom's autism limited his appreciation of the monumental importance Americans placed on skin color. But from the time he was young, he surely must have known he was the marvelous "Negro Boy Pianist"—after all, it was the publicity byline for much of his career and regularly announced at concerts. And Tom also seems to have understood the term "black." When Dr. Blackman told Tom his name, he asked him if he ever heard that name before. Tom replied, "Plenty of black men but no Blackman," suggested the doctor. At first the pun eluded Tom but after a while he responded with an appreciative "Lah! s-s-s-t! yes!"[4]

So Tom did understand that, just like the keys of the piano, people were black and white. Less obvious to him was the colorful array of racial slurs. In his literalness, Tom did not connect the dots and realize there were hundreds of less flattering synonyms for "black" or "Negro." A man raised on compliments never imagined the contempt his adoring audiences had for people like him, never realized that he was a member of a race his managers held in disdain. "Sometimes he would repeat conversations that he had picked up from his owners and managers which spoke of the black race in a disparaging way. He echoed their Southern contempt for the race. It was assumed by many that his feeling to his race became the same," concluded stagehand Frank Davis.

Linguistic nuance may have escaped Tom but his hypersensitive ear must have recognized that certain pieces attracted an applause that was different from the rest. It came from a particular part of the hall, the back or higher up in the gallery. It surged with a hearty roar, punctuated with a few whoops and shouts. In Iowa "there were a couple of seats filled with colored people, large and small, who felt a sort of claim on Tom," wrote the Dubuque fashion editor. So when he, in his rich bass baritone, sang the old spiritual *Them Golden Slippers I Want to Wear*, "they rose unanimously to their feet and had hard work to keep from joining in the chorus."[5] Also a great favorite amongst black audiences were his jangly imitations of that uniquely African-American instrument, the banjo.[6] But their identification with him went deeper than this. Revelation and vision were central pillars of the black church and the inspired rapture that overwhelmed Tom as he performed is captured in a poem by the Reverend James Corruthers:

> O Father, if to all could come
> The things revealed to poor Blind Tom,
> We, too, would clap our hands in glee,
> Rejoiced thy wondrous truths to see.
> The scales would leave our blinded eyes,
> And earth would be a paradise...
> For well we knew that where he stood,
> The blind musician talked with God;
> Nor did we doubt the silent prayer
> Was granted as we watched him there;
> For even as he turned to go,
> We heard him singing, sweet and low:
> '*A starry crown I'm a-goin' for to wear,*
> *A starry crown I'm a-goin' for to wear,*
> *A starry crown I'm agoin' for to wear—*
> *O, sinner, fare you well.*"[7]

But Reverend Corruthers's admiration was far from representative. Black intellectuals, trying to purge themselves from a history of subservience, kept Tom at arm's length. His high profile Rebel sympathies, unquestioned loyalty to his master and Jim Crow buffoonery were neither forgotten nor forgiven. Consequently, Blind Tom barely mustered a mention in the black press and on the rare occasion that he did, the tone was less than welcoming.

"Blind Tom is no longer the greatest musical prodigy living," declared *The Christian Recorder* as it heralded a new, northern-born, black musical prodigy also named Tom. "The original Blind Tom was of Southern Birth. Our Tom, who for certain reasons we call Blind Tom, but who is really our Northern Tom possesses all the singular and excellent musical qualities of the former, and we venture to say, he will command as great, if not greater admiration."[8]

By refusing to claim Blind Tom as "our Tom," they denied him his African-American identity and, in doing so, rejected the idea that his brand of buffoonery was an expression of authentic black culture. "The 'darky entertainer' is white," argued scholar Ralph Ellison in his 1964 landmark study, *Shadow and Act*. In other words, Tom was a caricature sapped of humanity, a figure of ridicule that enabled white American audiences to resolve the contradiction between their white supremacist and democratic instincts. But in disowning Tom, black critics missed something that was blindingly obvious to fifteen-year-old W.C. Handy. When he first saw Blind Tom in Florence, Alabama, it was 1888 or 89, and the young man who would go on to become the father of the blues was struck, not by Blind Tom's music, but something that in his world was unimaginable.

One morning, while on my way to school, I passed the Exchange Hotel and saw a heavy set man, very dark, sitting in a guest chair in front of the hotel—something I had never seen before. And when I reached the Florence District School I talked with my desk mate about what I had seen. He said to me "That's Blind Tom and I have got tickets to hear him play tonight." I went everywhere that Jim went, so we heard Blind Tom's piano recital. After the intermission, his manager requested anyone to come and play a piece on the piano and Blind Tom would immediately reproduce it. A very fine pianist, Miss Maggie Hugh Brock, played a number and all the time she was playing, Blind Tom's fingers were working, and as I remember, he had an unusual smile, even grin, as he listened. When she finished, Blind Tom said, "I'll play the number as the lady played it." Then he said, after playing, "I'll play the number as the lady should have played it." And that brought forth laughter. For me, that was the hit of the show.[9]

How in Jim Crow Alabama, wondered W. C. Handy, did Blind Tom sit in the front window of the best hotel in town like he owned the joint? And his blunt appraisal of Miss Brock's performance—how did he get away with such impertinence? There was simply no logical answer because one thing was certain in Florence, Alabama: no one, not even the most deferential, sycophantic Uncle Tom could jump Jim Crow.

This defiance was by no means an isolated event. For years, Tom had been pushing Southern belles off piano stools or commanding them to "hash" with impunity, even pummeling the occasional music teacher. In the racially oppressive South, such behavior made him an unlikely champion of black power. But among more educated northerners, less open to the mytho-magical possibilities of folk culture, the riddle of Blind Tom—a man who, on the one hand, toadied up to his master and, on the other, embodied the spirit of the Conjure Man and spoke without censure and acted as he pleased—was neither valued nor understood.

FAULTY FINGERING

"Blind Tom has returned to New York with his manager Mr. Bethune, to resume his studies under one of our most accomplished musical instructors," reported *The Musical Courier*. "His programme for next season will include concertos for the piano by Beethoven, Chopin and other great masters."[10] Professor Joseph Poznanski was the official reason why in 1875 and every year after, Blind Tom and John Bethune elected to spend their summers, not in Warrenton, but the sweltering humidity of New York.[11] And certainly Charleston-born Joseph Poznanski was well equipped for the job. A familiar name in the concert halls and assembly rooms of New York, he spent his youth studying music in Europe with his older brother, a violinist, under the virtuoso Henri Vieuxtemps. Now an organist and choir-master at St. Leo's Church, Poznanski worked closely with the New York Conservatory of Music and counted members of the Gottschalk family among his friends.[12]

If twenty-six-year-old Tom hungered for a tutor versed in the classi-

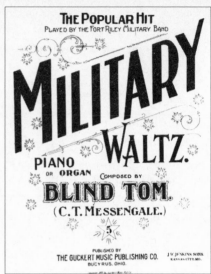

Two compositons by Blind Tom that were published under pseudonyms.

cal cannon, he surely did not anticipate the conditions that came with it. After one lesson Poznanski decreed that his fingering was faulty and insisted he change it. "A royal battle ensued that lasted two weeks," reported Norbonne Robinson. "Tom vowed and declared, with whole-hearted and picturesque profanity of which he had become master, that he would not change his fingering. In the end he was won over, but it took much persuasion." The results were impressive. Otto Spahr, who first met Tom when he was a prodigy of ten, saw him around this period and marveled at the superb technique he had now acquired.[13]

As other teachers had before him, Poznanski fed Tom eight or ten measures at a time. "We had two pianos in one room," he reported. "I would play for him and he would get up, walk around, stand on one foot, pull his hair, knock his head against the wall then sit down and play a very good imitation of what I had played with additions to it. His memory was something prodigious. He never forgot anything."[14]

Anna Tutein, who taught Tom a number of concert pieces in the 1880's, recalled how he would ask whether a note was a whole, half, quarter, eighth or sixteenth note, then apply it with pinpoint accuracy. His performances, she continued, were "by no means a mirror of the playing of others. He put in his own expression and exhibited much individuality. His octaves were very fine and clear and his great physical strength and elasticity made his playing forceful." (How different from the conclusion reached by Eugenie Abbot a decade earlier who felt, as she listened to him play *Die Forelle,* that it was like listening to her own performance.) While Anna Tutein hesitated to compare Tom to a master like Franz Liszt, she believed that he played "better than many white contemporary pianists who made great pretensions and who took years to learn what Tom could learn in a few hours." "In his ears and in his fingers Tom is the peer of some masterful musicians," agreed the novelist and occasional music critic Willa Cather. But for all the overtures to high culture, Tom was an instinctive crowd pleaser, wrapping up his lesson with Tutein by turning his back to the keyboard and playing the concerto she had taught him with his right hand playing the left part, and his left hand playing the right.[15]

As impressive as these bravura pieces were, they were only of secondary importance to John Bethune: Tom's show depended not on a welter of new showpieces, but a reliable formula of old standards and novelties that harkened back decades. Poznanski's primary function was to transcribe Blind Tom's compositions for the sheet music market which—thanks to the voracious appetites of hundreds of thousands of young ladies throughout the country who wore their accomplishments on the piano as a badge of refinement—was a lucrative source of income for the copyright holder (John Gunby Bethune). Pieces that were showy but not too difficult were in big demand, as were pictorial works that either captured nature in its dramatic splendor or wallowed in sticky sentiment.[16]

With the help of Professor Poznanski, Tom fed the machine, producing over one hundred pieces of sheet music—polkas, marches, nocturnes, descriptive pieces—most of which he never played on stage. Their names alone evoke their Romantic inflections: *Water in the Moonlight, Voices of the Waves, Cascade, Cyclone Gallop, Daylight* and *Rêve Charmant.*

Although Tom gladly claimed as his own pieces like *The Sewing Song*—his imitation of a sewing machine—a number of other compositions were, somewhat mysteriously, released under various pseudonyms. "He always had them written under other names than his own," remembered Joseph Poznanski.[17] Strange, as this breaks every rule of marketing and I can only imagine that his managers buried a nationally recognizable brand name like his with the utmost reluctance. This seems to be a rare instance where John's powers of persuasion failed him and Tom's considerable will ruled the day. Unable to deceive Tom even about the wording on the sheet music cover, John credited

Professor W.F. Raymond with composing *March Timpani*, J.C. Beckel with *Blind Tom's Mazurka* and C.T. Messengale with *Military Waltz*.

But why insist on the pseudonyms in the first place? *Military Waltz* was a popular hit for the Fort Riley Military Band while *March Timpani* was adopted by the All White Haverly's Mastodon Minstrel Company. As these pieces may have been intended for other musicians, perhaps these pseudonyms were Tom's way of getting around his aversion to other people stealing his harmonies. Maybe, too, it was a reflection of his creative process. These melodies are pretty standard fare and clearly not something whispered to Tom by machines, thunder or stars. More likely the impetus came from Professor Poznanski determined to squeeze a hit out him. Tom, quite reasonably, may not then have considered these works as genuine expressions of himself and may even have adopted the persona of a particular character as he composed it, to help him give voice to the music. After all, he played the parts of a fleet of music teachers—The Professor, Mrs. Flaherty and Dr. Smokeson—so why not composers too? When it came to the permutations of Tom's extraordinary mind, nothing was impossible. However, one pseudonym—François Sexalise—suggests that there may have been more to the move to New York than lessons with Professor Poznanski.

RESPECTABLE BLOODLINES

A Southern Gentleman John Gunby Bethune may have been, but an autocrat he was not. Stylishly dressed with a fine physique, he had a laid back ease about him, a devil-may-care indifference to the issues that vexed his father and spent his considerable leisure time, not championing points of principle, but accumulating the trappings of status and wealth. For cavaliers and steeplechasers nothing touched Warrenton, Virginia. For horse studs, it could only be Kentucky's bluegrass plains. John desired the best and could readily forgive the Yankees their sins against the South, if such pleasures could be found in the land of his former enemy. Neither was reason his guiding star. His nephew Norbonne Robinson described it as a touch of Celtic mysticism, an otherworldliness that allowed him to slide into Tom's imaginary world. "One Christmas," Robinson recounted, "Tom first heard the mention of Santa Claus and asked John who this Santa Claus was. 'Why Tom,' he replied, 'Santa Claus is like Dr. Smokeson.' That settled it with Tom. A comprehensive and appreciative grin covered his face." The two men understood each other perfectly.

Not all the Bethunes remember John so fondly. "My grandmother," recounted a great-great-great-grandson of General Bethune, "said that John Gunby exploited [Blind Tom] for his own financial gain."[18] Somewhere, it seems, a line had been drawn between General Bethune's seemingly acceptable conduct towards Tom and that of his son.

In 1875, John Bethune and his father appear to have disagreed over a matter of such importance that John took Blind Tom and left Warrenton for good. What they argued about is a matter of speculation though chances are it had something to do with John's taste for fine thoroughbreds and gambling.

By now John was forty-one years of age and unmarried. Perhaps he had never found the right girl. Perhaps he was never much interested in girls. Either way, as a highly eligible bachelor, he had passed up the chance to refine his own bloodlines and join houses with a Virginia belle of impeccable stature and breeding. This, surely, was what his father had hoped for him. Instead, the General's first-born son moved into a boarding house in New York City in the heart of a German migrant enclave on the Lower East Side (perhaps on the recommendation from German-born William Steinway of Steinway and Sons who reportedly gave Tom a piano; Tom later returned the honor by dedicating *Rêve Charmant* to him).

So much about John Bethune during this time is unknown, though any man with money, show business and racetrack connections like his was ideally placed to live an extravagantly dissolute life. With seven racetracks in its vicinity, New York offered access to the sport of kings almost every day of the week. And whether you were a society dilettante or big time buccaneer, August meant only one thing: Saratoga Springs. Gambling had transformed this rustic health spa northwest of New York into an opulent playground for the who's who of the Gilded Age. John Morrissey, the notorious gang leader of the Dead Rabbits, in partnership with August Belmont and Leonard Jerome, two pillars of the New York establishment, had built a racetrack on which horses owned by Wall Street speculators, Tammany Hall cronies and the sons of Brooklyn butchers raced alongside each other. "It was a strange tangle of crude, tough, corrupt circles of power," summed up one historian. "Where respectability began and ended did not always distinctly show." Everything was entwined and the permutations were immeasurable. Uniting them was a single overarching principle: everyone has a price.[19]

The only known picture of Blind Tom's guardian, John Gunby Bethune.

In the Saratoga racing season of 1873 and 1874, a thoroughbred by the name of *Blind Tom* was first, second or third past the post time and again. This *Blind Tom* was born in 1866, a year after the eponymous pianist began generating serious amounts of money in the north. Although John was not listed as the horse's owner, his partner at his Harrodsburg racing stable, T.J. Nichols, owned and trained *Blind Tom's* brother, *Day Star*, the 1878 Kentucky Derby winner.[*][20]

Somewhere between Saratoga's lavish casinos and racetrack was John Bethune. The divisions of Civil War, the insult of Reconstruction, all were forgotten in the thrill of the win. In August 1879, thirty-year-old Blind Tom was said to have accompanied him here, entertaining guests at one of the town's grand hotels. But where was he during the other years? If he was not with his guardian John or his manager Thomas Warhurst or in Warrenton with General Bethune, who was looking after him?

A RIDGE IN THE FLOORING

In old fashioned St. Mark's Place, just east of the bustling Bowery, stands a marble stooped dwelling that is a market spot in that noisy quarter of town, [reported the New York Sun]. At varying intervals

---

[*]*Blind Tom* was owned by Joseph J. O'Donohue and his career is a fine example of the racetrack's old boy network. A New Jersey businessman with substantial interests in the local docks, O'Donohue was also the City Chamberlain who regulated the docks and founding member of Tammany Hall.

daily the music of a sweet toned piano floats softly from the interior of
the old house and mingles a delightful harmony with the dull hum of
traffic in the populous thoroughfare. The fingers that so deftly touch
the keys are those of a strapping big Negro who sits at the piano in the
spacious back parlor. Every once in a while the stalwart African will
start up from his seat and rush out upon the porch and pace up and
down like an imprisoned animal, beating his chest and moaning
piteously . . . For hours everyday he tramps up and down the porch in
his slippered feet . . . [and] has worn a ridge in the flooring of the porch
near the hand rail by his restless promenade to and fro.[21]

By the 1870s, New York was among the loudest, most culturally
diverse and densely populated cities in the world. "Was there anything
ever known like it?" despaired one writer. "The condition of the traffic
of Broadway looks like one continual state of deadlock. Never is there
anything like the choking confusion and jostling, scuffling, blind bewil-
derment."[22] On one typical day, 7,811 horse-drawn vehicles were counted passing the corner of Broadway and Pine—huge lumbering hacks,
team-pulled drays heavy with freight and rickety, rumbling old stage-
coaches. Traffic noise made conversation nearly impossible as the sharp
clatter of the horses' iron shoes on the pavement tormented the ears.[23]

Blind Tom was not impressed. "How do you like New York?"
Susan Bethune once asked him. "I don't like it a bit," he replied. "Too
many fellow beings."[24] It was more than just the menacing stranger that
bothered him. The cacophony rendered the acoustic landscape a white
noise of conflicting sound waves and discordant, unpredictable bangs.
Tom was "morose and disliked society," concluded Professor Poznanski,
an assessment that would be robustly contested back in Warrenton.[25]
Tom's gloom seems to have more to do with the cluttered urban environment than people *per se*. And while he had no time for idle chatter,
he craved a less verbal, though very human, form of contact.

If a fleeting melody lingered in the air—the nearby bells of
Broadway's Grace Church as it pealed out a *Nearer My God To Thee*,
vocalists and pianists practicing in the neighboring Ninth Street flats, the
distant strains of a German beer garden or a band of street musicians
striking up a frivolous waltz—Tom would hungrily seize upon it and
burst into dance or echo it back with impeccable precision (although he
once bellowed to a tonally challenged singer that she ought to be
ashamed of herself). These musical threads connected him to his neighbors, many of whom, with more than a touch of pity, followed his musi-

cal conversations, watched him caper on the small balcony and grew anxious at any prolonged absence. One tenant showed a reporter from *The New York Sun* how he used his piccolo to keep a check on Tom:

> The speaker raised the piccolo to his lips and sent the notes of the pretty ballad My Nellie Blue Eyes floating over the porch. [After several minutes] there was a commotion in the parlor, the bolts of the big window were suddenly unlocked with a clang and Blind Tom plunged out into the porch and leaned over, with a smile lighting up his dusky face to catch the piccolo notes. When the ballad was finished he groped his way back to the piano and, pressing his fingers to the keys played the ballad himself and the high notes. Then he dived out on the porch again and waited anxiously for some more music from the piccolo player. A bird flew in the garden while he waited and, perching upon the branch that nodded near Tom, swelled its little throat in a sweet anthem to the sunshine and the balmy breezes. When the song ceased he went back to his piano and reproduced the notes with a fidelity that was marvelous. Then he shut the window and was seen no more that day on the porch.[26]

This was Tom's summertime world, his needs attended to by a thirty-five-year-old German divorcée known by the names Eliza or Elise Stutzbach. After ten years of low paid work—and the options available to a poorly educated immigrant woman were limited—the task of attending to Tom's needs, feeding him, keeping him clean and delivering him to his daily music lesson, was considerably less onerous than domestic service, laundry or needlework.

For her to do her job, John must have schooled Eliza in the secrets of managing Tom—the right balance of palaver and threats to soothe his outrage and leave him with the impression that he had had his way. Eliza soon mastered the technique, one stage hand commenting, after watching her deflect a tantrum, that "no one else in the world could have managed him."[27] In time she would become privy to a number of John's dirtier little secrets.

Meanwhile Tom paced up and down the ridge in the floor. No longer in communication with the stars, he was nonetheless absorbing sounds much closer to home: tip-toed patter, clinking glasses and suppressed giggles—the fizz of a heady cocktail that was brewing between his guardian and his landlady.

PART FOUR

FELLOW BEINGS

Blind Tom in 1898 at the age of fifty.

- 18 -

The Last American Slave

IN THE SUMMER OF 1882, PROFESSOR POZNANSKI TRANSCRIBED Blind Tom's new concert waltz, *Wellenklänge*—a sprightly echo of the ocean's waves that was published under the name François Sexalise and dedicated to his landlady Frau O. Stutzbach. The pseudonym he chose is different from the rest as "Sexalise" is not a surname, nor the name of a minstrel troupe or military band. It was, however, a remarkably apt description of the steamy state of affairs between John and Eliza, or Elise as she was also known. How the General must have fumed when he learned that in November that year his first-born son, a Southern gentleman of cavalier stock, had married a divorcée of no breeding, little class and dubious morality. What could have possessed him to enter into a legally binding contract with someone like her? Surely they weren't in love!

Whatever it was—and who can plumb the heart of anyone else—it did not seem to be too strong an

Tom chose to publish Wellenklänge *under the name of François Sexalise at the same time John was conducting an affair with his landlady Elise or Eliza.*

affection. Within weeks of marrying, John left his new bride and set off with Blind Tom for an eight month tour, without sending her so much as a letter, telegram or money order. On his return, he found himself locked out of the boarding house and his wife leaning from a second floor window, informing him with full-voiced fury that she was divorcing for "abandonment and non-support."

The couple next met in court. Although John professed to be still shaken by his wife's shameless mistreatment and disdain, he managed to drop a few bombshells of his own. Eliza was not his legal wife, his attorney told the court, as her divorce from her estranged husband Otto Stutzbach had not been finalized. This subsequently disqualified her to any of John's alimony. The judge agreed and John Bethune headed off to the nearest saloon for a much needed drink.

Eliza followed him through the door of this male preserve and proposed a reconciliation, if he was willing to financially support her. But John no longer wished to continue their marriage. Thus began a quarrel that was punctuated with a few shoves and whacks and only ended when a policeman forcibly removed them from the saloon. They were then placed before a judge who, to Eliza's continued outrage, again denied her alimony plea. John, however, departed "in glee"—as the newspapers reported the following day, an unwelcome bit of publicity that was sure to wipe the smile from his face.[1] The sorry affair was to turn Blind Tom off marriage for life, later telling a reporter that if he did 's-s-s-he might b-b-b-b-eat me and then the p-p-p-apers would be down on me."[2]

Three weeks later, Eliza exacted her revenge. By order of the Commons Plea Court—the papers again reported—she had John arrested for desertion and non-support. After shelling out $2,500 in bail money, he and Blind Tom relocated to Green's Hotel in Chestnut Street, Philadelphia—a lavishly appointed hotel with a famous Arctic-themed bar that came to embody the decadence of the "Gay Nineties."

Six months later, while Tom was on the road with Thomas Warhurst, the courts compelled John to return to New York to respond to yet another petition from his estranged wife. The animosity ran deep and both parties were ready to fight to the bitter end. Until this point, life had been good to John and never having to battle against the odds, he possibly imagined that the odds would always stay in his favor. But John was on a losing streak that would prove fatal. The next time he made headlines on February 16, 1884 was also the last:

A FATAL ACCIDENT

BLIND TOM'S MANAGER KILLED AT THE PW&B STATION

WILMINGTON, DELAWARE. John G Bethune, manager of the Blind Tom Concert Company, was killed at the railroad station a few minutes after 12 o'clock on Saturday. He was a passenger on the south bound express train due here at 11 o'clock but which was an hour late, and on his arrival, having a few spare minutes, went over to the Grand Union hotel to lunch. When he returned to the station the train was moving out and although warned not to do so, he attempted to jump on the platform of one of the cars. He missed his footing and after being dragged some distance was thrown beneath the car and fearfully mangled. His right leg and hip were crushed and his head was badly cut and bruised. Special Officer Thomas ran to the rescue but was unable to save him. The unfortunate man was dragged from beneath and gasping "oh my," died before a stretcher could be procured. The deceased was about fifty-five years of age.

Before dawn the next morning—on the 4:38 A.M. train—Eliza and her lawyer, Albrecht J. Lerche, arrived at Wilmington and began making applications for the body—but to no avail. The coroner held off his inquest until General Bethune arrived and released the body to him. As the train bearing John's remains pulled away, a local reporter was surprised to see his widow "rush from the gentlemen's waiting room and, halting between the railroad tracks, loudly bewail her loss. She re-entered the waiting room and paced excitedly to and fro wringing her hands and moaning."

Wary of her performance, the reporter followed her to the Registry of Wills and watched her subject a clerk to a storm of tears, legal bluster, entreaties and threats until her request was granted: a letter of administration showing that, as John's surviving spouse, she was entitled to his estate if—and this was a big if—he had died without a will. Next port of call was the coroner's office where, after more tears and bluster, Eliza won her demand to allow a local lawyer to search through the shreds of clothing that had been cut away from John's mutilated body.[3] Loud again were the protests when she was told that nothing of intrinsic value was found. In his empty eyeglass case, she insisted, was a valuable diamond that John always carried about with him—but in it the lawyer only found a ticket from New Jersey to Washington. When Eliza and her attorney Albrecht Lerche finally departed on the evening train, the local lawyer—who evidently felt like a vulture picking over the remains—confided to the reporter that he was greatly relieved to be rid of the case.[4]

The Wilmington Daily Commercial was not the only newspaper suspicious of this brash woman "claiming to be the dead man's wife," though no one thought to question Bethune's media savvy performance. He told reporters of Tom's "strong and almost worshipful devotion" for John and how the blind star "received the news of his death with intense expressions of sadness."[5] However, as these articles went to press Tom was in Wilson, North Carolina with Thomas Warhurst and Joseph Eubanks and they only knew what they read in the newspapers.

According to Eubanks, it was not until February 20th—six days after John's death—that they received a telegram from Bethune informing them of the tragedy and directing them to bring Blind Tom back to Warrenton, his first visit there in ten years. In the twelve days Tom remained there, Bethune had himself appointed as Tom's legal guardian. In an echo of the 1870 ruling, the accommodating Fauquier County judge again waived all legal requirements such as a physician's report and concluded that "if he was a lunatic in 1870, he was still a lunatic in 1884."[6] Warhurst and Eubanks then returned to North Carolina with Tom and picked up the threads of the tour.[7]

A few days later *The New York Post* reported that Blind Tom's mother was "living in a hovel in Virginia in destitution, and that his manager had squandered all his money." The paper cited Joseph Eubanks as the source of these damning revelations. With lightning efficiency, a retort was published from "E.Z.C. Judson" (the real name of notorious dime novelist, Ned Buntline) who dismissed Eubanks—a mere doorkeeper and baggage handler—and his remarks as "entirely gratuitous." Tom's mother resided now on General James N. Bethune's homestead in Muscogee County near Columbus, Georgia— the letter read—"amply provided for in house, money and land."[8] The only person not hiding behind an alias was the much-maligned Eubanks, who denied making any statements to anyone. Someone was putting words in his mouth, he insisted in his letter to the editor, for he always knew that Tom's mother lived in Columbus and not in Virginia.[9] Nevertheless, the seeds of doubt had been planted in the General's mind and Eubanks's services were promptly terminated.

Three weeks after John's death, his will was presented for probate and his entire estate was awarded to his father. For ill treatment and personal abuse, his "alleged wife" Eliza was cut off without a farthing. "She never had any genuine regard for me," read the will, "but was a heartless adventuress who sought to absorb my estate, the fruits of my savings during a bachelorhood of fifty years." At this, Eliza boldly attacked the attorneys with her parasol and "so outraged the solemnity of the occasion that the coroner had her forcibly ejected from the room"—or so claimed an article sourced by General Bethune. Then and there, he attested, Eliza vowed to avenge herself—the declaration of what was to be a most uncivil war.[10]

TOM'S BUGALOO

On a drizzly chilly date late in January in 1889 [reported Frank Davis, the unfortunate stagehand in the story he was about to relay] a young man, merely a ticket taker of the company, was leading the wonderful performer from the theatrical boarding house on Bulfinch Place to Horticultural Hall, where the daily concerts were given. A building was in process of construction on that side of Tremont Street and a temporary fence set out into the sidewalk. In his effort to prevent Tom from colliding with the pedestrian, [the stagehand] pushed Tom suddenly to the right and Tom ran into the fence.

Instantly there was a scene. The Negro swung a blind but powerful blow at his guide—a blow that caught the young man and sent him reeling. Then he stopped short there in the middle of the side walk, raised his sightless eyes, swung his bullet head and began to cry with the blubbering inconsolable cry of a child, "Mrs. Bethune," he wailed. The thin dark woman darted forward. "All right, Tom. Alright, I'm here. What's the matter?" she cried sharply. The Negro ceased his crying as suddenly as he began. "Mr. Davis was trying to take Tom to a lawyer," he whined. "I'll see that he don't," said the woman, "Now we'll go and find the piano."

The word "lawyer" became Tom's bugaloo. He never understood what a lawyer was but he associated it with trouble, which some might call a mark of intelligence rather than imbecility. Anything unpleasant in his mind was connected with a lawyer.[11]

For Tom, lawyers were more than trouble. The application of law was the very glue that bonded him to this guardian or that. In

April 1884, General Bethune was to administer yet another dose of that glue, traveling to Columbus with Tom in the hope of clarifying his lunatic status in the state of Georgia. On their tail were Eliza and her attorney Albrecht Lerche, who took the opportunity to visit Charity and enlighten her to the legal and moral implications of her son's insanity ruling.

If Eliza's previous performances are anything to go by, she painted a devastating picture of exploitation, abuse, ruthlessness and greed, a situation that so affronted her sense of justice and human decency, she felt compelled to travel the nine-hundred-mile journey south and persuade Charity to rise against her former master and deliver Tom from his clutches. Her plea evidently struck a chord in the old woman, who must have felt wounded by General Bethune's continued denial of her rights over Tom. Spurred on with a few encouraging words—assurances of financial security plus the prospect of a heart stirring reunion (hadn't Tom been singing *Mother Dear Mother, I Still Think of Thee* all these years?)—the eighty-three-year-old woman was persuaded to leave the Bethune farm, her home for over thirty-five years, and spearhead the campaign to free the last American slave.

When Bethune and Tom arrived in New Orleans for a concert a number of weeks later, Charity and her new attorney Albrecht Lerche were waiting for them, armed with a writ of *habeas corpus*. But their ambush failed. Bethune and Tom escaped and with them any chance Charity could quietly return to her Columbus home. With few options available to her, she agreed to relocate to New York, change her surname from Bethune to Wiggins and launch the legal attack from there.[12]

Over the next year, a revolving door of hearings, suits, appeals and petitions came before a pantheon of judges in three separate states, the two camps drawing wildly divergent portraits of Charity's life since the Civil War. In July 1885 Charity's legal team, which now included a very capable attorney by the name of Daniel Holland, wheeled out the big guns and successfully served a writ of *habeas corpus* on General Bethune, the attached petition itemizing a concise and damning list of abuses he had wrought on his ward:

> Tom was deprived of his liberty without due process of law; that he
> was exhibited for gain by his committee contrary to law; that he
> derived no such benefit of such gain or profit; that he was deprived

of access or intercourse with his mother and family; that he was subject to such cruel treatment that his mind was not allowed to develop; that he was intentionally kept in ignorance and prevented from knowing what is right; and that his committee knowingly and intentionally kept him in a state of imbecility for the purpose of making gain and profit out of his condition; that he was not a lunatic at the time he was committed and is not a lunatic at the present time; that he is entitled to his liberty because he is sane; that Bethune has been robbing him for twenty years under legal forms without [his mother's] consent or knowledge . . . That he was held in slavery and had not received the benefits of the emancipation laws of the United States; that he was held in involuntary servitude without due process of law.[13]

Bethune's main defense at the court hearing in Alexandria was Tom himself. If this was involuntary servitude, then why was Tom so anxious to stay with him—a message Tom fretfully repeated over and over in the witness stand: he wanted to go back to Warrenton and stay with General Bethune.[14] But the cross-examination systematically exposed the machinations behind his words. Tom was convinced that his mother was scheming to take away his piano and never allow him to play again, that she was in cahoots with a gang who would torment and abuse him. "The studied and, it seems, successful attempt to alienate the affections of the child from the mother is the crowning infamy of this business," concluded a *Musical Courier* article with disgust.[15] But it was the minefield of jurisdiction that was to save Bethune's bacon. The writ and the appeal were dismissed on technical grounds and Blind Tom returned to his beloved Warrenton—but not for long. Three months later he was performing to a large audience at the Fredericksburg Opera House, the first night of yet another nine-month-long tour.[16]

A war of words erupted in the nation's newspapers, its frontline running the length of Mason Dixon. *The Cleveland Gazette* was sickened by the outrageous miscarriage of justice. "The Bethunes have grown enormously rich off the proceeds of Tom's marvelous musical genius without a shadow of right in law and equity or common sense to appropriate it."[17] *The Atlanta Constitution* printed letters defending the Bethunes's honor, trust and fidelity. "Tom is devoted to the family and does not want to go anywhere else. All the professed sympathy for Tom has simply been manufactured by parties who are actively engaged in trying to get possession of him themselves and using his mother, an ignorant Negro, as a tool to accomplish their purpose."[18]

Southern papers' reporters portrayed Bethune as a remarkably well-preserved old man with long white hair and beard. "Shrewd" was a word never far from Charity's name, while her Irish-born lawyer Daniel Holland was said to have "gloried in the possession of a beer saloon." But it was Eliza who took the most savage drubbing: "a hard featured, coarse, aggressive looking woman enrobed in a flashy habiliment that would turn a paste diamond green with envy," was the appraisal of one Virginia newspaper.

Only the shadowy Albrecht Lerche somehow escaped not only their attentions, but history as well. The Prussian born solicitor has left few traces: an 1866 IRS record lists him as a factory worker making traveling bags, an 1880 naturalization record identifies him as attorney, while an 1884 *New York Times* article notes his role as chairman at a Tammany Hall meeting in the 23rd ward. Apart from the fact that his brother, a Carmelite priest, sued him over a disputed property on Manhattan's West 135th Street in 1893, little else about him is known. However, he seems to have been the one who instigated and financed Charity's legal challenge, confident he had the case, connections and wherewithal to deliver Blind Tom to his number one client, Eliza Bethune.

General Bethune may have dismissed the immigrant New Yorkers as "low class," but they understood matters of law. Thirty-three depositions later, Daniel Holland had cut a tidy path through the thorny bush of jurisdiction. "If the committee of one *non compos* changes his residence from the state where he was appointed [i.e., Virginia] to another state [i.e., New York] and takes the latter with him, the latter becomes a resident of the state to which they remove [i.e., New York] and retains such residence after the committee's death, even if he is afterwards taken to his original state [i.e., Virginia] and here appointed another committee," ruled the United States Circuit Court.[19] In other words, Thomas Wiggins—as he was now known by everyone except the Bethunes—was a citizen of New York and the battle for him could be waged there, in Lerche's sphere of power and patronage. In courts where democratically elected judges were aligned to political factions, in a city where the government was owned "body, pants and boots" by a vast political machine of which Lerche was a cog—Tammany Hall.

The shadowy Albrecht Lerche photographed with Blind Tom in 1898.

"I am confident that poor Tom will find that the laws of the United States will set right again the grievous wrong done to him and his parents," Lerche told *The Brooklyn Eagle* days before a hearing at which Bethune was to show cause why the estate and custody of Blind Tom should not be given to Charity Wiggins and why he should not pay to the court a portion of Blind Tom's earnings.[20] For almost a year, Bethune avoided answering the complainant's bill, claiming one extension after another. In the meantime, Lerche pursued other legal avenues.

He sought an insanity ruling for Tom. Eighteen months earlier, his legal team lambasted Bethune for using a dubious lunatic ruling to keep Tom enslaved—"he is entitled to his liberty because he is sane"—but now they had experienced a profound change of heart. In November of 1886, the New York Commissioner of Lunacy and Sheriff's jury heard testimonies from Charity Wiggins, Professor Joseph Poznanski, Joseph Eubanks and Albrecht Lerche and were persuaded that Blind Tom was mentally unsound and incapable of managing his own affairs.[21] In newspapers from coast to coast, the headline "Blind Tom Insane" became the source of a persistent rumor that Tom had suddenly and dramatically descended into madness.

The ruling must have stirred uncomfortable emotions in Charity, who considered her son a genius. But if she had misgivings about

Lerche's new strategy, she did not show it but instead exercised her right as the lunatic's next of kin and asked the court to have Eliza Bethune appointed as "the committee of the person and estate of Thomas Wiggins."[22] But did she fully understand the legal implications of her submission to the court? Did she realize that she was handing control of Tom's income and welfare to Eliza? And that once these rights were given away, they could not easily be reclaimed?

We can only speculate as how Daniel Holland and Albrecht Lerche presented this proposition to Charity. However, the court, in agreeing to her request, recognized a possible conflict of interest and imposed a stringent safeguard. Eliza would be given the guardianship of Tom on condition she pay a $25,000 bond to the court—a bond she would forfeit if it was proven she was errant in her duties. Eliza had nothing like that amount at her disposal, but thankfully Albrecht Lerche had four businessmen at hand who were prepared to act as her sureties. Without their assistance, she would never have met this condition. The bond now guaranteed, the guardianship was secured and the battle lines were redrawn: the struggle for Tom was no longer between former slave and master but daughter and father-in-law.

Six months later in May 1887, Eliza filed a petition in the U.S. Circuit Court alleging that Tom was wrongfully detained by General Bethune and Thomas Warhurst.[23] At the hearing in Baltimore, twelve weeks later, the judge ruled in Eliza's favor and ordered James N. Bethune to deliver Tom and the sum of $7,000 into her hands. Despite the sweltering heat, General Bethune took the news in his stride. "He refused a fan offered him, as well as a glass of water and for his comfort pulled out an old time looking pipe which he filled with plug tobacco, lit it and puffed away as if the thermometer was in the forties and not in the nineties."[24] But Bethune was proving to be a better actor than lawyer. The ruling was in fact a calamity and, over the next few weeks, he went into overdrive, appealing the judgment and courting the sympathy of the press.

The General's appeal was focused on two main points. The first concerned a cabal of faceless men who he believed had hatched a conspiracy against him. "Certain persons of [New York City] both known and unknown" had conspired with Eliza Bethune and Charity Wiggins to obtain possession of Blind Tom for their own corrupt ends. (False, wicked and libelous, retorted Lerche.) Bethune's petition did not elaborate further on his suspicions, but shifted his argument to Tom's welfare.[25] It was all a mistake about Tom being an idiot, Bethune confessed, and suggested that "feeble minded" would better describe him. Tom knew his mind well enough to know that he wanted to stay in Warrenton with the Bethune family, the people he had known and loved since childhood, and the court's decision to place him in Eliza's custody was causing him the utmost pain and alarm.[26]

But Bethune's arguments failed to persuade the judge. The order would stand and a date for the handover was set.

TROUBLE OF A SERIOUS NATURE

August was a sorrowful month in the Bethunes's Warrenton home. On August 16, 1885, the younger James and his wife buried their six-month-old daughter. Almost to the day the following year, they lost a second child. Now on August 16, 1887 James was to accompany Tom to an Alexandria court and hand him over to his new guardian. When he and Tom alighted the train at Alexandria that Tuesday morning, a crowd of onlookers was there to greet them, eager to know if the rumors were true—would there be trouble?

That was what the newspapers were predicting. Only two days earlier *The Washington Post* cautioned that "Tom was generally cheerful, talkative, even playful to his friends, while to a stranger, no statue was ever more impassive. In his happiest strains a strange voice will as effectively chill and change his spirits as if the freezing atmosphere of an iceberg had swept suddenly down upon him. Under such circumstances, as when infuriated, he is as intractable as the winds, and it is believed that being forced into new and distasteful relations will produce trouble of a serious nature."[27] "If he should refuse to go, as he has time and again averred, there will be a disturbance," warned *The New York Times*.[28]

So far, it looked as if the papers were right. The onlookers who escorted Tom to the courthouse were not long there before they saw Albrecht Lerche usher Charity into the courtroom. They watched as she greeted her son and saw her salutation be met with stony silence. "Tom ain't you going to speak to your mother?" she entreated, but Tom turned his back on her and refused to reply. However, Tom made his intentions clear to a local reporter: he was not going to New York, he wanted to stay with General Bethune and would fight them off. As members of the public squeezed into the overcrowded gallery, Tom "sat nervously in his chair, listening to every sound, apparently dreading the thought of being taken away."

At precisely midday the court swung into action and a court marshal ordered Tom to be turned over to his new committee. James Bethune obliged and, shooting poisonous glares at Lerche, told Tom: "I now deliver you to the court and you will be turned over to that thief. But remember that if these people get tired of you, you could come back to our house and you will always be taken care of." But Tom—as James Bethune had clearly hoped—refused to budge, and stated his case loud and clear—he did not want to be turned over to strangers!

The marshal called a recess hoping that a good meal and the immanent arrival of Eliza Bethune would ease Tom's anxieties. But as he tucked into his dinner, tensions upped a notch. James Bethune confronted Lerche, calling him a blackmailer who hounded his father and induced Charity to take Tom from his true friends by questionable means. Lerche shrugged off the abuse, sensing that this was not the time for conflict.

By three o'clock, Eliza still had not appeared so the marshal decided to turn Tom over to Lerche. But again Tom refused, raising his fists in defense and threatening to fight them all. The public gallery responded with howls of support and for a moment the much anticipated fight looked to become a reality, until a court attorney vowed to arrest the next heckler who dared Tom to fight. Finally, after much coaxing and promises that if he did not like his new home, he could return, Thomas Wiggins bade James Bethune goodbye, his parting words a vow never to touch the piano again until his return to Virginia.

It was not until James Bethune returned home to Warrenton alone that General Bethune realized that the pantomime he had rehearsed with Tom—the declarations of loyalty to General Bethune, the fight to the death—did not run according to script. The curtain had fallen on a show that had lasted almost thirty-five years.

During that time, Blind Tom had transformed the Bethune family. He founded their fortune, raised their social standing and brought a bit of showbiz glamour to their lives. Tom and the General's flight to Florida in the dying days of the war was now part of family legend, while his tender melodies, wild dancing, philosophical observations and bizarre routines had touched them all. And now he was gone, his absence leaving a hole in their lives as big as the hole in their bank balance.

If Bethune ever wondered if Tom's prodigious talent was God's way of rewarding him for saving the Wiggins family from the auction block, the thought may have crossed his mind that he was now being punished for profiteering from Tom at the Wiggins's expense. Hard on the heels of Tom's removal, auctioneers moved into Bethune's Warrenton home. To satisfy a legal bill, the court had levied his personal property and one by one his possessions—including Tom's Steinway grand—went under the hammer. General Bethune was bankrupt, his golden goose gone, the cavalier dream over. His only satisfaction lay in the knowledge that Eliza would never see the $7,000 the court had ordered him to pay her—or make a cent out of Tom. If the Bethune family version of events is to be believed, Tom was true to parting words: "After Mrs. (Eliza) Bethune legally gained possession of Tom, he refused to touch the piano and no persuasion could induce him to continue his concerts," wrote a Warrenton Old Timer.[29] General Bethune, at least, had convinced himself he had handed over a white elephant.

Within a few years, the family lost the Warrenton farm and the three generation of Bethunes living there were forced to rent a home in northeast Washington D.C. and survive on son James's modest income as a bookkeeper in the War Department. General Bethune spent his last years arguing points of theological principle and championing free trade. When he eventually died in 1895 at the age of ninety-two, the triumphs of his political career were almost eclipsed by a wave of interest in his former slave. "Death of Old Master Recalls Former Prodigy," read a *Washington Post* article days after Bethune was buried in the family plot in Columbus. In an ironic twist, the educated and cultivated Southern Gentleman became an historical footnote in the life of his "bestial" and "idiotic" slave.

- 19 -

"Tom is Non Compos Mentis"

BLIND TOM'S SEPARATION FROM THE BETHUNE FAMILY WAS FAR LESS TRAU-matic for him than it was for them. For all the bluster in the Alexandria courtroom, he boarded the 3:20 train and traveled to Washington with-out protest.[1] Already, in his single-minded and detached way, he had accepted whatever life dished out to him as if no alternative existed.

When he arrived in New York a few days later, newspaper head-lines rang out "Blind Tom is Free," heralding in a new era of justice and righteousness. "Although he has been in the public eye since he was five years old, he is returning to his mother's home with nothing but his wardrobe and a silver flute," observed *The New York Times*. "Now that he is in the care of a legally constituted guardian, whatever he will be able to earn above his expenses will inure to his own benefit."[2]

Eliza and her newly appointed manager Mr. Gibson—"a well set-up distinctly southern looking man with waxed goatee and moustache"—refashioned Tom's career according to the spirit of this new era. He was promoted as "the last slave to be set free by order of the Supreme Court of the United States" and his concert at Steinway Hall that November was his first "since freedom." Finally the black community could celebrate Tom as one of their own—which they did in their droves.

"Seldom in recent years have people turned out in such masses as on the occasion of Blind Tom and Mme. Selika's centennial concert under the auspices of Bethel Church on Wednesday evening," reported the *New York Age* in November 1887. "From the opening of the doors at

Take Notice!
The concert to celebrate
the centenary of the
Bethel AME Church
is announced in the
New York Age.

READ!   WHAT?
The Grandest Yet!
A DOUBLE TREAT, TWO CONCERTS IN ONE.
BY WHOM?
SELIKA
AND
Blind Tom.

Under the Auspices of BETHEL A. M. E. CHURCH,
(7 & Sullivan street) Rev. W. B. DERRICK, D.D., Pastor.

WHERE AND WHEN?
THESE TWO INIMITABLE MUSICAL PHENOMENONS
WILL APPEAR ON THE SAME DATE AND HOUR AT
STEINWAY HALL, Wednesday, November 23, 1887, at 8 P. M.

READ! TAKE NOTICE! As this is the first time in the history of the city that two of the world's leading musical wonders have appeared at the same date, place and hour, we invite all admirers of Music, Sweet Music, to be sure to attend, as such an event may never occur again in our day.

SELIKA, the unrivalled Prima Donna.
BLIND TOM, the Greatest Musical Enigma of the Century.

General Admission,   -   -   -   50 Cents.
Reserved Seats,   -   -   -   75 Cents.
oct29 4t

Steinway Hall there was a crush for seats, the galleries and floor were soon crowded. Among some of the noted people present was Hon. C.J. Taylor, U.S. Minister to Liberia, Mrs. Ex-President Roberts of Liberia and Hon. M.D. Basset of the Haitian Counsel, Bishop Disney of Canada, Rev. D. Arnott, secretary of the AME Church . . ."[3]

The concert was a spectacular return to the fold for the last American slave. Coloratura soprano Mme. Selika's trills and roulades and Blind Tom's arpeggios and octaves inspired such praise that a tour of the northeastern seaboard immediately followed. For the first time, Tom headed a lineup of African-American performers—Mme. Selika, ballad singer Harry Pepper, the cute and catchy Carrie Tutein and trombonist William L. Marsh—all to sellout crowds at popular prices.[4]

Next came an extravaganza at the Boston Music Hall alongside "no less than sixty colored celebrities," including the up-and-coming *prima donna* Sissieretta Jones, members of Haverly and Callander's minstrels, cornet virtuoso George W. Sharper, cellist Frederick Elliot Lewis, a full military band of forty uniformed musicians plus a drum corps of twenty. But the euphoric applause from the overwhelmingly black crowd was for thirty-nine-year-old Blind Tom: "He was encored again and again."[5]

Around this time, Tom met a young European pianist who was at the tail end of his own electrifying American tour. Eleven-year-old Josef Hofmann was already a startling prodigy: the dash, brilliance and accuracy of his execution, his ability to hear something once and know it forever, triggered a cascade of praise wherever he performed. "The great crowd was a whirl of excitement," reported *The Boston Globe* after his performance in that city. "The orchestra gave a fanfare, the men shouted and the ladies waves their handkerchiefs and there seemed to be no limit to the enthusiasm . . . Such brilliancy of execution, such self-command and independence, such intellectual appreciation of the task the performer has to accomplish . . . and the evident pleasure with which he plays added greatly to the enjoyment."[6]

The comparisons between Hofmann and Blind Tom were inevitable and brutal. "Here are two human brains endowed with what we call genius," wrote *The North American Review*. "In one case it was developed amid the congenial surroundings of an ancient European city—a musical centre of some repute. In the other case, it simply 'growed' like Topsy."[7]

The former and the reigning child prodigies tugged the audience's heartstrings in very different ways. After Hofmann played fifty-two concerts in ten weeks, the Society for Protection and Care of Children was inundated with complaints about his exploitation—an outrage that had never been extended to young Tom. Finally a benefactor intervened, offering the family $50,000 to take him off the stage and properly nurture his musical education. They accepted and Hofmann entered into "quiet and earnest study" with the great Russian virtuoso Anton Rubenstein, an opportunity he later described as the "greatest fortune in my life."[8] He grew up to be celebrated as one of the world's finest pianists, bringing a pared-back Modernist sensibility to Romantic bravura.

In the days before his return to Berlin, Blind Tom treated Hofmann to a private performance, at the end of which the young prodigy "seated himself at the pianoforte and reproduced with marvelous exactness one of the pieces Blind Tom had played him."[9] For months to come, Blind Tom would get his own back, delighting audiences with his imitations of Josef Hofmann.[10]

New lineup, new audiences, new influences, Eliza could systematically tick each box to prove that the sun was indeed rising on this new emancipated era in Tom's life. But why did Charity not feel as if she were basking in its warm rays? Where was the much promised money? The relationship with her son she had been so long denied? After relocating north and battling the courts for three years, had Charity simply moved from the frying pan to the fire?

A VERY HERCULES IN STATURE

"Blind Tom is extremely moral and religious in his habits and disposition. He says the *Lord's Prayer* in his room aloud, and is fond of reciting passages from the Holy Scriptures and will quickly order from the room anyone who uses profane or improper language in his presence,"[11] reported *The Ladies Home Journal*, words that surely evoked hoots of disbelief from those privy to Tom's full-blown profanity. But after accusing the Bethunes of neglecting Tom's religious education, Eliza needed to be doubly pious—and not only because Sunday was no longer a day of rest.

In the late nineteenth century, America was the world's fastest growing economy and a superpower *in utero*. This culture of unfettered *lassez-faire* and machine politics had given rise to a new generation of filthy rich, and even for small fish, the promise of wealth was only a kickback away. The core may have been rotten but the façade shimmered with virtue—the Tammany Hall crony eulogized democracy, the corrupt police chief defended law and order, Wall Street speculators upheld liberty, while Eliza championed Tom's freedom. Behind this illusion was a machine powered by its very opposite: patronage, bribery, monopoly and, in Tom's case, servitude. If Eliza and her attorney Albrecht Lerche had learned anything about survival during their time in the immigrant enclaves of New York, where votes were secured with an equal dose of thuggery and welfare, it was this simple principle.

Two of Eliza's former employees—tour manager A.H. Gott and stagehand Frank Davis—later wrote of their experiences with Blind Tom and neither reserved a single generous word for Eliza. In fact, their adjective of choice was exactly the same: sharp. Sharp eyed and sharp tongued. Worse than lacking General Bethune's infectious charm or John's laid back good humor, she remained impervious to the wonder and delights of Tom's amazing mind. "Mrs. Bethune owned Tom to all intents and purposes," reflected Frank Davis and likened her affections for him to those one might have for "a huge devoted but witless dog." "In his worst paroxysm of childish rage a sharp word from her would keep him quiet. 'Keep still Tom,' she would cry, just as one may snap at a dog who was misbehaving. He would quiet instantly, with a docile 'Yes Ma'am. Tom's keeping still, yes ma'am.'"[12]

Eliza herself would not disagree with the characterization. "Tom is merely an overgrown child," *The New York Sun* learned from her.

Blind Tom in 1880.
A man proud of his
achievements who once threw
a chair at his manager for
publicly calling him an "idiot."

"He has all the selfishness of a spoilt child and is jealous of any attention paid to anyone else in his presence. He has little natural affection and cares for those who minister directly to his wants."

Eliza insisted that Tom was immensely happy in his isolation, finding sufficient companionship in his piano. If he desired company, he still had his menagerie of characters on tap—most recently a gaggle of imaginary women—with whom he could hold receptions and discuss "the weather, new styles in dresses and like topics."[13] However, the recollections of A.H. Gott and Frank Davis reveal a man hankering for validation from the outside world, while being taken for a fool.

He was always craving to hear praise of his work and I used to go into the room every morning and read the newspaper notices to him, [remembered A.H. Gott]. They were usually very flattering and Tom was always immensely pleased. One day, when there had not been much applause the evening before, Tom was in wretched humor. He did not know it, but the house had been pretty slim and the newspaper notices very commonplace. I felt sorry for the darky and made up my mind to read him a good notice anyway, making one up as I went along. It went something like this:

"Blind Tom stood before the immense and cultured audience in all of his magnificence, a very Hercules in stature. The enormous building was packed to the doors and outside was a seething, struggling, perspiring mob of people, begging for even standing room, but several thousand disappointed people were turned away unable even to get in earshot of this prince of pianists. Tom's playing held the people spellbound from start to finish; the audience hesitated even to applause, so rapt were the listeners of this great master of harmony . . ."

You never saw anybody so tickled as Tom was. He sat their rubbing his hands together, drinking in every word and grinning ecstatically. Bye and bye I heard Tom walking the floor and repeating the stuff that I had fed him word for word, and he never stopped until he had gone through it, and I don't believe he misplaced a syllable.

A.H. Gott's tale has a less jovial side. From the days of Perry Oliver, Tom would deliver the introductory speech in the showman's high-pitched voice, declaring himself as a member of the "lowest ranks of humanity," while audiences smirked. This elaborate joke was not just about Tom, its comic point inseparable from his racial identity—and under Eliza's guardianship it became one of the show's crowning moments:

Mr. Gibson, his lecturer, used to announce to audiences that Tom was an imbecile, [recalled Frank Davis]—a statement to which the Negro took no exception until some one in his presence used the term in a slighting manner. Whereupon, at the next concert, he hurled a chair at Gibson's head when the phrase was reached. Mr. Gibson being wise, thereupon, slightly changed his phraseology and ever thereafter said in a complimentary tone "Tom, as you can plainly see, is not only a great pianist, but distinctly non compos mentis." At which Tom would grin voraciously and perhaps tried to stand on his head.

This became one of the Negro's points of pride. "Tom is *non compos mentis*," he would say proudly, when introduced to a stranger. To the day of his death he never learned the meaning of the Latin phrase.

Professor J. Jay Watson observed that "Tom possessed an enormous bump of what phrenologists called 'self-esteem'" and certainly, he was proud of his achievements and not prepared to denigrate himself for the sake of a laugh. He came onto stage every night, not as a willing scapegoat but as a musician who genuinely believed he was the wonder of the world, the greatest musical marvel of the age. But no matter how delicate his musical touch or brilliant his execution, to audiences he was always something of a buffoon whose dignity had been sacrificed on the popular stage. What he accepted as praise, they interpreted as ridicule.

THE MUSIC OF MACHINES

Nine months after Tom's so-called emancipation, Charity was back in Columbus, living with her daughter's family in a two roomed shotgun house. Eliza insisted it was the old woman's decision to leave. Even though she had provided her with apparel, board and sleeping apartments, Charity left St. Mark's Place secretly early one April morning "without any previous intimation of her intention to do so, or any dissatisfaction other than frequent demands for money" which, by Eliza's own admission, totaled just over one hundred dollars.[14]

Eliza put Charity's discontentment down to a basic incompatibility with Tom, telling *The Musical Courier* that once the novelty of their reunion had worn away it was clear that their tastes and temperaments were "so utterly at variance that there was little likelihood of them living happily together." It was now Tom's wish to sever all contact with his kin "for fear they may annoy him or prevent him from being the sole object of attention." Of course, Eliza was canny enough to add that she would continue to provide for Tom's family—and to an extent she did, sending Charity the occasional fifteen dollars or so.[15]

This was a rare moment where Eliza and General Bethune were at one, the two camps gleefully reporting a paucity of feeling between mother and son. "Fourscore years of life had made her a withered up, irritable old woman, set in her ways and not at all reconciled to the fact that the baby for whom she had mourned for so many years had turned into a prematurely aged man, fixed in his habits and strangely lacking in the natural affections he should have for her," reported a New York newspaper. "His mother came to live with him. He did not know her, while she was petrified of his outlandish gibberish and strange behavior, believing him possessed," reiterated a Washington paper.[16] "His old mother visited him once while he was in the north. He did not recognize her though," agreed a Columbus paper. "He declared she was not his mother and took no interest in her."[17] By negating Charity's emotional claim on her son, both Eliza and Bethune could justify their custodial claims on Tom. He was happier with anyone else but her.

However, it beggars belief that after two decades and a single meeting, Tom recognized Professor Ide of Frederick, Mr. Stoddard of Baltimore and Mr. E.D. Gallion of Lynchburg, but failed to identify his own mother, his main caretaker for his first five years. Of course it is a fiction, Charity confirming that he instantly recognized her at a reunion in 1885.[18] There is no point in pretending he was especially close to her, but that is hardly surprising. During the custody battle, Bethune waged a misinformation campaign against Charity that Eliza was to continue. In 1898, Charity told a reporter from *The Atlanta Constitution* how "someone" was "trying to prejudice her son against her:"

> I have been back from the North six years, I was there nine years, and I tell you, I got mighty homesick. A lady persuaded me to go—for they wanted me to help them get Thomas into other hands. I didn't do much in New York. They kept me out in the country a while. I got mighty tired of it and if they hadn't sent me back, I would have almost gone crazy.
>
> I think that Thomas ought to send me more letters. They tried to turn him against me in New York. One day he said "Mother you must go." I said, "What put that in your head?" He said, "If you don't go we will make you go." He put his hands out as if to shove me out. I said, "Thomas, who has been telling you this?" He said the people have and afterwards he was ashamed for the way he acted.[19]

Never one to passively accept her fate, eighty-seven-year-old Charity fought Eliza's smear campaign as much as her slim resources would allow. In May of 1888, she mounted a legal challenge that called into question the $1,076.69 that Eliza claimed were her total earnings from exhibiting Blind Tom. Charity petitioned the New York Supreme Court to fully examine Eliza's finances, which included two lawsuits she had instigated—one against General Bethune, the other against the Harrodsburg racing stable—plus the various debtors who were suing her for non-payment (most significantly Attorney Daniel Holland, who had not received a cent). If it was found that Eliza Bethune was not a proper and suitable person to continue as Tom's guardian, if she was acting prejudicially to Tom's well being and personal comfort, then—Charity's petition demanded—she should be removed from her position and forfeit the $25,000 bond she had guaranteed to the Supreme Court.[20]

The implications for Eliza were catastrophic. A ruling in Charity's favor would not only bankrupt her, but seriously upset a number of powerfully connected people who helped her secure Tom. The previous year General Bethune alleged that "certain persons both known and unknown" were conspiring to obtain possession of Blind Tom for their own corrupt ends—and the way things were shaping up, he was not far from wrong.

In the New York County Records Office there is a bundle of crumbling yellowed legal documents filed "In the Matter of Thomas Wiggins, commonly called Blind Tom, an Idiot." Scattered through its three hundred or so pages the surname Dempsey appears in a number of guises. There is a four-page affidavit from a "Guy C. Dempsey" listing the twenty-three-year-old man's assets and willingness to guarantee Eliza's $25,000 bond, a petition from his brother "John Aird Dempsey" suing Eliza for the sum of $523 and a court record acknowledging the receipt of affidavits from both Dempsey brothers attesting to Eliza's good character.

So who exactly were the Dempseys? From what I can ascertain, they were a New Jersey family of Irish extraction whose fortunes took a dramatic turn for the better in 1864 when their father, Dr. John Dempsey, joined a consortium of businessmen that won the franchise to lay railroad tracks from Houston Street to Avenue C. This bid was successful for one reason only: "Boss" Tweed— Tammany Hall's leader and New York's most corrupt politician— had been invited to join the board and take his slice of the action.

By the 1880's, Dr. Dempsey's adult children were part of New York's social set. Daughter Lavinia—whom the *New York Times* had caustically dubbed "Queen Lavinia of the Holland Dames" after she crowned herself such at an extravagant fancy dress ball at the Waldorf—staged royal parades, awash with pomp and pageantry, through the immigrant enclaves of the Lower East Side in aid of a children's charity she patronized.[21] Beside her on many an occasion was brother "Sir Knight" Guy Dempsey who, for all his aristocratic pretensions, continued to maintain strong links with the working class political faction to whom the family owed their wealth—Tammany Hall. Perhaps it was through Guy Dempsey's involvement with the socially minded Hickory Club, a wing of Tammany headed by Michael C. Murphy, the current health and future police commissioner, that he met Albrecht Lerche, a member of the twenty-fourth assembly district.

Guy Dempsey enjoyed all the benefits that came with being a Tammany Man. In 1900, after two decades of the high life, he was declared bankrupt, but with a little help from his friends, he was soon appointed Deputy Tax Commissioner in Brooklyn's Borough of Richmond. There his wealth was quickly restored, despite (or perhaps because of) a history of procedural irregularities.

To this résumé, Guy Dempsey could add bond surety to Blind Tom's guardian, a favor he bestowed in 1886. Shortly after lending Eliza his considerable financial clout, Dempsey asked a favor of her. Would she employ his brother John as the advance agent for Blind Tom's exhibitions? Even though he had no experience in show business, Eliza agreed (did she have a choice?). Very quickly it became apparent that brother John had no intention of working for his $28 per week, seeing it more as an opportunity to rack up expenses—$523 in the first ten weeks. The stunt was styled on a tactic widely used by the city's politicians to grease their palms—a contractor submitting a grossly inflated bill to the city, then kicking the difference back to the politician in cash. Eliza, perhaps naive to the terms and conditions that implicitly came with Guy Dempsey's guarantee, sacked his brother and refused to pay the bill. In no time she learned the error of her ways. During a concert at Lakewood, New Jersey, she was served papers by a man acting as John Dempsey's solicitor but who, in fact, was a con man wanted for larceny. Despite Carlton H. Betts's lack of legal training, he was canny enough to ensure that until the matter was resolved, Eliza could not exhibit Blind Tom.

In the midst of this saga, Charity mounted her legal challenge. Suddenly the disputed $523 paled in comparison to the $25,000 now at stake. United under fire, the Dempsey family put Eliza in contact with a lawyer and politician by the name of George H. Foster to ward off the attack. A man forged by big city politics, Foster had both contacts and clout. A one-time Republican reformer, he jumped ship to Tammany Hall and, in no time, was elected President of the Board of Aldermen. This committee, initially created to cap the outrageous abuses of Boss Tweed, was now a vehicle to drive Tammany's agenda. Police pay raises, the licensing of street stands, the electrification of the 4th Avenue horse car line all required the blessing of the Board in general and President Foster in particular. Even a concert at Irving Hall (where Blind Tom had often played) risked strike action unless the Board received their comps. "Mr. Foster seems to be a man dis-

Charity Wiggins at the age of 99 outside her daughter's cottage in Columbus.

posed to magnify his office and overrate the importance of the body over which he presides," scorned *The New York Times* the same month he represented Eliza in court. "The majority of the [present Board of Aldermen] are of such a character that the public interests are the very last thing they think or care about. What they desire to promote is the opportunity for jobbery and what they wish to protect is the power and influence of pothouse politicians."[22]

Tammany Hall had its fingers in just about every pie. A faction of the Democratic Party who claimed to champion the voice of the immigrants and impoverished, it was a well-oiled political machine that demanded and received unwavering obedience from boardroom to street. In poorer neighborhoods like Eliza's, district leaders—Mafia-styled fixers—attended to local grievances: securing jobs, paying rents arrears, putting up bail and, on election day, hiring carriages to take the lame, sick and blind to vote. "It's philanthropy, but it's politics, too—mighty good politics," recalled one Tammany apparatchik. "The poor are the most grateful people in the world and, let me tell you, they have more friends in the neighborhood than the rich have in theirs." After delivering the votes that cinched the election victory, the mayor could expect a list of city appointments from the Tammany boss and, from here, the appointees could begin to capitalize on the grand opportunities that came their way, skimming the cream from almost every phase of New York life.[23] It was this machine that the illiterate, eighty-seven-year-old former slave was now up against. The case had all the makings of a David and Goliath struggle—but this was Gotham, and here Goliaths were guaranteed to win.

On July 15, 1888, Supreme Court Justice George P. Andrews (who was indebted to Tammany Hall for his nomination) and Justice A.R. Lawrence (a County Democrat, who depended on Tammany's support to further his political ambitions) considered the petition of Charity Wiggins. And then they considered the affidavits submitted by George Foster—statements from Guy C. Dempsey, John A. Dempsey and con man Carlton H. Betts, all of whom vouched for Eliza's good character. After due consideration, the judges ruled in Eliza's favor. Charity's application was denied and the $25,000 was safe.[24] The President of the Board of Aldermen was one lawyer Eliza would never forget to pay.

Impoverished by this single legal effort, Charity returned to Columbus, bitter but wiser in the ways of the Yankee world. Certainly there had been some highlights. The months she traveled with Blind Tom "was as near heaven as she will ever get this side of the real heaven" but mostly she felt duped, abused and manipulated. "They stole him from me," she told a Columbus reporter "When I was in New York I signed away my rights. They won't let Thomas come to see me and I am not allowed to see him."[25]

And she never did, even in 1901 when Tom, *en route* to Montgomery, stopped off in Columbus for a few hours. His nephews and nieces were invited to spend time with him, Tom entertaining them by "jumping around like a Juney bug" and strumming an old tin pan, but Charity was not made welcome.[26] A photograph captures her outside her daughter's cottage in Columbus, composed in a plain cotton dress, scarf wrapped around her head, a gentleness in her eyes belying the trouble in her heart. She died the following year at the age of one hundred, proud of her son to the end, a genius who had "yet to be produced by the entire white race."[27]

Netherworld

ON THE NIGHT OF MAY 30, 1889, BLIND TOM PLAYED HIS REGULAR show at the Bijou Theater in Penn Street, Pittsburgh to a slim house, most people kept away by yet another day of torrential rain (which, unbeknownst to everyone, was mixing with the thick blanket of pollution that permanently hung over the city to create an early example of acid rain). Friday morning, the downpour had not abated and Tom, Eliza and their latest manager, James Marvin, battled their way to Union Street Railway Depot and boarded the 12:05 train for the iron and steel town of Johnstown where Tom was billed to play that night.[1]

Two hundred miles east, Southfork Dam—a recreational lake owned by Pittsburgh's wealthiest industrial magnates—was feeling the brunt of a maintenance problem its owners had elected to ignore. A pear-shaped bulge in the dam's spillway hung out over the narrow Conemaugh valley as it strained to contain the waters of a four-hundred-acre lake that was full to capacity and rising. Jets of water punched through the mud and boulder wall; the overflow topped the rim, taking with it huge lumps of masonry. The dam wall was disintegrating before the engineers' helpless eyes.

A deafening roar ripped the air. Like twin gates, the spillway split open, unleashing an uncontrollable torrent of water, twenty million tons strong. The deluge struck the farmlands below like a hammer. Villages were smashed to fragments in the blink of an eye: houses and barns were crushed like eggshells; twenty ton locomotives were flung from their tracks, tossed skyward, sucked back and belched out in bits. The avalanche of death hurtled towards the center of Johnstown at a mile a minute.

The wave descended on the town, ripping iron structures from their foundations, detonating foundries on impact, unstoppable until it ran smack into a stone viaduct flanked by two steep hills, one hundred thousand tons of mangled wreckage slamming in behind it. Trapped, the floodwater sucked back into town, collided onto itself and spiraled into a violent whirlpool that ground the center of Johnstown into oblivion, a giant millstone pulverizing every house, theater, shop, court-house, street car, gas light and pavement to nothing. The flotsam and jetsam then exploded into flames and burnt throughout the night. Thus the lives of 2,209 people were washed away.[2]

The Columbus Enquirer Sun reported: "From all indications it is more than probable that we have seen and heard Blind Tom, the famous Negro Pianist, for the last time. His body and that of his manager is believed to be among the thousands of unidentified dead in the ill-fated valley of Johnstown and being strangers, and more-over one of them being a colored man, it is likely their bodies were buried with the rest of the nameless dead."[3]

But it was all a case of mistaken identity. Blind Tom was still very much alive and his management made some efforts to counter the reports. "Tom's attorney, Albrecht J. Lerche, accompanied the party to Freeport, Pennsylvania where they gave a performance at the Grand Opera House on Friday evening," relayed *The Washington Post*. "He was to have played at the Johnstown Opera House the next night. After Friday's performance at Freeport they intended tak-ing a train for Altoona but hearing of the disaster took the Erie rail-road, which brought them to Jamestown, where an engagement was filled last Monday."[4]

But the message failed to get through. In Johnstown, a small marble tablet bearing the date and the fact of Tom's death was laid at the site of the mass grave. For the next two decades, no one was exactly sure if Blind Tom was dead or alive.[5] It was a situation that rather suited his guardian, who, under the welter of lawsuits and depositions from an increasingly irate Daniel Holland, preferred to simply disappear. "7 St. Marks Place had been abandoned by Eliza Bethune," the beleaguered attorney complained to the court, "she has since had no office or place of residence therein and plaintiff charges that her absence is with a view and intent to evade the orders of this court."[6]

THE ORIGINAL BLIND TOM

"Please inform me whether Blind Tom is still alive and, if so, does he perform in public?" one reader asked *The Chicago Tribune* in 1890. There were plenty answers, but no two were the same. Yes, he was dead. No, he was in retirement or dying in a New York asylum or had just played in Michigan or was living in poverty, broken in health, dangerously insane and under restraint, or traveling and performing with all his old vigor or was being shunted from one grasping attorney to another.[7]

In fact, Blind Tom was in one of three places: touring the far-flung regions of Canada and America, holed up in an apartment on East 22nd Street, or passing summers under lock and key with Eliza and her new husband at their country retreat in the Navesink Highlands of New Jersey. (Yes indeed: Albrecht Lerche secretly married Eliza in 1890.)

In all but one of the seven years following the Johnstown Flood, Tom spent six to nine months on the road playing the large and small towns of Michigan, Minnesota, Illinois, Iowa, Ohio, Indiana, Kansas, Louisiana, Mississippi, Tennessee, Alabama, North Carolina, South Carolina, Kentucky, New Jersey, Ontario, Pennsylvania, Colorado, Maryland, Nebraska, Utah, Washington, Oregon, California, Texas and Arkansas.[8]

When the show rolled into town, the first reaction almost always was the same: suspicion. This was not the real Blind Tom—he was dead. This must be an impostor. To fill the near empty halls, his management began offering a thousand dollars—no, make it five thousand dollars—to anyone who could prove that he was not the original Blind Tom. And as soon as Tom began to wow the curious with his imitations of trains, banjos and bagpipes, members of the older generation could gladly confirm that he was indeed the legendary Blind Tom—although a legend now well past his prime.

Blind Tom's historical performance at Steinway Hall and meeting with Josef Hofmann masked something that, by now, was painfully obvious to Eliza. Blind Tom's show business currency was slipping and had been for years. His scaled down stage antics and worn out repertoire no longer dazzled sophisticated Gilded Age audiences hooked on two steps, cakewalks and coon songs. In the march of progress, Blind Tom had been left behind, a solitary, isolated figure who knew nothing of the marvels on display at the 1893 Chicago World's Fair— Beaux Arts elegance, electrical gadgetry, Ferris wheels, hamburgers, soda pop and ragtime (at least in the saloons and sporting houses surrounding the site). Although African-American culture had been largely excluded from the official program, black musicians descended on Chicago in their droves, among them a twenty-five-year-old pianist named Scott Joplin. Five years on Joplin's *Maple Leaf Rag* would electrify the country, its upbeat, jaggedy sound capturing the mood of the cranked-up, chaotic times. Meanwhile Tom seemed to wallow in sentiment, a relic of bygone era. "*Delta Kappa Epsilon March* was in vogue before the days of Sousa," scorned a critic of Blind Tom's selection;[9] *The Maiden's Prayer* was an "old threadbare thing which was the proud ambition of our mothers to play at their graduation exercises" said another.[10]

Why Eliza did not overhaul Blind Tom's repertoire is unclear. He voiced no objections to the newfangled sounds and technology of the electric age. On the contrary, he was fascinated. "One of Tom's most exciting recent experiences was his first encounter in *The North American* reading room with a gramophone and large musical box known as the *Regina*," reported the magazine of fifty-two-year-old Tom. "The latter particularly reduced him almost to a delirium of ecstasy. He sat close to it and insisted on hearing its entire repertoire and astonished his manager and audience by playing some selections at his next concert. Blind Tom rattling off the latest popular march, Blind Tom playing *Florodora* was a novelty."[11] Edison's telephone and Marconi's wireless must also have been greeted with a musical reply from Tom, but there would be other more unpredictable ones too: a flourish inspired by the onomatopoeiaic zipper perhaps, the ding-a-ding of a cash register or the typewriter's clack.

One phenomenon that did not pass by Tom was Ignacy Paderewski. More than just the latest bravura pianist from Europe to take the country by storm, he was the biggest attraction New York had ever seen. Ladies adored him and Tom, too, was a fan, incorporating *Chant d'Amour* into his repertoire and naming his dog after the Polish star. Tom seems to have been amongst the tens of thousands who flocked to his show but was "so affected" he had to be removed from the hall before the concert was over. If it only took a street band for Tom to break into a peculiar dance that seemed to bring "every nerve into action," the poetic intensity of Paderewski's performance must have had him bouncing along the aisles. Despite this admiration, the two never met—unsurprising considering that Paderewski was something of a lion and Tom, a dinosaur. While Paderewski's three American tours generated close to half a million dollars, Eliza was forced to trawl the continent with Blind Tom year in, year out, charging fifty and seventy-five cents a ticket—the same price the Bethunes were asking thirty-three years earlier.[12]

The concert had now been pared back and Tom delivered what was virtually a one-man show. "There was something of deep pathos in the scene the poor blind Negro presented on stage last night," wrote *The Nashville American* in 1892. "No one accompanied before the curtain. He walked about the stage and spoke in words and accents about Blind Tom just as his old manager did. He explained what Tom was going to do each time and then proceeded to do it."[13] Previous managers had gratified his urge to usurp the showman's role by giving him the opening speech and the introduction to *The Battle of Manassas*. Now he presented the show from beginning to end, taking on the voice, mannerisms and stage patter of one—if not all—of his previous managers. Whether this was a concession to Tom's demands, or an effort by Eliza to play up his oddness, or just a way to save money, it certainly was cause for much bewildered comment. Now as he jumped to his feet and applauded himself, he would explain to the audience "that it was just a part of his imitative ways and trusted that it gave no one offence."[14] During the spelling challenge in Toronto, someone gave him the word "Nordheimer." He paused and in a moment of "ruffled dignity, gravely and reproachfully said that he must be given legitimate words." Even in interviews after the show, he maintained the showman's solemnity, one time praising the citizens of Galveston for "nobly supporting him" and saying that he was certain "they appreciated and understood the highest attainments of classical music." And, of course, no show would pass without Tom proudly declaring that he was "not only a great pianist, but distinctly *non compos mentis*."[15]

"He is a human phonograph, a sort of animated memory, with sound producing power," concluded Willa Cather in the *Nebraska State Journal*. "It was a strange sight to see him walk out on stage with his own lips—another man's words—introduce himself and talk quietly about his own idiocy. There was an insanity, a grotesque horribleness about it that was interestingly unpleasant. One laughs at the man's queer actions, and yet, after all, the sight is not laughable. It brings us too near to the things that we sane people do not like to think of."

While Tom confounded them on stage, Eliza sat by the doorkeeper, keeping her sharp eye on every cent.[16] It was no accident that the grueling tour schedule omitted Georgia, Virginia and New York City: three places where she and Tom were sure to encounter those dreaded "lawyers." But despite every precaution, some of them managed to beat their way to her door. In Louisville, the receipts of four concerts were seized to pay an attorney whom she had appointed many years earlier to investigate the liquidity of the Harrodsburg racing stable (it was bankrupt). In 1893 the still unresolved claim by Daniel Holland damn near hounded them off the road, while later one of Lerche's former legal partners—more fixated on avenging their treachery than recouping his legal fees—tracked her down in Oklahoma Territory.[17] But for Eliza the real challenge was the monotony: traveling vast distances in slow moving trains, adhering to Tom's strict mealtime schedule in a town where every kitchen was closed, and keeping a zealous watch over him lest some "lawyer" turn up with a claim on him. But there was light at the end of the tunnel: every concert was taking her one step closer to her dream.

THE MYSTERY OF NAVESINK

NEW YORK, JANUARY 3, 1894. Blind Tom, who for more than three years has been supposed to be dead, is an unwilling prisoner in an East Side tenement. No one is ever admitted to the prison, not even the grocery boy. His basket is placed outside the rear door of the apartment and the grocery boy goes away. Then the door is opened, either by the former Mrs. Bethune or by A.J. Lerche her husband, who stealthily emerges and, hastily snatching up the articles, disappears inside. The mysterious conduct of the couple is the talk of the neighborhood.

As to the furnishings of Blind Tom's apartments, little is known, as no stranger is ever admitted. There is a piano, upon which Tom is heard playing at all hours of the day. The neighbors have never guessed the identity of the pianist. Whenever Tom plays, the tenants crowd into the hallways and listen with rapt attention. Sometimes he sings, and his voice blends splendidly with the piano's notes. A dozen attempts to gain access to the rooms have been without success. Repeated knockings at the door were of no avail although it was known Mrs. Lerche was inside.[18]

This *Atlanta Constitution* exclusive is not the fruit of an intrepid reporter's investigation, but the work of a private detective hired by Irene Ackerman, executrix of the estate of Attorney Daniel Holland, the now-deceased legal brains behind Blind Tom's "emancipation." For six years now, Eliza had been evading a court order to pay Ackerman $3,304.75,[19] swearing she had earned nothing from exhibiting Blind Tom. Ackerman could now prove that the Lerches had purchased 123 acres of woodland property at Navesink Highlands for the sum of $33,000, and she was petitioning for Eliza to be charged with contempt.

Although Ackerman's allegations were true, the Supreme Court Judge (who just so happened to be a loyal friend of Tammany's head honcho, Richard Croker) ruled in Eliza's favor. "Eliza Bethune has, at her own expense and risk, given concerts at which the said idiot assisted, playing upon the piano musical selections so heard by him," was Judge Traux's take on the situation.[20] However, a combination of lost revenue and bad press finally persuaded Eliza to settle with Irene Ackerman. She, above all, understood the value of appearances, dishing up a sugar-coated treat to a reporter from *The Ladies Home Journal* when he visited their Navesink home:

> One of Tom's greatest pleasure is his daily bath in the Shrewsbury River. In the warm weather when the tide is favorable, he dons his bathing suit, walks down to the shore from the house and ducks and paddles about and splashes in the water. He can take a few strokes but labors under the pleasing illusion he is a long distance swimmer. He became a favorite with the children who sometimes lead him to the water and watch him bathe. At first he did not take kindly to this agreeable diversion . . . but has come to be very fond of his bath, enjoying it hugely.[21]

Without doubt, the Lerches's rambling country home in the wilds of Navesink gave Tom a taste of nature he had not savored since Warrenton: a forest-clad headland flanked by Sandy Hook Bay on one side, and the Shrewsbury River on the other, the seasons rising and fading in leaf, blossom and bird.[22] And everywhere—wrote a *Harpers* reporter—"the eternal waves, the everlasting hills and all over, a dreadful silence, broken only by the faint beating of the distant surf and the ripple of the nearby river."[23]

As long as there was music in the air—the rhythmic chant of the waves, seagulls circling the fishing boats as they lolled at the mouth of the Shrewsbury each night, the distant rousing strains of Bellevue Resort's famous brass band—time weighed nothing at all. "He sits in the open and mimics bird and beast," Lerche told a reporter.[24] Absorbed in the eternal now, Tom had nothing else to desire and, just as the thunder spoke to him in Georgia, so the ocean spoke to him here. "His best [composition] was a piece entitled *What the Wind and the Waves Told Tom* in which he imitates the whistle of the wind, roar of the waves, howl of the storm and crash of the thunder," reported *The New York Sun*[25]—a piece that possibly evolved into *Water in the Moonlight*. Published in 1894 under his own name, it is a powerfully visual title for a blind man to choose. Perhaps the "second sighted" Tom had taken delight in the same exquisite image enjoyed by a travel writer a few years earlier. "We sat on the sands and saw the moon rising, orbed like the sun, large, round and ruddy, from the eastern sea, drawing a second moon out from the deep; and lo', a thousand little waves ran out to meet her, lifting silver crests to greet her."[26]

No matter how great the majesty of nature, nothing could divest the Lerches of their deep-rooted paranoia. The story of the children flocking around Tom as he bathed in the Shrewsbury is at odds with the experiences of a reporter from *The Philadelphia Sunday Press* named Harry-Dele Hallmark.

Queer stories have been brought to the cities by the Highlanders, awesome tales of a crazy Negro who lives in a hermitage. He frightens the children into crying and the older people into running. They say that at evening time in the lonely woods one would come upon a man who would suddenly fling both hands into the air, making weird sounds with his lips, rolling his great eyes around in an appalling manner. The boy who waves a flag at the railroad curve along the shore tells of this same Negro appearing on the little platform to take the train. Swede and Italian laborers were loafing around the platform when the queer black man suddenly jumped into the air and applauded wildly, bowing and crying "Bravo! Bravo!"

To shriek and run seems to have been all the Highlanders did . . . and the slogan of the old plantation hands that "somebody's hoodooed" seems to be gaining ground in the Highlands of Navesink. Such were the rumors.

In November of 1897, Hallmark decided to unravel the "mystery of Navesink" and, after a long train journey in the driving rain with multiple connections on "other side of town stations," the somewhat pompous, even camp, reporter rolled up to Navesink's "desolate surf beaten wooden promontory" thinking the worst was behind him. But the day's great challenges had only begun. Stranded at the train station, he struggled to find anyone prepared to drive him to the Lerches's fortress home in the highland woods. But "the Frenchman and his wife"—as the couple were known—were held in such terror "that even persuasion by coin of the realm couldn't reason the butcher into driving me to the house in his wagon."

Eventually Hallmark persuaded a young man with a raw boned horse to take him there and as they traveled through the woods, the young man eagerly relayed one creepy tale after another. The Lerches had purchased the adjoining boat club to prevent access by sea—he told him—while the woods around the house had been allowed to grow tangled and disordered. "Ten small dogs were constituted as a staff of militia; one especial, venomous, yellow mongrel told to watch approach by land and water." Hallmark felt his bravado fade with each new tale. "The queer part of it is that one somehow catches the spirit of the villagers and for the life of you, the approach to the house is uncanny."

Despite his misgivings Hallmark soldiered on, his driver making a detour to the uninhabited end of the house to avoid the dogs. But the strategy failed and Hallmark was besieged by the canine militia, who barked and snapped at his heels. Not far behind came "a personage in a workman's suit of blue homespun," who roared at him and ordered him to remain where he was. "We could hear bolts being slid and saw windows shut and waited—the raw boned horse, the eager young man and I."

Once Hallmark established who he was—a reporter from a major newspaper—Albrecht Lerche turned out to be "extremely affable" and, although he did not invite him into the house, was happy to answer any questions about the legendary Blind Tom. He drew Hallmark a charming picture of Tom's life in Navesink—a world filled with imaginary characters and moments of glory relived time and again. "The piano in the hallway is his resting place for hours, and for years he has lived his public life over in daily private rehearsals: he makes his bow, goes to the instrument, plays the old tunes, and jumping up

Tom with his dog Paderewski in the garden at Navesink Heights.

bows and applauds and bravos heartily. In the pleasant weather he tires of the piano and sitting in the grounds, plays an imaginary pianoforte in the air, imitating perfectly the sounds, then bows his thanks to the birds and dogs." Hallmark expressed his desire to meet with the legendary performer but Lerche shook his head—Blind Tom was away right now, he regretfully told him, and so was his wife.

Hallmark left the meeting in triumph. "I had chased the hoodoo, decided a mystery, answered a public question. I had met the enemy and he was mine. I had squarely cornered him and interviewed him. I learnt all there was to learn. I was laudable self-congratulatory. The eager boy listened. 'But you didn't see Blind Tom,' he said. 'But I told you he wasn't there,' I replied. And the eager boy answered, 'That's where you got left. He was peeping out of a bolted window upstairs.'"

Hallmark underestimated Lerche just as General Bethune had many years earlier. The secretive German had come a long way since his days as a factory worker and this was perhaps one reason why: urbane, smooth-tongued Americans did not take the ambitions of a heavily accented, working class man that seriously. But he, more than they, understood the machinations of power and had forged the connections and worked the system so that now he was the country gent (albeit in a blue workman's suit) while the Bethunes traded on passed glories.

But time would soon render his earthly achievements inconsequential. Five years after his meeting with Hallmark, Albrecht Lerche was dead, leaving his widow to take care of the aging "idiot" to whom she was legally bound—the $25,000 bond that Guy Dempsey had guaranteed the court perhaps the only thing saving Tom from desititution. Whether she liked it or not, Eliza had little choice but to keep her nose down and attend to the needs of the man once heralded as "The Most Marvelous Musical Genius Living" while he performed, cheered and bowed to an empty room.

Thunderstorm Requiem

As the owner and manager of the Orpheum—the largest chain of vaudeville theaters in the country—Percy G. Williams had his work cut out for him. Every Monday he needed to find a showstopping headline act, two other performers of a little less celebrity plus a motley assortment of comedians, animal acts, magicians, contortionists, singers, musicians and actors to outshine his many rivals.

It was a crowded marketplace. Vaudeville was to the Gilded Age generation what the minstrel show had been to their grandparents—the bedrock of popular entertainment. With the gradual demise of minstrelsy, white comics dropped the blackface and, turning to the immigrant enclaves for inspiration, gave voice to the next generation of one-dimensional ethnic stereotypes: the sharp-witted Jew, the song-loving Italian, the opium-smoking Chinese and the drunken Irishman. Topical these variety acts may have been, respectable they were not, the comics often performing alongside scantily clad showgirls in theaters where alcohol flowed and prostitutes worked the upper balconies. It was only when a New York impresario moved to an uptown theater in the late 80's, his eye on the ladies who flocked to the department stores of nearby Broadway, that the show was given a makeover. Variety was re-christened "variety" and grew up to be the classy, respectable, clean-as-a-whistle double of its rough edged, downtown twin.

Within a decade, vaudeville was an industry every bit as mechanized as any assembly line. The three kings of vaudeville—Percy G.

Williams, B.F. Keith and E.F. Albee—offered non-stop family enter-tainment for twelve hours a day in theaters that matched the Imperial or Savoy for luxury. For twenty-five cents, these sumptuous vaude-ville palaces enabled working folk living in filthy streets and crowded tenements to be royalty for a day.

For the theater owners, there was no escaping reality. With the boom in vaudeville, entertainers' fees had skyrocketed and the search for new star-studded attractions was relentless. To stay on top, Percy Williams had agents scouring the theaters of Europe with a fine-tooth comb and personally oversaw the engagement of all headline acts.[1]

In late 1903 he made an exception to this rule. A vaudevillian of some standing mentioned to Williams that he knew Blind Tom to be alive—he had just seen him in Navesink Heights. At the mere men-tion of his name, Williams knew this was exactly the type of star he had been looking for: a household name who had mysteriously vanished from sight and an act respectable enough to lure an older audience to his theaters for the first time. Warm fuzzy nostalgia, a nod to high culture, a good few belly laughs and a jumble of perplexing, unanswerable questions—Blind Tom was perfect. Immediately the entrepreneur sent an agent to New Jersey to secure the fifty-five-year-old pianist as the headline act for next week's show.

It was an arrangement that ideally suited the recently widowed Eliza Lerche. No other branch of entertainment was as flush with money as vaudeville—feature acts could earn anywhere between $800 and $3,000 a week. It took up to twenty-two weeks to complete the circuits of the three vaudeville giants while the United Booking Office (very kindly waiving their White Only policy) could keep Blind Tom working in another hundred houses. As the adage ran: in vaudeville, if you had seventeen good minutes, you had seventeen good years.

In December 1903, Blind Tom headlined the show at Brooklyn's Orpheum Theater, presenting an abridged mix of light classics, imi-tations, novelties and confoundingly odd behavior. Audiences were large, tantalized by a publicity campaign that proved that while Percy Williams was a man of the future—tailoring popular entertain-ment to suit the fast paced world of urban, multi-ethnic audiences—he was not lacking a good dose of the old-fashioned Barnumesque.

Employing a bombast not heard since the days of Perry Oliver, Williams told readers of a Brooklyn tabloid that "all the mysteries of the keyboard are his own to learn, not by science, for he has never been

The Orpheum's lineup for December 1903.

taught."[2] Tom's post-flood mystery years became even more mysterious. "Blind Tom has been killed in the Johnstown Flood, he has died of consumption and his brain has been analyzed by an eminent doctor for a Manhattan 'newspaper.' Once he fell down an elevator, several times he has lost his life in train wrecks and on one occasion he leapt from the Eads Bridge at St. Louis. But despite these numerous tragedies, Blind Tom is still alive."[3]

A letter to the editor, with an address that later proved to be a vacant lot, charged Percy Williams with charlatanism ("I know for a positive fact that the original Blind Tom was a victim of the Johnstown Flood. I was one of a party of rescuers who identified Blind Tom and as such he was buried. The inscription on his tombstone in the Johnstown Cemetery will prove this.") Thus providing Williams with the opportunity of offering $1,000 to anyone who could prove that his Blind Tom was not the real one.[4]

Once the initial flurry of his comeback died down, Tom became a cog in the vaudeville machine, touring first the Orpheum circuit, then the Keith, both tours crossing the continent. Thomas Warhurst's daughter visited him after one of these shows and the two talked of old friends, after which she concluded Tom "seemed happier than he had been for a long time."[5]

Also working the Orpheum circuit around this time, was an up-and-coming magician and escapologist by the name of Harry Houdini whose contempt for self-proclaimed psychics and mediums would only deepen with age. After scrutinizing Blind Tom's novelty acts, he recognized the fingerprints of The Great Houdin (whom he had also in honored in his name) and believed he could explain the source of Tom's mysterious powers. Spiritualists had long contended that Tom was in communication with spirits and channeling higher powers—claims that deeply irritated Houdini. So when he published his tirade against the supernatural in 1924, *A Magician Among the Spirits,* Blind Tom inevitably came in for some flak and Houdini denounced Tom's inexplicable powers of "second sight" as "psychic fraud."[6] Though their names are now linked by controversy, in 1905 Tom was unaware of Houdini's scrutiny and gave him no more thought than he would any other vaudevillian—if he indeed ever heard his name at all.

A year into his vaudeville career, Tom's health began to deteriorate. In December 1904, *The Chicago Tribune* announced a last minute change to the lineup at Hyde and Behman's. Actress Jessie Millward would replace Blind Tom as the headline act, as the star had been "stricken with paralysis."[7] A stroke, perhaps? Over the next year his appearances were few and far between and by late 1905—after a career spanning forty years—Tom disappeared from public view for good.

"ALL GONE MISSUS"

June 14, 1908. Three weeks ago, as Blind Tom sat before his piano, he suddenly fell and dropped face downwards on the floor. Mrs. Lerche who had cared for him for over twenty years, ran in the room and helping him up, found that his whole right side was paralyzed. But Tom couldn't understand that he was different and soon went back to his piano. When he found that his right hand could not strike the keys he said with his voice quavering "Tom's fingers won't play."

Again and again he tried. Finally when he realized it was useless, his big blind eyes filled with tears and he wept like a child. Each day he returned to the piano and started some favorite piece. Discords came quickly however and then, with tear-moistened cheek, he would rise and pace the floor until late into the night. His old mistress sought to comfort him but he would only sob out, "Tom's fingers won't play no mo."

Last Saturday night Tom went to his piano and began softly his old lullaby Down by the Suwannee River but his voice broke. Sobbing he rose and said "I'm done; all gone missus." The next she heard was a faint cry and a thump near the bathroom door. He dropped dead from a second shock. Dr. Charles Gilchrist was summoned but he said that his services were too late.[8]

Is this a scene from a vaudeville melodrama or a reliable account of Blind Tom's last days? However one reads it, Eliza's version of events is the only one available for the simple fact that she was virtually the only person who saw him. Cloistered away in a tenement on 12th Street in Hoboken, New Jersey, the fifty other families in the block knew of him only by rumor and conjecture. In the five years she had lived there, Eliza never put her name on the doorplate, had removed the electric doorbell and refused to answer the door. Nobody was allowed inside except for a young man who, more than likely, was one of Eliza's nephews, Anton or Otto Ess.

One tenant had briefly glimpsed Blind Tom as Eliza led him to a closed carriage when they left for their Navesink summer home.

Another spotted a veiled man entering the building and assumed Tom was disfigured. On several occasions the janitor, attending to a matter in the apartment, heard him moving around the bedroom. But it was the piano music that finally convinced the tenants that their mysterious neighbor was truly the great Blind Tom. Up until two months before his death, they were accustomed to hearing exquisite piano music at all hours of the day and night. Then it stopped. By this estimation, eight weeks must have passed between Tom's first stroke and the mortal one.[9]

With the announcement of Blind Tom's death came the glare of media scrutiny. A flock of reporters hovered outside the tenement as the body was taken to Campbell's Undertakers. Eliza's physician informed the press pack that after the service, Tom's own funeral march would be played on the chapel organ. "This composition is said to be of uncommon merit, a passage of a great deal of sonority is immediately followed by a passage of such lightness and gaiety that the effect produced is one of pathos," enthused a *New York Times* reporter who knew enough about Blind Tom to wonder if it was the same piece he played at John Bethune's funeral a number of years ago.[10] *The Ladies Home Journal* had first mentioned this alleged funeral requiem in an article written fifteen years after John's death; but no one else has ever referred to its existence. However, the description of the piece does match the Washington lady's description of *What the Stars Told Tom*—"after a prelude of most exquisite chords, he suddenly burst into such brilliant, such wildly gay, at one moment, and at the next such heartbreaking melodies as never heard below the stars."

On the afternoon of June 16, in an undertaker's chapel on Hoboken's 23rd Street, twenty-five people—including reporters from *The New York Herald, Times, World* and *Sun*—filed past Tom's open coffin. The Reverend G.W. Downs of the 18th Street Methodist Church read a brief service, three modest wreaths were laid and *Nearer My God to Thee* then struck up on the chapel's organ.[11] But where was the funeral march, wondered the *Times* reporter, where was the tribute to Tom's musical genius? Was the great marvel of the nineteenth century to be honored with nothing more than the "wheezing notes of a time-worn melodeon"?

Although the identity of the *Times* reporter is unknown, his disappointment is clear. He had seen Blind Tom in concert often enough to appreciate the mark that the blind pianist had made on the collective imagination. No other performer in nineteenth century America had aroused as much curiosity. Routinely compared with monsters and maestros, gorgons and angels, spirits and beasts, Tom seemed to embody two irreconcilable opposites—within him two beings, disconnected and polarized, were vying for power.

However, many members of the public also sensed that Tom was powerfully connected. When Mark Twain first encountered Tom on a train in 1868, he saw a man not just echoing the train but howling along in unison. So absolute was his absorption in it, the boundary where Tom ended and the locomotive began was indistinguishable. He was the train. In the same way, he was the storm, the machine, the maelstrom of battle.

Other eyewitnesses believed the connection went even deeper than this. After the Washington lady watched him dance under the night sky, then listened to him play what the stars had told him, she felt "as though his genius had found its way back to the Creator— as if the liberated soul on wing to heaven carried the enrapt and wandering senses into the presence of God's 'choir invisible.'" "His love of melody seems to ravish his entire being," echoed a white Southern critic, "and his soul seems to be in ecstasy of the Heaven-born concert of sweet sounds."[12] Preacher James Curruthers agreed, opining that if we all saw the things revealed to Blind Tom, then "creed and color, tongue and clime/ Would melt away like morning rime."

Was it possible—as these eyewitnesses are suggesting—that through music and sound, Tom was able to experience the underlying unity of all things? Did his savant powers exempt him from the dualistic mode of perception—the state of mind that separates subject from object and prevents us from recognizing the "I" in the "other"? Did his deep empathy for music allow him to return to a Garden of Eden—so to speak—to a time before The Fall where, blind to his own nakedness, he could revel in the state of grace?

"The name Blind Tom is a sort of myth to us all," summed up one lady.[13] "Our age has not produced an equal," a critic agreed.[14] As audiences struggled to reconcile his many aspects, they instinctively began to ponder what it is to be human and wonder at the mystery of life. They came to acknowledge that the source of Tom's inspiration, the fury of his passion lay somewhere outside the limits of their perception, in the bigger picture, the greater whole.

The sendoff in the undertaker's chapel was everything that Blind Tom was not—piecemeal, soulless, mechanical and dull. As the *Times* reporter endured the drone of the wheezy melodeon, he felt the sting of this final insult until nature chimed in with a tribute of her own.

A clap of thunder drowned out the offending whine. Sheets of rain pounded the roof, the wind roared high and tree branches lashed the stain glass windows. As the coffin was carried down the chapel aisle, it was not the dreary organ that could be heard. Instead, "the music of the elements sounded in the ears of the company gathered to pay tribute to the Negro musician." Finally a fitting sendoff for the man "who loved the swish of tree boughs and leaves in the wind and the howl of the blast under the eaves and the patter of the rain against the window pane."[15]

The reporter knew he had witnessed a convergence of music and nature ripe with significance, resonant with symbolism. An old black Granny who recognized in infant Tom's misty opaline eyes the gift of "second sight" would have nodded approvingly. Ah yes, a sign—proof he was in communication with the spirit world. Equally, an autistic savant with a razor sharp memory and lifetime of dispassionate observation might show it to be nothing more than a statistical inevitability. But how was a modern man, a worldly newspaper reporter, to make sense of what he had just witnessed? Should he conclude that the two events were somehow connected? Or recognize that the urge to link them was merely an expression of a mind searching for meaning, for wholeness? What was the answer to the riddle of Blind Tom when even the most straightforward questions had no clear-cut answers, as he discovered when he asked the young woman at the melodeon what happened to the promised funeral march. "Did he write a funeral march?" was her vacant reply.

Front-page reports of Blind Tom's death in papers across the country stirred up a storm of memories. In the following weeks, musician Otto Spahr, journalist Henry Watterson, stage hand Frank Davis, theater manager A.H. Gott, 7th Ohio Cavalry veteran Mr. D. Boon and Thomas Warhurst's daughter all felt compelled to write of their encounters with the prodigy. But in black newspapers tributes were thin on the ground. Three weeks after his death, *The New York Age* reflected, somewhat guiltily, on their muted response to the passing of the most famous black performer of the Civil War generation:

> In every section of the country, the big daily papers regarded Tom's death as a great loss and expressed themselves accordingly. Negro editors did not express any great sorrow over his death but commented relative to the amount of money he made during his life and what, if any, he left at his death. What Blind Tom accomplished in an artistic way and the amount of good he did in showing the musical possibilities of his race was not mentioned.
>
> It must be remembered that he was born a slave with no business qualifications nor independence of spirit to combat the commercial world. His blindness made him even more dependant. It must not be overlooked that Blind Tom was taken by his master when very young and turned over to an instructor; that the musical prodigy developed a fondness as well as an unlimited confidence in his master, which was perfectly natural. After slavery days, he did not pine for a change—he was satisfied, as were many slaves who had been given their freedom, but who were well content to remain with their former masters. The independence of spirit that now characterizes the race in many quarters was then absent. Conditions were vastly different to what they are today.[16]

The disquiet felt by many black editors and intellectuals would soften with time. Indeed, if not for the efforts of an African-American reporter fifteen years later, the final chapter of Blind Tom's burial could never be told. Every mainstream report of Tom's funeral ended with the image of the funeral party making its way through the belting rain to Brooklyn's Evergreen Cemetery. At Eliza's behest, it was to be a private burial—she, her daughter and two nephews the only mourners around his graveside. The reason—as *The Chicago Defender's* Charles T. Magill was to discover in 1922—was not to show their grief but cover their shame.

> In an ill-kept, unmarked grave, over-run by weeds, lies the remains of Blind Tom, a man who during his lifetime made three different fortunes for white people. The spot is called Pleasant Hill in section D of Evergreen Cemetery, Brooklyn and was found only after a careful perusal of the records, and then a two hours search. This man, whose earnings ran into the hundreds of thousands of dollars, has been laid

away in conditions but one degree better than a pauper. The section
of the Evergreen where lies his body is the poorest and most forlorn
part of the burying ground. If Blind Tom died "unwept, unhonored
and unsung," certainly he has been buried in that manner.[17]

As McGill also revealed, Eliza did her utmost to write the
Wiggins family out of the picture. "Mother's name: Margaret" she
informed the Bureau of Vital Statistics in Hoboken, her final nega-
tion of the bond between Tom and Charity. She knew the family
were disappointed that Tom was not buried in his hometown of
Columbus but if any of them dared show their faces looking for an
inheritance, they were in for a fight.[18]

The Wiggins family, possibly drawing on the hard lessons learnt by
Charity, never came knocking on Eliza's door (assuming they could
find it) but remained living in and around Columbus, some traveling
north to Brooklyn during the great migration of the twenties, others to
different parts of the South. No matter how far they scattered, their
pride in their famous uncle lived on. "I known it all my life," said Blind
Tom's great grand-niece, the elder Emma Jefferson. "Because we would
talk about it. I heard my grandmother talk about it."[19]

Eliza was remembered with little affection by her own family.
She survived Tom by two years, dying at the age of seventy a wealthy
woman although not, it seems, a happy one. She, who had been
pointedly excluded from John Bethune's will, knew the frustration of
being disinherited. On her deathbed in May 1910, the old lady was
sufficiently disenchanted with her daughter Marie Jahn and sister
Clara Ess to leave them nothing from an estate valued at $150,000.
The two contested the will, arguing that an outsider had manipulated
Eliza, but to no avail.[20] Her two nephews, Anton and Otto, were left
$1,000 a piece and the rest of the money was given, in equal
amounts, to five homes for the aged in the New York and Jersey
area. The house in Navesink no longer stands. Today the land is part
of Hartshorne Woods Park although the air still rings with the music
of the waves that once spoke to Blind Tom.

RECLAMATION RITES

"Listen to Things/More often than Beings/Hear the voice of
fire/Hear the voice of water/Listen in the wind/To the sighs of the
bush/This is the ancestors breathing," wrote Senegalese poet and sto-

ryteller, Birago Diop, articulating so beautifully the continuity of life and death in the indigenous religions of Africa.[21] This continuity is also expressed in the two ceremonies that are traditionally bestowed on the dead. The first—the burial—severs the link between physical body and the life force that once inhabited it. The immortal twin is sent away—to a grove, the other side of a deep river or the waters of the abyss—where it remains for months, even years, until ushered back with a second ceremony, a homecoming or reclamation rite that welcomes it into the community of ancestors.

It was a rite that General Bethune's youngest daughter, Fanny, almost certainly knew nothing about. The only one of the Bethune children who never married, after the family lost the Warrenton farm, Aunt Fanny lived her life as a guest in the homes of her brothers and sisters from Arizona to Georgia to Washington D.C. Throughout the 1890's she took a room in Warrenton for the summer and nostalgically relived a lost cause and time. "Miss Fanny Bethune has in press an original march dedicated to the Confederate Veterans. It will soon be on sale at the drug store," a local newspaper reported in 1896. "She was one of the mistresses of Blind Tom and this was one of the choice bits he delighted to play."[22] Re-issuing Blind Tom's favorite pieces—which they may have played together during the summer nights in Warrenton—was not enough to reconcile Fanny to the grief of losing him. In 1928, at the age of eighty-one, she set about remedying this once and for all and initiated a second burial for Blind Tom. Her reasons were essentially the same as a native African's: this was to be a homecoming, a reclamation.

Courtesy of the thousands of black porters who worked the railroad network, back copies of the banned *Chicago Defender*—a radical publication in the Jim Crow South—were routinely smuggled below the Mason-Dixon line and somewhere along the line Charles T. Magill's exposé of Blind Tom's shabby burial seems to have found its way into Fanny's hands. Haunted by the thought of Tom lying "unhonored, unwept and unsung" in an unmarked grave, it became her dying wish to bring Tom back to what she considered his rightful burial place—the Bethune family plot in Columbus's Linwood Cemetery. It was the same plot where she, in a few short months, would also be laid to rest and perhaps she envisaged that their two bodies would return to earth side by side, their dust co-mingling as their music once did in the Warrenton air.

Maxmillian Bethune Wellborne, a kinsman of the Bethunes and Governor of the Federal Reserve Bank of Atlanta, remembers Fanny speaking of her plans to bring Tom home. As he listened, did he not feel compelled to remind her of a few realities about the New South: twenty years on from the Supreme Court's Plessy v Ferguson ruling, the region had hardened along "separate but equal" lines. The Ku Klux Klan were in ascendancy, lynchings were on the rise and nothing could whip up a mob faster than the whiff of racial miscegenation. Although Cousin Fanny's respectability was beyond question, he knew that her desire to be buried alongside a black man would raise more than an eyebrow.

Whatever gentle persuasion Wellborne may have offered her, Fanny could not be swayed. According to one version of events, Tom's body was shipped from Brooklyn to Columbus without issue, but was turned away at Linwood Cemetery—it would be an insult to the memory of Confederate veterans buried there to have a black man in their midst, cemetery officials ruled. As a favor to Fanny Bethune's family, a neighbor allowed Tom's remains to be buried in a quiet corner of his plantation, Westmoreland, and two blank granite stones were placed at the head and foot of the improvised grave.[23] Fanny intended this to be a temporary measure and appointed a local man by the name of Jesse Moore to get around Linwood Cemetery's strict segregation policy and ensure that Tom's remains would be disinterred from the Westmoreland plantation to the family grave.

A few weeks later, Fanny was dead and Jesse Moore—released from his nigh-impossible contract—left Blind Tom where he lay in Westmoreland, his second unmarked grave.

This situation was somewhat rectified in 1954, when the Georgia Historical Commission erected a historical marker two hundred feet west of the Westmoreland grave that paid tribute to Tom's "native genius." But another twenty-two years would pass before a proper headstone was laid, a Bicentennial initiative of the 34th Medical Battalion at nearby Fort Benning. Permission was granted by the plantation's new owner Therese Dismuke, local stonemason Ed Stovall donated the marker and the 34th's Bruce Bergstresser and Bill Walton prepared the site, hacking away at the blank granite tombstone that, over the years, had become entwined with the roots of a nearby cedar tree.

On February 10, 1976 the dedication ceremony took place. Blind

Blind Tom's niece, Elnora Walker (seated) and members of her family at the Westmoreland Plantation in 1976 before the newly unveiled headstone that marked her famous uncle's grave.

Tom's niece, ninety-two-year-old Elnora Walker, was invited to raise the cloth that covered the new marker. But at the last moment—recalled Bill Walton—the elderly Therese Dismuke stepped out of the crowd and lifted the cloth. The grab for glory was brushed over with typical Southern grace, the official photos crediting Elnora Walker with the unveiling and nothing more ever being written or said.[24]

However this was not the only fact modified for public consumption. In the early 1950's—possibly in the groundswell of interest leading up to the erection of the 1954 marker—Georgia's State Librarian, Ella May Thornton, wrote to the Evergreen Cemetery in Brooklyn in an effort to confirm the details of Tom's disinterment. The answer she received must have taken her by surprise. "Our records indicate Blind Tom was interred in the abovementioned grave on June 15, 1908. His remains are still interred in that grave although there is no memorial marking his burial place." In November 1938—the letter continued—a man by the name of Gustav Lohlien was interred in the same grave although Thomas Wiggins had not been removed.

Ella May Thornton greeted the news with skepticism. "I believe Blind Tom was disinterred before Lohlien was buried in the same grave," she wrote by hand at the bottom of the letter.[25] Frankly, what else was she to think? That the person Fanny appointed to disinter the body went through the elaborate charade of pretending to ship Tom's body back to the South? It was far easier to suppose that no documentation existed because a corrupt Yankee had pocketed a bribe and allowed the body to be removed without any official authorization.

But for Ella May Thornton the implications went deeper than sectional pride. "It is touching to find evidence of the lasting affection of the Bethune Family," she wrote of Fanny's dying wish. If Tom was still in the cold Brooklyn ground, what would become of the love story she had mapped out in her mind—master's daughter meets, then loses her musical slave. How could she now get him back?

So while the citizens of Columbus marked what was, quite possibly, an empty grave, the grave bearing Thomas Wiggins's body lay untouched for the remainder of the century. Passing this patch of ground in Evergreen Cemetery on countless occasions was a Brooklyn-based concert pianist with a growing interest in the elusive Blind Tom. It was not until 2001, when John Davis was recording an album of Tom's music, that he discovered Charles T. Magill's article and realized that the man whose music he was so absorbed in was buried a mere fifteen-minute drive from his own home. Davis then made contact with a number of Tom's descendants and, together, they set about righting this long-standing wrong.

"One of the more unusual deliveries made last week to the Evergreen Cemetery came in a truck from Steinway & Sons," reported *The New Yorker* in July 2002. "The piano—an ebony grand—was set up on a square of AstroTurf under a tent in the cemetery's Pleasant Hill section. Nearby, a small, festively dressed crowd gathered around a granite tombstone—also freshly delivered—commemorating the death, ninety-four years ago, of Thomas Greene Wiggins."[26]

Blind Tom may have uttered a few blunt words when the crowd sang, less than tunefully, *O God, Our Help in Ages Past*. But he surely would have reveled in the high praise. As the strains of his own *Rêve Charmant* floated through the summer air, his descendants—nieces Emma Jefferson and Olivia Jackson—could now feel satisfied that they had finally reclaimed their great-great uncle from the waters of oblivion, paving the way for his entry back into popular consciousness to join the pantheon of American stage legends. In the roll of thunder, the clack of a train, the voice of the waves, his essence would live on.

The Real Blind Tom

THERE IS ANOTHER PIECE TO THE JIGSAW OF BLIND TOM'S LIFE. IT IS BY no means the final piece nor does it lock neatly into any of the others. However, along with Cousin Lizzie Bethune's tale of Charity's visit to the Columbus Fireman Parade, Orson Fowler's descriptions of Tom's spectacular "T" pirouettes and the Washington lady's recollection of his wild dance in the starry rose garden, it is among my favorites. It fits somewhere in the Hoboken years—that bleak solitary time Tom spent locked up in a tenement, the prisoner of a cold and indifferent guardian.

As the rain drenched funeral party set off to the cemetery to bury Tom in June of 1908, the mourners at the Campbell's Undertaking Room began to debate whether or not the body in the coffin was the real Blind Tom. A white actor whose career went back to Civil War times had frequently met Tom on his travels and was adamant it was the same man. "I first met him thirty-five years ago and he looks about the same as he did then." An elderly black lady from Maryland, two Harlem women and *The Times* reporter, all who had seen Tom perform many times, agreed. It was the same face, although considering Blind Tom had been a household name for close to half a century, he looked much younger than they supposed.[1] But a "strong accented," "low class" English woman who refused to give her name, believed otherwise:

I know the man who was buried here today, [she told a New York newspaper]. That's not the famous Blind Tom. I know that Negro from when I was hard up not that many years ago, I did a turn with him in several Hoboken music halls. He called himself Blind Tom but I do not believe he was the real Blind Tom. He had often spoke to me about the real Blind Tom and told me many of his peculiarities. He told me Blind Tom was an imbecile while this man was unusually intelligent. He often spoke of his desire to go to Europe and told me the other Blind Tom had been fortunate enough to go there and play before royalty. He lived in Hoboken and was brought to the theatre every night by a young man about twenty. For some years he had been playing in different music halls in Hoboken.[2]

It is possible that the English actress had made up her story. But for me, details like the Hoboken address, the preoccupation with Europe and the presence of the young man are too coincidental to dismiss her story outright. Something in what she claimed was true, or at least partially true. Clearly she was wrong about the body inside the coffin not being the real Blind Tom, as the five other witnesses positively identified him. Which begs the question, if the man inside the coffin was the man she knew from the Hoboken music hall, could there be a hidden chapter to Tom's final years?

Hoboken was famous for its music halls and every weekend Manhattan ferries disgorged thousands of revelers onto the main strip—many of them boisterous young men determined to play the night as hard as the week they had just worked. A notoriously tough audience, they came to Hoboken—not for the light dramas on offer at the Lyric or the Germanic Society's music recital—but for the lewd jokes, ribald skits and bevy of leggy showgirls at burlesque theaters like The Star, The Flora and The Bijou. Was this the type of music hall that the English woman worked in when she was hard up? Was it in these salacious surrounds that she met the famous Blind Tom? And the young man she referred to, was he the same young man seen going in and out of Eliza's apartment?

Nobody in Eliza's family ever wrote down their memories of Tom, although whenever a reporter managed to beat their way to the Lerches' door, the vitality of Tom's imaginary world was always mentioned. The Bethune family, too, recall the long hours Tom spent in the guise of characters like Dr. Smokeson and Mrs. Flaherty, which he did with such sincerity that the Washington lady opined that it would "induce the belief of a dual state of existence." And for decades, hundreds of thousands of people across North America were confounded by Tom's nightly rendition of Uncle Charlie, Senator Douglas and the pompous and grandiose showman. Tom had created an imaginary world—awash with musical triumphs, rapturous applause, exacting music professors and gossiping women—that was as real to him as the four walls that contained him. Was it possible that after a lifetime of role-playing both on and off the stage, he had created a menagerie of fully formed characters, rich with biographical detail, and could assume their identity with effortless conviction?

I say this because the English actress encountered a "Blind Tom" who was not always muttering snatches of other people's conversations, did not stammer when he spoke or compulsively bounce on one foot. Rather, he was someone of unusual intelligence who possessed a detailed knowledge of the "imbecile" Tom. Could it be that in among Tom's stable of imaginary friends was a character who also went by the name "Blind Tom"—an urbane, erudite gentleman with the gravitas of Dr. Smokeson, the dignity of The Professor and the pizzazz of The Showman, who enthralled the showgirls with his sublime musical touch, dazzled them with his feats of memory and politely answered their questions about the "imbecile" Blind Tom? In short, did Tom develop an alter ego of himself? Or was this the real Blind Tom?

The Blind Tom the English actress knew was a familiar face in the backstages of a number of Hoboken music halls. However, audiences barely knew he was there. There was no banner emblazoned with his name, no publicity to tantalize the public, no impresario to welcome him on stage. Instead he was stationed behind the piano at the foot of the stage, obscured from an audience busy whooping and howling the chorus line. Here, in relative anonymity, he could finally explore one of the simple pleasures of music that after five decades of performing was virtually unknown to him—playing music with other people. As house pianist, he could have spurred on the dancing girls, accompanied the singers, punctuated the gags of the comedians, filled in the black holes and blunders and, perhaps, in between shows, jammed along with the house band. (He always longed to play with a brass band.) Perhaps Tom had finally found a way to be part of the fun and not the object of fun. Perhaps in a bawdy Hoboken burlesque, he discovered that strangers were just other people.

Speculative, I know, but the fantasy of him surrounded by musicians of equal stature is also shared by one of his few genuine

Dizzy Gillespie plays When the Saints Go Marching In *at one of two gravesites claimed to be Blind Tom's. This one is in Columbus, Georga, the other is in Brooklyn's Greenwood Cemetery.*

friends: Norbonne Robinson—the boy who for eight unbroken summers played, clowned and joked with Tom then drifted off to sleep listening to him extract heaven from the keyboards:

> One dream I have often indulged: I would love to take Tom to a jam session in Harlem. I would have Art Tatum, Count Basie, Earl Hines, Duke Ellington, Teddy Wilson, and the late Fats Waller each giving a rendition of that piece he considered most characteristically his own. As a finale I would have Tom who, were he alive, would be well versed in jazz, boogie-woogie and swing, cut loose with his own interpretation of these modern manifestations of music.

Perhaps Tom was already doing something a little like that in a music hall in Hoboken—witnessing, deciphering, channelling and embracing the world around him with wholehearted enthusiasm, just as he had been doing since he first discovered the piano as a four-year-old child.

Notes

CHAPTER 1: A GOOD BREEDING WOMAN

1.   Rebecca Harding, "Blind Tom" *AM*, November, 1862
2.   "Edison and his Inventions," *Scribners Monthly*, Vol 18, Issue 2 June, 1879
3.   Etta B. Worsley *Columbus on Chattahoochee*, 1951
4.   "Blind Tom," *AC*, Nov 27, 1886
5.   "Mother of Blind Tom Passes Away," *The Sunny South*, 1902
6.   "Interview with Mrs. Walker," Thomas Wiggins aka Blind Tom, Black History Series, *The Columbus Times*, 1974

7. GN Vol IV Pt 3 P332
8. GN Vol IV Pt 4 P300
9. Theodore Dwight Weld, *American Slavery As It Is: Testimony of a Thousand Witnesses,* 1839
10. "The Death of Mrs Lamar," *Columbus (Ga) Daily Enquirer Sun* Feb 14, 1895
11. "Mother of Blind Tom Passes Away," *The Sunny South,* 1902
12. Solomon Northup, *Twelve Years a Slave,* New York, 1855
13. Avery, Isaac Erwin, *Idle Comments,* Charlotte NC, 1905
14. Louis Hughes, *Thirty Years a Slave: From Bondage to Freedom,* 1897.
15. 1870 Census of Muscogee County, Georgia
16. GN Vol IV Pt 2 P 304
17. GN Vol IV Pt 1 P 168
18. J.S. Buckingham, *The Slave States of America,* 1842
19. SSL
20. Henry R. Goetchius "Columbus Ga and General Henry L. Benning" *The Georgia Historical Quarterly,* Vol 3 No 1 March, 1919.
21. Etta B. Worsley *Columbus on Chattahoochee,* 1951
22. Leon Harris interview with Emma Jefferson, CNN, April 3, 2002 Play Highlights Blind Slave Musician www.geoffandwen.com/Blind/newsarticle
23. Undated petition, SP918 NYCRO
24. 1870 Census of Muscogee County
25. 1870 Census of Muscogee County
26. "Silhouettes," AC, October 23, 1942
27. Edward Seguin, *Idiocy & its Treatment by the Physiological Method,* 1866
28. Letter from Mother to Daughter, Feb 1856, Georgia State Archives
29. "Mother of Blind Tom Passes Away," *The Sunny South,* 1902
30. J.S. Buckingham, *The Slave States of America,* 1842
31. "Another Lovely Residence for Sale," *Columbus Times & Sentential,* Jan 26 or 27, 1851
32. *Columbus Times & Sentential,* July 5, 1844
33. *Columbus Times & Sentential,* Dec 24, 1850
34. Another Lovely Residence for Sale, *Columbus Times & Sentential,* Jan 26 or 27, 1851
35. Nancy Telfair, *A History of Columbus 1828-1928,* 1929
36. GN Vol IV Pt 1 P 88
37. J.S. Buckingham, *The Slave States of America,* 1842

CHAPTER 2: EVERY INCH A SOUTHERN GENTLEMAN

1 NR
2. "Argument of James N. Bethune before the Supreme Court," CS, July 21, 1859
3. "Reception of General Bethune," *Columbus Daily Sun,* July 1, 1859
4. "Death of General James N Bethune in Washington: A Very Remarkable Man" WP Feb 13, 1895.
5. Anon, *An Historical and Genealogical Account of the Bethunes of the Island of Skye,* 1893
6. E. Merton Coulter, *College Life in the Old South,* 1928
7. "Silhouettes," AC, October 23, 1942.
8. 1850 Census, www.ancestry.com
9. Letter from Mother to Daughter, Feb 1856, Georgia State Archives
10. "A Very Remarkable Man," WP, January 27, 1895
11. "Prospectus of The Corner Stone," CS, October 14, 1856
12. "The Dissolution of the Union as a Matter of Interest to the South," CS, 1856
13. J.S. Buckingham, *The Slave States of America,* 1842
14. "The Justice and Simplicity of Free Trade & Direct Taxation," CS, Feb 3, 1859
15. Helen Ione Green, "Politics in Georgia, 1853-54, The Ordeal of Howell Cobb," *Georgia Historical Society,* 1946 p196

16 J.S. Buckingham, *The Slave States of America*, 1842, p183
17 Donald G. Mathews "The Abolitionists on Slavery: the Critique Behind the Social Movement" *The Journal of Southern History* Vol 33, No 2, May 1967
18 "The Justice and Simplicity of Free Trade & Direct Taxation," *CS*, Feb 3, 1859
19 *CS*, Feb 3, 1859
20 *Cincinnati Daily Commercial*, July 21, 1865

CHAPTER 3: NO ORDINARY CHILD

1. GN Vol IV Pt 1 P 100
2. SSL
3. GN Vol IV Part 2 P 123
4. SSL
5. Allan W. Snyder and D. John Mitchel, "Is Integer Arithmetic Fundamental to Mental Processing?: The Mind's Secret Arithmetic," *Biological Sciences,* Vol. 266, No. 1419 (Mar. 22, 1999), pp. 587-592, The Royal Society
6. Dr. Anette Ingsholt, *Blindness, Mental Retardation and Autism,* National Institute for Blind and Partially Sighted Children and Youth, Denmark, 2006
7. David S. Viscott "A Musical Idiot Savant" *Psychiatry,* 32:494-515, 1969
8. Quote by Ebenezer Davis, cited in Mark M. Smith's *Listening to the Nineteenth Century,* 2001
9. GN Vol IV Pt 3 P 17
10. Katherine Hines Mahan, *History of Music in Columbus, 1828-1928*, p46
    "Black sheep, black sheep, Where you left yo lammy?
    Way down yonder in the valley.
    Buzzards and ole butterflies are peckin' out his eyes,
    And the po' lil sheep say mammy mammy."
11 GN Vol IV Pt 2 P 57
12 Tempie Herndon Durham, *North Carolina Narratives*, Vol XI, Pt 1 P 285
13 GN Vol IV Pt 1 P 77
14 Katherine Hines Mahan, *History of Music in Columbus, 1828-1928*, p46
15 Etta B. Worsley, *Columbus on the Chattahoochee,* 1951
16 Lawrence W. Levine, *Black Culture & Black Consciousness,* 1978 p6
17. SSL
18. GN Vol IV Pt 2 P 99
19. GN Vol IV Pt 3 P 206
20. GN Vol IV Pt 1 p 46
21. "Interview with Mrs Julia Lee of Colombus Ga," May 1, 1953, *Mildred Stock Collection, MARBD, SCRBC.*
22. Letter from H.J. Wiesel, *DMJ* January 24, 1863
23. William Osler Langley, "Blind Tom: A Child of Melody," *The Theater in Columbus*
24. "The Choir," *CS*, date obscured
25. GN, Vol IV Pt 2 P 26-27
26. Cited in Levine p26—Natalie Curtis Brown, "Negro Music at Birth," *Musical Quarterly 5*, 1919 p88
27. Cited in Levine P 27—Clifton Joseph Furness, "Communal Music Among Arabians and Negroes," *Musical Quarterly*, Issue 16, 1930
28. GN Vol IV Pt 4 p321
29. GN Vol IV P 2 p235
30. GN Vol IV Pt 2 p82
31. NR
32. Edouard Seguin, *Idiocy & its Treatment by the Physiological Method,* 1866
33. NR
34. SLTGB
35. SSL

CHAPTER 4: UNWRITTEN LEGEND

1. "Afraid of Gifted Son," *WP*, Jan 25, 1903
2. Louise Dooley, "In the World Of Music," *AC*, Aug 2, 1903
3. "Blind Tom Bethune, Death of His Old Master Recalls Prodigy," *WP*, Feb 14, 1895
4. "She's the Mother of Blind Tom," *AC*, Nov 6, 1898
5. Henry Watterson, "Blind Tom," *Louisville Courier-Journal*, June 16, 1908, p4
6. SSL
7. "Blind Tom Bethune, Death of His Old Master Recalls Prodigy," *WP*, Feb 14, 1895
8. MM Dauphin & Hattie Taylor, "Blind Tom," *The American Slave: A Composite Autobiography*, Vol 3, 1977, p53.
9. E. Merton Coulter, *College Life in the Old South*, 1928
10. C. Sharp, "Blind Tom: How the Wonderful Negro Idiot Conducted Himself," *AC*, Sept 1, 1887
11. C. Sharp, "Blind Tom: How the Wonderful Negro Idiot Conducted Himself," *AC*, Sept 1, 1887
12. SSL
13. "Blind Tom Bethune, Death of His Old Master Recalls Prodigy," *WP*, Feb 14, 1895
14. "Wonderful Blind Tom," *WP*, Nov 28, 1866
15. NR
16. M.M. Dauphin & Hattie Taylor, "Blind Tom," *The American Slave: A Composite Autobiography*, Vol 3, 1977, P 53
17. SSL
18. James Monroe Trotter, *Music and Some Highly Musical People*, 1882
19. Letter from Mother to Daughter, Feb 1856, Georgia State Archives
20. H.E. Scudder, "A Leaf from My Notebook," *Sword and Pen Magazine*, Dec 12, 1888
21. Emmet R. Calhoun, "Blind Tom Musical Prodigy" *Birmingham News,* undated
22. "Afraid of Gifted Son," *WP*, Jan 25, 1903
23. *AM*, Nov 1862

CHAPTER 5: SECOND SIGHT

1. Ray Broadus Browne, *Popular Beliefs and Practices from Alabama*, 1958
2. GN Vol IV Pt 3 P 345
3. SLTGB
4. Lousie Dooley, "In the World Of Music," *AC*, Aug 2, 1903
5. Maya Deren, *Divine Horsemen: Voodoo Gods of Haiti*, 1970
6. SSL
7. Henry R. Goetchius, "Columbus Ga and General Henry L Benning," *The Georgia Historical Quarterly,* Vol 3 No 1, March 1919.
8. David Evan, "Black Fife and Drum Music in Mississippi," *Mississippi Folklore Register*, No 3, Fall 1972
9. Julia D. Owen, "Letters From Etude Friends" *The Etude* Nov *1941*
10. GN Vol IV Pt 2 P 168
11. GN Vol IV Pt 2 P 158
12. William Wells Brown, *My Southern Home: The South and Its People*, 1880
13. "The Habeas Corpus in the Case of Blind Tom" *Cincinnati Enquirer*, July 22, 1865

CHAPTER 6: STAR OF THE MUSICAL WORLD

1. *Atlanta Daily Intelligencer*, October 20, 1857
2. "Wonderful Blind Tom," *WP*, Nov 28, 1886
3. Letter from Mother to Daughter, Feb 1856, Georgia State Archives
4. *Federal Union*, Milledgeville, Nov 6, 1855
5. Otto Spahr "A Reminiscence Of Blind Tom," *AC*, Aug 17, 1908
6. "Blind Tom and the Japanese," *DMJ*, June 9 1860

7. Letter from "Sallie," Elkton (Va), Aug 29 1860, Private Collection.
8. Robert C. Toll, *On With The Show,* New York, 1976
9. *AM,* Nov 1862
10. *Atlanta Daily Intelligencer,* October 20, 1857
11. Otto Spahr, "A Reminiscence Of Blind Tom," *AC,* Aug 17, 1908
12. *Cincinnati Gazette,* July 21, 1865
13. Henry Watterson, "Blind Tom," *Louisville Courier Journal,* June 16, 1908
14. M.M. Dauphin & Hattie Taylor, "Blind Tom," *The American Slave: A Composite Autobiography,* Vol 3, 1977
15. "Blind Tom Bethune, Death of His Old Master Recalls Prodigy," *WP,* Feb 14, 1895
16. Carl Frederick Wittke, *Tambo and Bones,* 1930
17. *The London Musical Standard,* Aug 4, 1866
18. Carl Frederick Wittke, *Tambo and Bones,* 1930
19. *The Albany (N.Y.) Argus,* January 1866
20. SSL
21. *DJM,* Feb 11, 1860, reprinted from the *Charleston Courier,* Jan 24 1860
22. *AM,* Nov 1862

CHAPTER 7: THE SHOWMAN & THE MAGICIAN

1. "Bad Accident" *CS,* December 6,1855
2. "Death of Benjamin T Bethune," *CS,* July 2, 1855
3. "Death of Mrs Bethune," *Columbus Enquirer,* May 22, 1858
4. "Death of P.H. Oliver," *Weekly Sumter Republican,* August 12, 1871
5. Phineas T. Barnum, *Struggles and Triumphs,* 1927
6. Letter from H.J. Wiesel, *DMJ,* Jan 24, 1863
7. Reprint of Ad for Charleston Concert, *DMJ,* Feb 11, 1860
8. "A Black Prodigy of the Musical World," *CT,* June 15, 1860, Reprinted from *The Baltimore Patriot*
9. "A Blind Negro Pianist," *CT,* Feb 7, 1860
10. *AM,* November 1862
11. *DMJ,* Dec 6, 1862
12. Letter from H.J Wiesel, *DMJ,* Jan 24, 1863
13. *DMJ,* Dec 6, 1862
14. "More About Blind Tom" *DMJ,* Dec 6, 1862
15. *Musical Independent* April 1869
16. St. Louis May 1861, no publication given, *Scrapbook,* Boston, 1918
17. St. Louis May 1861, no publication given, *Scrapbook,* Boston, 1918
18. Rev. C.M. Verdel, "Personal Recollections of BT the Musical Wonder," *Wesleyan Christian Advocate,* undated.
19. Oliver Sacks, *An Anthropologist on Mars,* 1995 p 228
20. Henry Watterson, "Blind Tom," *Louisville Courier-Journal,* June 16, 1908

CHAPTER 8: SHE USED TO WASH MY FACE

1. Letter from H.J. Wiesel, *DMJ,* Jan 24, 1863
2. C. Sharp, "Blind Tom: How the Wonderful Negro Idiot Conducted Himself," *AC,* Sept 1, 1887
3. "Blind Tom"s Wonderful Memory" *NYT,* April 4, 1881
4. "Blind Tom With Mind Clouded Displays A Marvelous Memory" *The North American,* June 8, 1901
5. J. Frank Davis, "Blind Tom," *Human Life,* August 1908
6. *Metronome,* August 1908
7. Virginia Compton-Clay, *A Belle of the Fifties,* New York, 1905
8. *Metronome,* August 1908
9. J. Frank Davis, "Blind Tom," *Human Life,* August 1908

10. "Blind Tom," *American Phrenological Journal*, New York, December 1865
11. Jim Sinclair "Bridging the Gaps: An Inside-out view of Autism (Or Do You Know What I Don"t)" in E. Schopler & GB Mestibov, (eds) *High Functioning Individuals with Autism*, 1992
12. Tito Mukhopadhyay, *Breaking the Silence, My Life, The World & Autism*, 2000
13. *SLTGB*
14. Katherine Pope Merritt, "Blind Tom a Musical Prodigy of Ante Bellum Georgia," *Atlanta Journal*, March 23, 1934

CHAPTER 9: SOME FELLOW MIGHT STEAL ME

1. Nathaniel Hawthorne, "Chiefly about War Matters," *AM*, July 1862
2. Forty years after the event Henry Watterson dates this meeting "at Washington and in the autumn of 1860." This date does not tally with other records that identify Tom's being in Washington during May and June of 1860.
3. Henry Watterson, "Blind Tom," *Louisville Courier-Journal*, June 16, 1908
4. "Blind Tom and the Japanese," *DMJ*, June 12, 1860. Sara Pryor (wife of a firebrand Congressman Roger A Pryor) recalls that Washington society "lost its head" when the first Japanese Embassy visited the city. "There was something ridiculous in the way it behaved. So many fêtes were given to the Japanese, so many dinners, so many receptions, we were worn out attending them." Sara Rice Pryor, *My Day, Reminiscences of a Long Life*, 1908 p146.
5. Elise K. Kirk, *Music At The White House: A History of the American Spirit*, 1860
6. Virginia Compton-Clay, *A Belle of the Fifties*, 1905
7. Sara Rice Pryor, *My Day; Reminiscences of a Long Life*, 1909
8. Emerson D. Fike, *The Presidential Campaign of 1860*, 1911
9. Henry Villard, *New York Herald Tribune*, August 21, 1858
10. Blind Tom, *CT*, Sept 30, 1879
11. NR
12. George Fort Milton, *The Eve of Conflict: Stephen A Douglas and The Needless War*, 1934
13. *Cincinnati Daily Gazette*, April 30, 1860
14. "The Abduction of Blind Tom," *Columbus Daily Sun*, July 21, 1860
15. Rebecca Latimer Felton, *Country Life in Georgia in the Days of My Youth*, 1919
16. *New Albany Daily Ledger*, July 1865
17. "Blind Tom in New York," *Columbus Weekly Sun*, Feb 5, 1861
18. "More Aid and Comfort," *NYT*, Jan 25, 1861
19. *Columbus Daily Sun*, January 31, 1861
20. *Cincinnati Commercial*, July 20 1865, Reprinted *CT*, July 22, 1865
21. *Cincinnati Gazette*, July 21, 1865

CHAPTER 10: THUNDER OF WAR

1. Harrison Berry, *Slavery and Abolitionism as Viewed by a Georgia Slave*, 1861
2. Joseph Le Conte, *The Autobiography of Joseph Le Conte*, 1903
3. Gretna Green, "Recollections of Blind Tom in 1865," *Atlanta Journal*, June 24, 1934
4. *Savannah Morning News*, Nov 9, 1861
5. "Patriotic and Liberal Proposition," *Columbus Enquirer*, July 25 1861
6. *Southern Confederacy*, Dec 17, 1961
7. Mary Polk Branch, *Memoirs of a Southern Woman: Within the Lines*, 1912
8. Kenneth Coleman, *Confederate Athens*, 1967
9. *Fayetteville Observer*, May 19, 1862
10. S. Frederick Starr, *Bamboula!, The Life and Times of Louis Moreau Gottschalk*, 1995
11. L.M. Gottschalk, Edited by Jeanne Behrend, *Notes of a Pianist*, 1996
12. "Richmond June 20," *The Charleston Mercury*, June 24, 1861.
13. Ella May Thornton, "The Mystery of Blind Tom" *Georgia Review*, Winter 1961

14. Letter to the Editor, *AC*, Oct 24, 1942
15. Katherine Pope Merritt, "Blind Tom a Musical Prodigy of Ante Bellum Georgia," *Atlanta Journal*, March 23, 1934
16. Tom Stoddard, "Blind Tom Slave Genius" *Storyville*, No. 28, 1970
17. Henry Watterson, "Blind Tom," *Louisville Courier-Journal*, June 16, 1908
18. *Nashville American*, Dec 6, 1877
19. M.M. Dauphin & Hattie Taylor, "Blind Tom," *The American Slave: A Composite Autobiography*, Vol 3, 1977
20. H.E. Scudder, "A Leaf from My Notebook," *Sword and Pen Magazine*, Dec 12, 1888

CHAPTER 11: HOME SWEET HOME

1. *Cincinnati Enquirer,* July 21, 1865
2. Letter dated April 23, 1862, *TMCP*
3. Letter dated May 16, 1861 from brother Robert, *TMCP*
4. Letter dated Sept 30, 1862, Lexington Ky, *TMCP*
5. Compiled Service Records of Confederate Soldiers Who Served in Organizations from the State of Georgia Military Unit, Dept of War, NARA
6. Charles Quintard, *The Memoir and Civil War Diary of Charles Todd Quintard*, Edited by Sam Davis Elliott, 2003
7. Marshall and Jean Stearns, *Jazz Dance: the Story of American Vernacular Dance*, 1968
8. *Cincinnati Enquirer*, July 22, 1865
9. 1870 Census, County of Muscogee, P175
10. "Mother of Blind Tom Passes Away," *The Sunny South*, 1902
11. *Columbus Enquirer*, May 10, 1864
12. Frances Woolfolk Wallace, May 18, 1864 entry, *A Diary, March 19-August 25, 1864*, Documenting the South, UNC-CH. www.docsouth.unc.edu
13. Frances Woolfolk Wallace, April 10, 1864 entry, *A Diary, March 19-August 25, 1864*, Documenting the South, UNC-CH. www.docsouth.unc.edu
14. "Letter from Ollie to Grandma, Vicksburg Feb 25, 1924," Vertical File, WC Bradley Memorial Library, Columbus Georgia.
15. Bell Irwin Wiley, *The Life of Johnny Reb: The Common Soldier of the Confederacy*, 1979
16. Extracts from an unidentified clipping found in the Music Room of the New York Public Library".
17. SSL, *Albany (N.Y.) Argus*, January 1866.
18. David S. Viscott "A Musical Idiot Savant" *Psychiatry*, 32:494-515, 1969
19. *Cincinnati Times*, June 20, 1865
20. GN, Vol IV Pt 4, P 329
21. *Cincinnati Daily Commercial*, July 24, 1865
22. *Cincinnati Enquirer* July 21, 1865
23. *Cincinnati Enquirer* July 20, 1865

CHAPTER 12: FIAH UP DE ENGINES!

1. Howard N .Monnet (ed), ""The Awfulest Tom I Ever Seen": A Letter from Sherman"s Army," *Civil War History 8*, 1862
2. GN Vol IV Pt 2 P 30
3. Inez Hunt, *The Story of Blind Tom*, 1972
4. *"Letter from John G Bethune to Confederate Secretary of State, Judah P Benjamin,"* Oct 18, 1864, NARA
5. *"Selected Records of the War Department Relating to Confederate Prisoners of War 1861-1865,"* NARA
6. Rebecca Latimer Felton, *Country Life in Georgia in the Days of My Youth*, Documenting the South, UNC-CH. www.docsouth.unc.edu
7. Louise C. Barfield, *History Of Harris County, Georgia 1827-1971*, 1976

8. David P. Conyngham, *Sherman"s March Through the South*, 1865
9. GN Vol IV Pt 1 P2
10. *Cincinnati Enquirer*, July 22, 1865
11. "Atlantian Heard Blind Tom," *Atlanta Journal*, June 24, 1934
12. GN Vol IV Pt 4 P24
13. M.M. Dauphin & Hattie Taylor, "Blind Tom," *The American Slave: A Composite Autobiography*, Vol 3, 1977
14. Rebecca Latimer Felton, *Country Life in Georgia*, 1980
15. D. Boon, "An Early Concert By Blind Tom," *New York Sun*, June 27, 1908
16. "Atlantian Heard Blind Tom," *Atlanta Journal*, June 24, 1934
17. "Atlantian Heard Blind Tom," *Atlanta Journal*, June 24, 1934
18. *NYT*, Aug 12, 1887
19. *SSL*, Reprint of article from *The Public Ledger*, September 27, 1865
20. *The Washington Bee*, February 5, 1887
21. "Dispute over Blind Tom," *NYT*, June 16, 1908

CHAPTER 13: YANKEE JUSTICE

1. "On the Record," *A National Archives Publication*, Sept 1979
2. Marion B. Lucas, "Camp Nelson, Kentucky, During the Civil War: Cradle of Liberty or Refugee Death Camp," *The Filson Club Historical Quarterly*, Oct 1989
3. *Cincinnati Times*, July 20, 1865
4. *Cincinnati Daily Commercial*, July 20, 1865
5. *Cincinnati Daily Commercial*, July 20, 1865
6. Peter H. Clark, *Black Brigade of Cincinnati: Being a Report of Its Labors and a Muster-Roll of Its Members*, 1864
7. *Cincinnati Enquirer*, July 21, 1865
8. *Cincinnati Enquirer*, July 22, 1865
9. *Cincinnati Times*, July 20, 1865
10. *Cincinnati Gazette*, July 21, 1865
11. *Cincinnati Enquirer*, July 22, 1865
12. *Cincinnati Daily Commercial*, July 24, 1865
13. *Cincinnati Times*, July 24, 1865
14. Nancy Telfair, *A History of Columbus 1828-1928*, Columbus, 1929
15. *Columbus Enquirer*, July 7, 1866
16. Daniel F. Littlefield, Jr. and Patricia Washington McGraw, *The Arkansas Freeman, 1869-1870—Birth of the Black Press in Arkansas*, Vol 40, No 1, 1979

CHAPTER14: THE GREAT MUSICAL MYSTERY

1. "Blind Tom," *American Phrenological Journal*, New York, December 1865
2. NR
3. H.E. Scudder, "A Leaf from My Notebook," *Sword and Pen Magazine*, Dec 12, 1888
4. *Cincinnati Daily Commercial*, July 20, 1865
5. *Manchester Courier*, September 26, 1866
6. H.E. Scudder, "A Leaf from My Notebook," *Sword and Pen Magazine*, Dec 12, 1888
7. *The London Musical Standard*, Oct 13,1866, p 222
8. H.E. Scudder, "A Leaf from My Notebook," *Sword and Pen Magazine*, Dec 12, 1888
9. Edward Seguin, *Idiocy & its Treatment by the Physiological Method*, 1866
10. *Cincinnati Gazette*, July 20, 1865
11. Edward Seguin, *Idiocy & its Treatment by the Physiological Method*, 1866
12. H.E. Scudder, "A Leaf from My Notebook," *Sword and Pen Magazine*, Dec 12, 1888
13. "How I Heard Blind Tom," *People Magazine*, Nov 2, 1867
14. *Philadelphia Inquirer*, December 27, 1865
15. Death of Edward Seguin, *NYT*, October 29, 1880
16. Edward Seguin, *Idiocy & its Treatment by the Physiological Method*, 1866

17. H.E. Scudder, "A Leaf from My Notebook," *Sword and Pen Magazine*, Dec 12, 1888
18. William Osler Langley, "Blind Tom: A Child of Melody," *The Theater in Columbus*.
19. H.E. Scudder, "A Leaf from My Notebook," *Sword and Pen Magazine*, Dec 12, 1888
20. Mark Twain Project, Clemenss "Spelling Match" Speech, 1875 www.marktwainproject.org
21. H.E. Scudder, "A Leaf from My Notebook," *Sword and Pen Magazine*, Dec 12, 1888
22. "Blind Tom," *American Phrenological Journal*, New York, December 1865
23. "Extracts from an unidentified clipping found in the Music Room of the New York Public Library," *Mildred Stock Collection, MARBD, SCRBC.*
24. *Albany (N.Y.) Argus,* January 1866 cited in *SSL*
25 *Musical Messenger,* Oct 1892
26. *The Aquarian Theosophist,* Vol IV #10 Supplement, August 17, 2004
27. *New York Tribune*, May 2, 1868
28. *The London Times*, August 18, 1866
29. *The London Times,* July 23, 1866
30. L. De Hegermann-Lindencrone *In the Courts of Memory 1858-1875* www.gutenburg.org
31. "Antics of Blind Tom" *WP*, Feb 21, 1897
32. *SSL*, Testimonials, Philadelphia, Sept 16, 1865
33. *SSL*, Testimonials, Letter from Charles Halle, Letter from I Moscheles, 1866
34. *Musical Messenger,* October 1892
35. *SSL, The Dundee Advertiser*
36. *Musical Independent,* April 1869
37. Harold C. Schonberg, *The Great Pianists*, 1963, p178
38. Charles Halle & Marie Halle, *The Life and Letters of Sir Charles Halle*, 1896
39. Eugenie B. Abbott, "The Miraculous Case of Blind Tom," *Etude*, v58, 1940

CHAPTER 15: HEAVENLY TONES

1. M. Louise Evans, "Old Timer tells History of Blind Tom," July 13, 1850, No Publication Listed, Vertical Files The Warrenton Library, Fauquier County
2. Edward Scobie, *Black Britannia: A History of Blacks in Britain*, 1973
3. M. Louise Evans, *Stirring Story of Warrenton Steeplechase in 1875 Told,* No Publication noted, April 21, 1949, Blind Tom Bethune File, Warrenton Library
4. NR
5. "The Story Of Blind Tom," *WP,* Aug 14, 1887
6. "Antics of Blind Tom," *WP*, Feb 21, 1897
7. NR
8. Mme. Anna Amalie Tutein, "The Phenomenon of Blind Tom," *The Etude,* Feb 1918
9. "Antics of Blind Tom," *WP*, Feb 21, 1897
10. Felicitas D. Goodman & Nana Nauwald, *Ecstatic Trance*, 2003
11. Maya Deren, *Divine Horsemen, Voodoo Gods of Haiti*, 1970
12. "Antics of Blind Tom," *WP*, Feb 21, 1897
13. Charity Wiggins, "Response to Petition of James N Bethune," Aug 11, 1887, SP918 NYCRO
14. *Musical Courier,* July 22, 1885
15. *Detroit Free Press*, July 25, 1889
16. "Blind Tom in Retirement," *The New York Sun*, April 15, 1897
17. NR
18. "How I Heard Blind Tom," *People Magazine*, Nov 2, 1867
19. "Blind Tom The Pianist," *CT,* July 22, 1865
20. *Columbus Enquirer*, April 20, 1864
21. *Cincinnati Gazette*, July 21, 1865
22. J. Frank Davis, "Blind Tom," *Human Life,* August 1908
23. "Antics of Blind Tom" *WP*, Feb 21, 1897
24. NR

25. "Experiences with a Prodigy, Medina, New York, September 14 1896," No publication cited, *Scrapbook*, Boston, 1918

CHAPTER 16: PERPETUAL MOTION

1. NR
2. "Letter from Mark Twain, Hartford, Conn, July, 1869," *San Francisco Alta California*, August 1, 1869
3. Henry Holt, *Garrulities of an Octogenarian Editor,* 1923
4. *The Washington Bee*, February 5, 1887
5. C. Sharp, "Blind Tom: How the Wonderful Negro Idiot Conducted Himself," *AC*, Sept 1, 1887
6. *The Washington Bee*, February 5, 1887
7. "Statement by Joseph Eubanks," Aug 20, 1885, SP918 NYCRO
8. *CT*, August 8, 1869
9. J. Frank Davis, "Blind Tom," *Human Life*, August 1908
10. "Same Blind Tom of Yore," *Nashville American*, Jan 23 1892
11. "Blind Tom as He Is Today," *Ladies Home Journal*, Sept 1898
12. J. Frank Davis, "Blind Tom," *Human Life*, August 1908
13. "Antics of Blind Tom," *WP*, Feb 21, 1897
14. "Blind Tom," *AC*, Nov 27, 1886
15. *CT*, August 8, 1869
16. *Metronome*, August 1908
17. J. Frank Davis, "Blind Tom," *Human Life*, August 1908
18. Musical, *BG*, June 1, 1882
19. The City, *CT*, June 17, 1875
20. "Blind Tom Concert," *CT*, Jan 19 1869
21. "Blind Tom," *Sedalia Missouri Daily Democrat*, April 15, 1872
22. *New York Sun*, Nov 26, 1873
23. "Blind Tom Discomfited Old Joe," *The Chicago Defender,* Nov 18, 1922
24. Mme. Anna Amalie Tutien, "The Phenomenon of Blind Tom," *The Etude,* Feb 1918
25. *DJM*, Sept 2, 1865
26. NR
27. Carrie Jacobs-Bond, *The Roads of Melody* 1927
28. *Nashville Daily American*, Dec 7, 1877
29. "Blind Tom at Raleigh," *AC*, Feb 20, 1876
30. "Recollections of Blind Tom"s performance in Columbus Ga, Feb 10 1879," *Columbus Ledger Enquirer,* Nov 9, 1941
31. "She"s the mother of Blind Tom," *AC,* Nov 6, 1898; "Thomas Wiggins Niece Never Heard Him Played," *Columbus Ledger Enquirer,* June 5 1975
32. "Thomas Wiggins Niece Never Heard Him Played," *Columbus Ledger Enquirer,* June 5, 1975
33. Julia D Owen, "Letters From Etude Friends," *The Etude,* Nov 1941
34. M. Fuell, *Blind Boone: His Early Life and Achievements,* 1915; NT Gentry, "Blind Boone and John Lange, Jr.," *Missouri Historical Review,* xxxiv, 1940; G.T. Ashley *Reminiscences of a Circuit Rider,* 1941; Madge Harrah, *The Incomparable Blind Boone*, Negro Digest, July 1961; "Wayne B. Allen: Blind Boone's Last Manager," *Ragtimer*, Sept–Oct 1969; W Parrish "Blind Boone's Ragtime," *Missouri Life*, vii/5, 1979.
35. *Musical Courier*, July 22, 1885
36. Blind Tom, *AC*, Nov 27, 1886

CHAPTER 17: THE THINGS REVEALED

1. "Experiences with a Prodigy, Medina New York, September 14, 1896," no publication cited, *Scrapbook*, Boston, 1918
2. "Atlantian Heard Blind Tom," *Atlanta Journal,* June 24, 1934

3. Louise Barfield, *Harris County History of Harris County*, Georgia, 1827-1961, 1961
4. *Cincinnati Gazette*, July 21, 1865
5. *CT*, August 8, 1869
6. William Osler Langley, "Blind Tom: A Child of Melody," *The Theater in Columbus*
7. James Carruthers, *Blind Tom Singing*, Southern Workman, May 1901
8. "Blind Tom—One Marvel Succeeds Another," *Christian Recorder*, Feb 2, 1867
9. Interview with W.C. Handy, May 2, 1953, *Mildred Stock Collection, MARBD, SCRBC*.
10. *Musical Courier*, July 9, 1880
11. *Musical Courier*, July 9, 1880
12. "Death of Isaac B. Poznanski," *NYT*, Jul 19, 1896; "Amusements" *NYT*, Oct 13, 1870
13. Otto Spahr "A Reminiscence Of Blind Tom," *AC*, Aug 17, 1908
14. "Wonderful Blind Tom," *WP*, Nov 28, 1886
15. Mme. Anna Amalie Tutein, "The Phenomenon of Blind Tom," *The Etude*, Feb 1918
16. Robert Offergeld & Edward A. Berlin, "The Music of Democratic Sociability," *Gottschalk & Company*. www.newworldrecords.org/linernotes
17. "Wonderful Blind Tom" *WP* Nov 28, 1886
18. "The Melby's are Vacationing in a Family Tree," *Columbus Ledger*, Aug 21, 1974
19. John Dizikes, *Yankee Doodle Dandy, The life & times of Tod Sloan*, 2004; Anita Leslie, *The Remarkable Mr Jones*, 1954
20. www.pedigreequery.com; daystar@everything2.com
21. *New York Sun*, July 7, 1888
22. "The Future of New York," *The Galaxy*, Vol 9, Issue 4, p548
23. "Carriage Horses," *History: Urban Pollution*, www.allcreatures.org
24. NR
25. Blind Tom, *AC*, Nov 27, 1886
26. "The Pianist Blind Tom," *Cleveland Gazette*, 4 August, 1888
27. J. Frank Davis, "Blind Tom," *Human Life*, August 1908

CHAPTER 18: THE LAST AMERICAN SLAVE

1. "Determined to Have Alimony," *NYT*, July 28, 1883
2. *Detroit Free Press*, July 25 1889
3. *Wilmington Daily Commercial*, Feb 20, 1884
4. *Wilmington Daily Commercial*, Feb 21, 1884
5. "Death of Blind Tom"s Master," *AC*, Feb 19, 1884
6. "Is Blind Tom a Slave?," *Musical Courier*, July 22, 1885
7. SP918 NYCRO
8. "Blind Tom and his Accounts," *WP*, March 6, 1884
9. "Blind Tom & His Friends," *WP*, April 3, 1884
10. "Cutting of his Alleged Wife," *NYT*, March 13, 1884; "The Story of Blind Tom," *WP*, Aug 14 1887
11. J. Frank Davis, "Blind Tom," *Human Life*, August 1908
12. "Blind Tom in Court," *AC*, April 12, 1885; *Musical Courier*, July 22, 1885
13. *Musical Courier*, July 22, 1885
14. "The Custody of Blind Tom," *NYT*, July 11, 1885
15. *Musical Courier*, July 22, 1885
16. *Baltimore Sun*, July 11, 1885
17. "Blind Tom a Slave," *Cleveland Gazette*, Aug 1, 1885
18. *Musical Courier*, Aug 12, 1885
19. Circuit Court, ED Virginia Oct 2, 1886, *Federal Reporter*, Vol 29, First Series
20. "Blind Tom still a Slave," *Brooklyn Eagle*, Oct 4, 1885
21. "Blind Tom," *AC*, Nov 27, 1886
22. "Blind Tom," *AC* Nov 27, 1886
23. "Fighting for Blind Tom," *NYT*, May 8, 1887
24. "Blind Tom is Free," *NYT*, July 31, 1887
25. Petition by James N. Bethune, August 5, 1887, SP918 NYCRO

26. "Blind Tom Again," *Alexandria Gazette*, Aug 1, 1887; "Wants to Take Care of Blind Tom," *NYT*, Aug 12, 1887
27. "The Story Of Blind Tom," *WP*, Aug 14, 1887
28. *NYT*, Aug 12, 1887
29. M. Louise Evans, "Old Timer tells History of Blind Tom," July 13, 1850, No Publication Listed, Vertical Files The Warrenton Library, Fauquier County

CHAPTER19: TOM IS NON COMPOS MENTIS

1. *Alexandria Gazette*, Aug 16, 1887
2. "Blind Tom"s Return," *NYT*, Aug 18, 1887
3. "Celebrations at Bethel," *New York Age*, Nov 26, 1887
4. "Sunday Concerts" *BG*, Nov 27, 1887
5. "Tonight"s Concerts," *BG*, January 1, 1888
6. "Howard's Gossip," *BG*, Dec 1, 1887
7. *The North American Review*, Vol 146, Issue 375, Feb 1888
8. Josef Hofmann, "The Proper Musical Education of Children," *Polish Music Journal* Vol. 6, No. 1, Summer 2003
9. "Howard's Gossip," *BG*, March 29, 1888
10. *The Daily True American*, April 19, 1888
11. "Blind Tom as He is Today," *LHJ*, September 1898
12. J. Frank Davis "Blind Tom," *Human Life*, August 1908
13. "Blind Tom in Retirement," *New York Sun*, April 15, 1897
14. "Affidavit by Eliza Bethune," July 19 1888, SP918 NYCRO
15. "Blind Tom in Retirement" *New York Sun*, April 15, 1897
16. "Afraid of Gifted Son," *WP*, Jan 25, 1903
17. Lousie Dooley "In the World Of Music" *AC*, Aug 2, 1903
18. "Wonderful Blind Tom," *WP*, Nov 28, 1886
19. "She's the mother of Blind Tom" *AC*, Nov 6 1898
20. "Petition by Charity Wiggins," May 21, 1888, SP918 NYCRO
21. "Queen Dazzles East Side," *NYT*, Jan 6, 1899
22. *NYT* March 16 1888; Aldermen & Street Stands *NYT*, Dec 14 1888; "The Aldermen and Franchises," *NYT* May 22 1888; "The Mayor and the Aldermen," *NYT*, March 16 1888.
23. M.R. Werner, *Tammany Hall*, 1928
24. "At a Special Term of the Supreme Court," July 15, 1888, SP918 NYCRO
25. "Blind Tom"s Mother Deplored the Separation," *Columbus Times Industrial Index*, Thirty-second Annual, Columbus. Reprint of *Columbus Enquirer Sun* article, October 1900
26. "Blind Tom"s Mother is Sad," *AC*, Jun 9, 1901
27. William Osler Langley, "Blind Tom: A Child of Melody," *The Theater in Columbus*

CHAPTER 20: NETHERWORLD

1. "Blind Tom Reported Dead," *Columbus Daily Enquirer Sun*, June 12, 1889
2. Willis Fletcher Johnson, *History of the Johnstown Flood*, 1889
3. "Blind Tom Reported Dead," *Columbus Daily Enquirer Sun*, June 12, 1889
4. "Blind Tom Not Dead," *WP*, June 10, 1889
5. "Blind Tom Lives," *AC*, Jan 4, 1894
6. Petition from Daniel Holland, dated Nov 16, 1892, SP918 NYCRO
7. "Blind Tom Alive," *CT*, Nov 17, 1890; *Fredericksburg Freelance*, Nov 24, 1891; "Blind Tom's Whereabouts," *CT*, Sept 16 1889; "Blind Tom Robbed," *Cleveland Gazette*, Jan 31 1891; *Musical Courier*, Dec 30 1891; *Providence Herald*, Sept 21 1901
8. For details of Blind Tom's tour itinerary of these states see Geneva Handy Southall, *Blind Tom, The Black Pianist-Composer (1849-1908)*, 1999
9. *Keith's Theatre, Vaudeville*, April 18 1905, No publication cited, *Scrapbook*, Boston 1918

10. "Blind Tom as He is Today," *LHJ*, September 1898
11. "Blind Tom With Mind Clouded Displays A Marvelous Memory," *The North American*, June 8, 1901
12. *BG*, Feb 5, 1899
13. "Same Blind Tom Of Yore," *New York Dramatic News*, Jan 23, 1892
14. Keith"s Theatre, Vaudeville, April 18 1905, no publication cited, *Scrapbook*, Boston, 1918
15. *Toronto World*, April 27, 1889; *Galveston County Daily News*, March 25, 1895 Cited in Southall, 1999
16. Willa Cather, *Nebraska State Journal*, May 18, 1895
17. SP918 NYCRO
18. "Blind Tom Lives," *AC*, Jan 4, 1894
19. "Blind Tom's Guardian" *WP*, Dec 27, 1893
20. "Special Session of the NYSC," Nov 20, 1888, SP918 NYCRO
21. "Blind Tom as He is Today," *LHJ*, September 1898
22. Harry-Dele Hallmark, "A Master of Melody in Hermitage," *Philadelphia Sunday Press*, Dec 5 1897
23. "The Navesink Highlands," *Harpers New Monthly Magazine*, June 1879
24. Harry-Dele Hallmark, "A Master of Melody in Hermitage" *Philadelphia Sunday Press*, December 5, 1897
25. "Blind Tom in Retirement," *New York Sun*, April 15, 1897
26. "The Navesink Highlands," *Harpers New Monthly Magazine*, June 1879

CHAPTER 21: THUNDERSTORM REQUIEM

1. Percy G. Williams, "Vaudeville & Vaudevillians," *Saturday Evening Post*, June 5, 1909
2. "Blind Tom is Found Alive in Jersey Town," unidentified publication, Dec 21, 1903, clipping seen in 42nd Street Library, Music Room.
3. *Brooklyn Eagle*, Dec 29, 1903
4. "Blind Tom Is An Issue: Did he Die At Johnstown," *Brooklyn Eagle*, Dec 27, 1903
5. *Metronome*, August 1908
6. Harry Houdini, *A Magician Among The Spirits*, 1924
7. Vaudeville, *CT*, 18 December, 1904
8. "Blind Tom Story Told by NY World," *Columbus Enquirer Sun,* June 17, 1908
9. "Funeral 1908," unidentified and undated publication, *Scrapbook*, Boston, 1918
10. "Blind Tom Pianist Dies of a Stroke," *NYT,* June 15, 1908
11. "Blind Tom A Mystery," *WP*, June 17, 1908
12. *Daily State Journal*, Montgomery Alabama, Feb 21, 1872
13. "Letter from Margaret Huber to Ella May Thornton," *Ella May Thornton Archive*, Georgia Room, UGa
14. *Daily State Journal*, Montgomery Alabama, Feb 21, 1872
15. "Dispute over Blind Tom," *NYT,* June 16, 1908
16. "Blind Tom," *New York Age*, July 2, 1908
17. Charles T. Magill, "Blind Tom, Unresolved Problem in Musical History," *Chicago Defender,* 1922/VIII/19
18. "Blind Tom was a member of a family of Twenty-Three," *AC*, Jun 16, 1908
19. "Leon Harris interview with Emma Jefferson," *CNN*, April 3, 2002 Play Highlights Blind Slave Musician www.geoffandwen.com/Blind/newsarticle
20. "Mrs. Lerche's Will Stands," *NYT,* May 26, 1911
21. Ellen Conroy Kennedy (ed), *The Negritude Poets*, 1989
22. *The True Index of Warrenton*, July 4, 1897
23. Etta B. Worsley, *Columbus on the Chattahoochee*, 1951
24. Bill Walton, personal correspondence with Barbara Schmidt, October 2001, http://twainquotes.com/archangelsmystery.html
25. "Letter from Evergreen Cemetery to Ella May Thornton," *Ella May Thornton Archive*, Georgia Room UGa

26. Elizabeth Kolbert, "Blind Tom"s Tombstone," *The New Yorker*, July 15, 2002

CHAPTER 22: EPILOGUE - THE REAL BLIND TOM

1. "Funeral 1908," unidentified and undated publication, *Scrapbook*, Boston, 1918; Reprinted as "Blind Tom a Mystery," *WP*, June 17, 1908

SECONDARY SOURCES

Deren, Maya, *Divine Horsemen, Voodoo Gods of Haiti*, 1953
Dizikes, John, *Yankee Doodle Dandy: The life and Times of Tod Sloan*, 2002
Eaton, Clement, *The Waning of the Old Southern Civilization 1860 –1880s*, 1868
Frith, Uta, *Autism: Explaining the Enigma*, 1989
Genovese, Eugene, *Roll Jordan Roll*, 1976
Goff, Philip and Harvey, Paul (Eds), *Themes in Religion and American Culture*, 2004
Levine, Lawrence, *Black Culture and Black Consciousness*, 1978
Nadel, Stanley, *Little Germany: Ethnicity, Religion and Class in New York City 1845-1880*, 1990
Raboteau, Albert J., *Slave Religion: The "Invisible Institution" in the Antebellum South*, 1978
Sargant, William, *Battle for the Mind*, 1957
Schonberg, Harold C, *The Great Pianists*, 1963
Southall, Geneva Handy, *Blind Tom: The Post-Civil War Enslavement of a Black Musical Genius*, 1979; *The Continuing Enslavement of Blind Tom, the Black Pianist Composers*, 1983; *Blind Tom, the Black Pianist-Composer*, 1999.
Smith, Mark M., *Listening to the Nineteenth Century*, 2000
Stearns, Marshall and Stearns, Jean, *Jazz Dance: The Story of American Vernacular Dance*, 1968
Wiley, Irwin Bell, *The Life of Johnny Reb: The Common Soldier of the Confederacy*, Baton Rouge, 1979
Williams, Peter (ed), *America's Religion, From their Origins to the Twenty First Century*, 2002

PHOTO CREDITS

Page 2: *Blind Tom in 1882*, by George K. Warren, Courtesy of National Portrait Gallery, Smithsonian Institution/Art Resource, NY; p. 8: *Sketches In the Life*, British Library; p. 14: *Oliver Gallop Sheet Music Cover*, LOC; p. 19: *Portrait of Charity Wiggins*, Columbus Enquirer; p. 23: *Notice placed by Wiley Jones*; p. 31: *Portrait of General Bethune*, WP; p. 39: *Plantation Melodies*, LOC; p. 52: *Blind Tom holding Rainstorm*, Photographs and Prints Division, Schomburg Center for Research in Black Culture, The New York Public Library, Astor, Lenox and Tilden Foundations; p. 57: *Shango Figure*, Fowler Museum at UCLA; p. 62: *Blind Tom at Ten*, Private Collection; p. 69: *Alexander Stephens*, LOC; p. 69: *Robert Toombs*, LOC; p. 77: *Blind Tom Poster*, NARA; Vocal Composition, LOC; p. 87: *"Robert Heller" poster*; p. 102: *Blind Tom Seated 1865*, University of Minnesota Special Collections; p. 107: *Harriet Lane*, LOC; p. 107: *Stephen A. Douglas* LOC; p. 115: *Temperance Hall Benefit*, Columbus Daily Sun; p. 115: *1861 Charleston Benefit*, Southern Confederacy; p. 118: *Blind Tom Benefit*, Charleston Mercury; p. 129: *Blind Tom 1865*, Twainquotes; p. 149: *Blind Tom etching*, Harpers Magazine; p. 158: *Blind Tom Sitting Portrait*, Private Collection; p. 161: *Louis Moreau Gottschalk*; p. 167: *Tom L'Aveugle*, Private Collection; p. 174: *Blind Tom and General Bethune*, Twainquotes; p. 185: *Blind Tom Standing Portrait*, Private Collection; p. 190: *Mechanics Hall Program*, Private Collection; p. 195: *Blind Tom Sketch*, James Monroe Trotter; p. 195: *Blind Boone at 15*, Missouri Historical Society; p. 198: *Blind Tom at Grand Piano*, Private Collection; p. 222: *March Timpani*, LOC; p. 222: *Military Waltz*, LOC; p. 206: *John Bethune sketch*, WP; p. 210: *Blind Tom at piano*, Harpers; p. 211: *Wellenklange*, LOC; p. 219: *Blind Tom and Lerche*, Harpers; p. 225: *Selika and Blind Tom*, New York Age; p. 228: *Blind Tom in 1880*, LOC; p. 234: *Charity in 1900*, CSU Archives; p. 245: *Blind Tom with dog*, Harpers; p. 249: *Orpheum announcement*, Brooklyn Eagle; p. 259: *Blind Tom dedication*, Henry Stallings Jnr/Twainquotes; p. 264: *Dizzy Gillespie at graveside*, Twainquotes.

ACKNOWLEDGMENTS

In the Rare Books and Manuscripts Department of the Boston Public Library there is a scrapbook, a slim notebook, dedicated to Blind Tom. Pasted onto each page is a clipping—Blind Tom's return to the vaudeville stage, the recollections of A.H. Gott and Thomas Warhurst's daughter— and reading through this disconnected narrative, a picture of Tom begins to emerge. But as to the identity of the person who scoured the newspapers, compiled the clippings and assembled the scrapbook, there are no clues. But it is to that individual—and the handful of Blind Tom aficionados over the century—to whom I am deeply grateful. They are a lineage of sorts. Although these writers and researchers worked without knowledge of each other, they were united in purpose—to document the life of the man known to the world as "Blind Tom."

The Chicago Defender's Charles T. Magill was the first to look beyond the showman's spiel, his investigations in 1924 crucially establishing the place and circumstance of Tom's burial. Less known are the efforts of Wellbourne Victor Jenkins, a black Atlanta man who, in the early 1940's, wrote to The Atlanta Constitution seeking out stories about Blind Tom with a view to writing a biography. He never did, but his inquiries stimulated a storm of memories amongst the paper's readers, many of which have been included in this book.

A decade later, Georgia State Librarian Ella May Thornton also became smitten with Blind Tom. Over a period of years, she and an assistant began tracking down articles and sheet music, compiling bibliographies, as well as conducting interviews with the Bethune family. The results can now be found in two archive boxes now lodged in the Georgia Room at the University of Georgia.

Roughly about the same time in the Bronx, a writer by the name of Mildred Stock—author of Ira Aldridge: The Negro Tragedian—embarked on a similar journey. Although her proposed book Blind Tom: Genius of the Chattahoochee never eventuated, she uncovered some wonderfully insight-ful articles and conducted interviews with Tom's great niece, Julia Lee and blues legend, W.C. Handy. I thank the Stock family and the Manuscripts,

Archives & Rare Books Division of the Schomburg Center for Research in Black Culture for allowing me to use this material.

In 1974, as part of their Black History Series, *The Columbus Times* in Georgia produced a special feature on Blind Tom packed with photographs, interviews, memoirs and scraps of detail. Whether this was drawn from a private collection or a part of the newspaper's library, I do not know—but whoever undertook this project, I am most grateful.

Between the years 1979 and 1999, Dr. Geneva Handy Southall, a Professor in Afro-American Studies at the University of Minnesota, produced a three volume work on Blind Tom which, for the first time, set out his life in rich chronological detail. This has been a fantastic reference for me and, without it, my task would have been considerably harder. For her pioneering research and dedication to memory of Blind Tom, I am truly thankful.

I am indebted, too, to Inez Hunt who in 1972 published *The Story Of Blind Tom*, a children's book based on stories that Susan Bethune told her son, Norbonne Robinson. Her book was most helpful in bringing psychological dimension to Tom and General Bethune's flight to Florida.

The public's awareness of Blind Tom made a great leap forward when concert pianist John Davis released *John Davis plays Blind Tom*. For me it was a delight and a revelation to hear Blind Tom's music played by someone of Davis' caliber. I thank him too for initiating efforts to place a marker on Blind Tom's Brooklyn grave.

Until the launch of www.blindtom.org this year, Blind Tom's presence on the web was, by and large, courtesy of the efforts of Barbara Schmidt. An offshoot of a site dedicated to Mark Twain, (www.twainquotes.com /archangels.html) the pages have been a valuable focal point for bringing together stories, images and the music of Blind Tom. I thank her too for helping me track down some illustrations.

In the last year there has been another flurry of research into the life of Tom. Many thanks to Susan Berlowitz for her ingenuity and eagle-eyed persistence; Bruce Abrams of the New York County Clerk's Office, for his encyclopedic memory; Americus' intrepid archivist, Alan Anderson for his generosity; Ceceile Kay Ritcher for her strategic thinking; Michael Fairchild for his patience; Chris Hudson for his precision; and Rod Clare for his enthusiasm.

The deepest gratitude is reserved for my dear friend John O'Brien, whose incisive editorial advice—always delivered with good humor, honesty and tact—has encouraged me to reign in my excesses and reach for more. Special thanks to Martin Sharp, who first introduced me to Blind Tom many years ago and Paul Lovell, Mark Parsons, Brian Powers and Jim McKechnie for their insights and help over the years.

This is the first book I have written and for making it a reality, I am indebted to the support, advice and enthusiasm of both my agent Robert Astle and editor David Shoemaker as well as the staff at The Overlook Press.

My conversations with Adam Ockelford of the Royal National Institute for the Blind and Professor Allan Synder of The Centre for the Mind were both enlightening and added greatly to my understanding of the inner workings of Tom's mind. Extended discussions with Amanda Handel and Amy Johansen about nineteenth century piano music and the dynamics of performance deepened my appreciation of music and musicianship. My conversation with The Honorable George Greene—an avid Blind Tom collector—was a rare treat.

I also wish to thank, and apologize to, Charity's descendants. It was never my intention to publish this book without making contact with them, and my numerous attempts to do so from Australia were unsuccessful. I would have loved to hear their stories about Charity and Tom and hopefully some day I will.

And finally, to David, Jasmine and Indigo—my husband and two daughters—for their patience, love and inspiration.

Index